The Spanish Civil War

BERG EUROPEAN STUDIES SERIES

GENERAL EDITOR: **Brian Nelson** (Monash University, Melbourne)

ADVISORY BOARD: Michael Biddiss (University of Reading), John Flower (University of Exeter), Paul Michael Lützeler (Washington University, St. Louis), David Roberts (Monash University, Melbourne), Tony Judt (New York University), Walter Veit (Monash University, Melbourne)

Marko Pavlyshyn (ed.), *Glasnost in Context*

David Roberts and Philip Thomson (eds.), *The Modern German Historical Novel*

Brian Nelson (ed.), *Naturalism in the European Novel*

Brian Nelson, David Roberts and Walter Veit (eds.), *The Idea of Europe*

Dieter Freundlieb and Wayne Hudson (eds.), *Reason and Its Other: Rationality in Modern German Philosophy and Culture*

Forthcoming

Mirna Cicioni and Nicole Prunster (eds.), *Visions and Revisions: Women in Italian Culture*

THE SPANISH CIVIL WAR

A Cultural and Historical Reader

edited by

ALUN KENWOOD

BERG

Providence / Oxford

Published in 1993 by
Berg Publishers, Inc.
Editorial offices:
221 Waterman Street, Providence, RI 02906, U.S.A.
150 Cowley Road, Oxford OX4 1JJ, UK

A CIP catalogue record for this book is available from the British Library

Library of Congress Cataloging-in-Publication Data

The Spanish Civil War : a cultural and historical reader / edited by
    Alun Kenwood.
        p.   cm.
    Includes translations of extracts from French and Spanish.
    Includes bibliographical references and index.
    ISBN 0–85496–318–9 (cloth). — ISBN 0–85496–338–3 (paper)
    1. Spain—History—Civil War, 1936–1939. 2. Nationalism—Spain
—History—20th century. 3. Spain—History—Civil War, 1936–1939
—Fiction. I. Kenwood, Alun.
DP269.9627 1992
946.081—dc20   92–10649
                                                                   CIP

Preface

The outbreak of Civil War in Spain in July 1936 unleashed a whirlwind of destruction, persecution, and horror that over three years shattered the nation and claimed the lives of more than half-a-million Spaniards. The ideological confrontation, the ferocity of the conflict, and the intense commitment of the participants establish the war as a landmark in modern European history and help to explain the stimulus it gave to the imagination of writers and artists from the 1930s onward.

The Introduction sets the war in its historical context and surveys the Spanish and other national responses to the conflict. The Anthology of Texts consists of key historical documents and extracts selected from the work of representative writers from Europe, the United States, and the Hispanic world. They portray the political, social, and military history of the conflict; the horrors of modern warfare; the ideologies and illusions, the hopes and despair of the participants; the international dimensions of the upheaval; and the extraordinary idealism and creative energy of the period. The Glossary provides a brief description of the leading figures and political parties mentioned in the text. All items marked with an asterisk appear in the Glossary; only the first mention of the item is indicated in this way. The List of Anthologized Texts provides a summary of the sources used in the anthology. The original source of all new translations is given in the original language, and all excerpts translated by Alun Kenwood and Colin Nettelbeck appear in Berg house style, which includes the anglicization of Spanish place names. Several authors do not appear in the List of Anthologized Texts because their work was first published in an anthology or periodical; the title of the anthology or periodical is included instead.

The Anthology of Texts has been based primarily on material from the war years, 1936–1939. It offers the widest representative selection of Hispanic material yet available in English translation; a much fuller and more balanced representation of Nationalist writing than is to be found in any other anthology of its type; and a considerable amount of French and Spanish material translated into English for the first time.

I would like to express my sincere gratitude to my colleague and the general editor of the Berg European Studies Series, Professor Brian Nelson, for his encouragement and helpful comments on the manuscript. I am also indebted to other colleagues who have contributed in different ways to this anthology: Elaine Barry, Kevin Foster, David Garrioch, John Leonard, Colin Nettelbeck, and Pavel Petr.

Alun Kenwood

Chronological Table of Events

1873–74	First Spanish Republic.
1879	Formation of the Spanish Socialist party.
1882	Foundation of the Socialist Trade Union, the UGT.*
1885–1923	Constitutional monarchy of Alfonso XIII.*
1898	Spanish-American War and loss of the overseas empire.
1910	Foundation of the Anarchist Trade Union, the CNT.*
1917–23	Social unrest, Anarchist terrorism and government repression in Barcelona and Andalusia.
1923–30	Dictatorship of General Miguel Primo de Rivera.*
May 1926	General strike in the U.K.
1928	Antonio de Oliveira Salazar becomes head of the "New State" in Portugal.
Oct. 1929	Wall Street crash and start of the Great Depression.
1930	Fall of the Primo de Rivera dictatorship.
1931	
14 Apr.	Second Spanish Republic proclaimed. Alfonso XIII goes into exile.
28 June	Left-wing majority elected to the Cortes.*
Aug.	National government formed in the U.K.
Sep.	U.K. abandons the Gold Standard.
Oct.	Manuel Azaña* appointed prime minister after Niceto Alcalá Zamora* resigns over anticlerical articles in the new constitution.
Dec.	Alcalá Zamora elected president of the Republic.
1932	
Jan.	Dissolution of the Jesuits. CNT general strikes. Divorce legalized.
July	Salazar appointed premier in Portugal. Nazis win 230 seats in *Reichstag* election.
Aug.	First military uprising by General José Sanjurjo* fails.
Sep.	Agrarian law reform and Catalan Statute approved by the Cortes.
1933	
Jan.	Anarchist revolts in Barcelona. Peasant unrest in the south culminates in the massacre of Anarchists in Casas Viejas.

Feb.	Fascist coup by Engelbert Dollfuss in Austria.
Mar.	Right-wing Catholic party, the CEDA,* founded by José María Gil Robles.* Religious reform bill passed, proposing lay education and closure of church schools.
	Franklin Delano Roosevelt elected president in U.S.
	Dollfuss becomes dictator in Austria.
	Mass unemployment in Germany, U.K., and U.S.
Oct.	The Spanish Falange, an authoritarian right-wing party modelled on Italian and German lines, founded by General Primo de Rivera's son, José Antonio Primo de Rivera.*
	Germany quits the League of Nations.
Nov.	Spanish right-wing parties gain a victory in the general elections over a divided Left.
Dec.	Anarchist uprisings in Catalonia and Aragon.
	Mass unemployment in Europe and in U.S.

1934

Feb.	The Falange merge with the right-wing JONS* party.
	Socialist insurrection in Vienna crushed.
Mar.	A four-week general strike, led by Buenaventura Durruti,* begins in Saragossa.
Apr.	General Sanjurjo and his fellow-conspirators given amnesty.
June	First meeting of Adolf Hitler and Benito Mussolini.
	Rural unrest in southern Spain. Street fighting in Madrid and the north in protest against the central government.
July	Attempted Nazi *putsch* in Austria. Dollfuss murdered.
Aug.	Following the death of Paul von Hindenburg, Hitler becomes head of state.
	Mussolini agrees to train Carlist* militias, or *requetés.**
	Miners' uprising in Asturias is crushed by General Francisco Franco* and the Foreign Legion. The failure of the risings in Madrid and Barcelona leads to severe repression.

1935

July	VII Comintern Congress approves Popular Front tactics in Spain.
Sep.	Formation of Trotskyist, anticommunist political party, the POUM.* The government crisis leads to the announcement of new elections.
Oct.	Italy invades Abyssinia.
	The League of Nations proposes economic sanctions against Italy.

1936

Feb.	The Popular Front elected to government. Amnesty granted to prisoners from the 1934 Asturias rising.
Mar.	The Falange banned and José Antonio Primo de Rivera arrested. Church burnings. Land seizures in the south. Street

fighting between Left and Right. Army ultimatum to Azaña on disorder.

Germany occupies the Rhineland.

Apr. General strikes and demonstrations throughout Spain.

Socialist and Communist youth movements merge in unified Socialist youth group, the JSU.*

General Emilio Mola* continues with his plans for a military uprising.

May Azaña named president of the Republic.

June Socialist Léon Blum heads the Popular Front in France.

The Italian conquest of Abyssinia completed.

12 June Lieutenant José Castillo, an officer in the Republican Assault Guards,* is assassinated by Falangists. The Monarchist leader José Calvo Sotelo* is murdered in revenge.

17–20 July Military risings in Morocco and Spain.

18 July Insurgents successful in Morocco and Seville.

19–20 July The military rising defeated in Madrid and Barcelona.

Hitler agrees to support the insurgents (later known as the Nationalists).

Anti-Fascist militias formed in Barcelona.

Committee of National Defense established by the Nationalists in Burgos.

20 July General Sanjurjo killed in air crash.

The British Labor party expresses its support for the Republic, while the Conservative government under Stanley Baldwin remains uncommitted.

21 July The siege of the Alcazar in Toledo begins.

The rebel rising in Almeria is crushed.

25 July The first shipment of French planes reaches Spain.

26 July The Comintern agrees to seek volunteers and funds to aid the Republic.

Hitler agrees to Franco's request for military aid.

30 July The airlift of the Army of Africa to mainland Spain begins.

2 Aug. Blum's cabinet splits and France announces a policy of nonintervention in the Spanish war.

8 Aug. France closes its border with Spain.

9 Aug. Merida falls to the rebels.

12 Aug. The first International Brigade volunteers reach Spain.

14 Aug. The Nationalists capture Badajoz and massacre the Republicans. Terror and counterterror within the country.

15 Aug. Britain bans the export of arms to Spain.

19 Aug. Murder of poet Federico García Lorca.

24 Aug. Soviet Union's first ambassador to Spain arrives in Madrid.

Germany, Portugal, and Italy agree "in principle" to a proposal for nonintervention.

28 Aug. First aerial bombardment of Madrid.

4 Sep.	Francisco Largo Caballero* forms a government of Republicans, Socialists, and Communists.
	The Stalin purge trials begin. Recruiting for the International Brigades approved.
5 Sep.	The Nationalists take Irun and close the border with France.
7 Sep.	First autonomous Basque government formed under the Republic.
9 Sep.	First meeting of Non-Intervention Committee in London.
13 Sep.	San Sebastian falls.
27 Sep.	The Nationalists take Toledo and end the siege of the Alcazar.
29 Sep.	Franco named head of state and commander in chief of the Nationalist forces.
30 Sep.	The Republican government creates the Popular Army.
1 Oct.	The Republican government approves Basque autonomy.
	The British Labor party rejects the Communist party's application to affiliate.
	Sir Oswald Mosley, leader of the British Union of Fascists, stirs up anti-Semitic feeling in London.
12 Oct.	The first Soviet aid for the Republic arrives.
6 Nov.	Republican government flees from Madrid to Valencia.
7–8 Nov.	All-out assault on Madrid, but the city is saved by the peoples' militias and the International Brigades.
	Roosevelt reelected president of U.S.
15–17 Nov.	The Condor Legion, a squadron of the German airforce, in action.
18 Nov.	Germany and Italy recognize Franco's regime.
20 Nov.	The Falangist leader, José Antonio Primo de Rivera, executed in Alicante.
23 Nov.	The battle for Madrid ends in stalemate.
17 Dec.	The POUM ousted from the Catalan government at Communist insistence.
22–23 Dec.	Italian "volunteers" arrive in Spain to help the Nationalists.
1937	
6 Jan.	U.S. forbids the export of arms to Spain.
5–24 Feb.	Jarama battle: renewed Nationalist assault on Madrid is thwarted.
7–8 Feb.	Malaga captured by Italian-aided Nationalists.
14 Feb.	The POUM and a militant Anarchist group, the FAI,* demonstrate in Barcelona in favor of social revolution before victory in the war.
20 Feb.	The Non-Intervention Committee forbids the enlistment of volunteers to serve in Spain.
8–18 Mar.	Battle of Guadalajara. The Popular Army, with the International Brigades, routs the Italian Corps.

THE SPANISH CIVIL WAR

A Cultural and Historical Reader

edited by

ALUN KENWOOD

BERG

Providence / Oxford

Published in 1993 by
Berg Publishers, Inc.
Editorial offices:
221 Waterman Street, Providence, RI 02906, U.S.A.
150 Cowley Road, Oxford OX4 1JJ, UK

A CIP catalogue record for this book is available from the British Library.

Library of Congress Cataloging-in-Publication Data

The Spanish Civil War : a cultural and historical reader / edited by
   Alun Kenwood.
      p.   cm.
   Includes translations of extracts from French and Spanish.
   Includes bibliographical references and index.
   ISBN 0–85496–318–9 (cloth). — ISBN 0–85496–338–3 (paper)
   1. Spain—History—Civil War, 1936–1939. 2. Nationalism—Spain
—History—20th century. 3. Spain—History—Civil War, 1936–1939
—Fiction. I. Kenwood, Alun.
   DP269.9627   1992
946.081—dc20   92–10649
                                                  CIP

Contents

Preface

The outbreak of Civil War in Spain in July 1936 unleashed a whirlwind of destruction, persecution, and horror that over three years shattered the nation and claimed the lives of more than half-a-million Spaniards. The ideological confrontation, the ferocity of the conflict, and the intense commitment of the participants establish the war as a landmark in modern European history and help to explain the stimulus it gave to the imagination of writers and artists from the 1930s onward.

The Introduction sets the war in its historical context and surveys the Spanish and other national responses to the conflict. The Anthology of Texts consists of key historical documents and extracts selected from the work of representative writers from Europe, the United States, and the Hispanic world. They portray the political, social, and military history of the conflict; the horrors of modern warfare; the ideologies and illusions, the hopes and despair of the participants; the international dimensions of the upheaval; and the extraordinary idealism and creative energy of the period. The Glossary provides a brief description of the leading figures and political parties mentioned in the text. All items marked with an asterisk appear in the Glossary; only the first mention of the item is indicated in this way. The List of Anthologized Texts provides a summary of the sources used in the anthology. The original source of all new translations is given in the original language, and all excerpts translated by Alun Kenwood and Colin Nettelbeck appear in Berg house style, which includes the anglicization of Spanish place names. Several authors do not appear in the List of Anthologized Texts because their work was first published in an anthology or periodical; the title of the anthology or periodical is included instead.

The Anthology of Texts has been based primarily on material from the war years, 1936–1939. It offers the widest representative selection of Hispanic material yet available in English translation; a much fuller and more balanced representation of Nationalist writing than is to be found in any other anthology of its type; and a considerable amount of French and Spanish material translated into English for the first time.

I would like to express my sincere gratitude to my colleague and the general editor of the Berg European Studies Series, Professor Brian Nelson, for his encouragement and helpful comments on the manuscript. I am also indebted to other colleagues who have contributed in different ways to this anthology: Elaine Barry, Kevin Foster, David Garrioch, John Leonard, Colin Nettelbeck, and Pavel Petr.

Alun Kenwood

Chronological Table of Events

1873–74	First Spanish Republic.
1879	Formation of the Spanish Socialist party.
1882	Foundation of the Socialist Trade Union, the UGT.*
1885–1923	Constitutional monarchy of Alfonso XIII.*
1898	Spanish-American War and loss of the overseas empire.
1910	Foundation of the Anarchist Trade Union, the CNT.*
1917–23	Social unrest, Anarchist terrorism and government repression in Barcelona and Andalusia.
1923–30	Dictatorship of General Miguel Primo de Rivera.*
May 1926	General strike in the U.K.
1928	Antonio de Oliveira Salazar becomes head of the "New State" in Portugal.
Oct. 1929	Wall Street crash and start of the Great Depression.
1930	Fall of the Primo de Rivera dictatorship.
1931	
14 Apr.	Second Spanish Republic proclaimed. Alfonso XIII goes into exile.
28 June	Left-wing majority elected to the Cortes.*
Aug.	National government formed in the U.K.
Sep.	U.K. abandons the Gold Standard.
Oct.	Manuel Azaña* appointed prime minister after Niceto Alcalá Zamora* resigns over anticlerical articles in the new constitution.
Dec.	Alcalá Zamora elected president of the Republic.
1932	
Jan.	Dissolution of the Jesuits. CNT general strikes. Divorce legalized.
July	Salazar appointed premier in Portugal. Nazis win 230 seats in *Reichstag* election.
Aug.	First military uprising by General José Sanjurjo* fails.
Sep.	Agrarian law reform and Catalan Statute approved by the Cortes.
1933	
Jan.	Anarchist revolts in Barcelona. Peasant unrest in the south culminates in the massacre of Anarchists in Casas Viejas.

Feb.	Fascist coup by Engelbert Dollfuss in Austria.
Mar.	Right-wing Catholic party, the CEDA,* founded by José María Gil Robles.* Religious reform bill passed, proposing lay education and closure of church schools.
	Franklin Delano Roosevelt elected president in U.S.
	Dollfuss becomes dictator in Austria.
	Mass unemployment in Germany, U.K., and U.S.
Oct.	The Spanish Falange, an authoritarian right-wing party modelled on Italian and German lines, founded by General Primo de Rivera's son, José Antonio Primo de Rivera.*
	Germany quits the League of Nations.
Nov.	Spanish right-wing parties gain a victory in the general elections over a divided Left.
Dec.	Anarchist uprisings in Catalonia and Aragon.
	Mass unemployment in Europe and in U.S.

1934

Feb.	The Falange merge with the right-wing JONS* party.
	Socialist insurrection in Vienna crushed.
Mar.	A four-week general strike, led by Buenaventura Durruti,* begins in Saragossa.
Apr.	General Sanjurjo and his fellow-conspirators given amnesty.
June	First meeting of Adolf Hitler and Benito Mussolini.
	Rural unrest in southern Spain. Street fighting in Madrid and the north in protest against the central government.
July	Attempted Nazi *putsch* in Austria. Dollfuss murdered.
Aug.	Following the death of Paul von Hindenburg, Hitler becomes head of state.
	Mussolini agrees to train Carlist* militias, or *requetés.**
	Miners' uprising in Asturias is crushed by General Francisco Franco* and the Foreign Legion. The failure of the risings in Madrid and Barcelona leads to severe repression.

1935

July	VII Comintern Congress approves Popular Front tactics in Spain.
Sep.	Formation of Trotskyist, anticommunist political party, the POUM.* The government crisis leads to the announcement of new elections.
Oct.	Italy invades Abyssinia.
	The League of Nations proposes economic sanctions against Italy.

1936

Feb.	The Popular Front elected to government. Amnesty granted to prisoners from the 1934 Asturias rising.
Mar.	The Falange banned and José Antonio Primo de Rivera arrested. Church burnings. Land seizures in the south. Street

	fighting between Left and Right. Army ultimatum to Azaña on disorder.
	Germany occupies the Rhineland.
Apr.	General strikes and demonstrations throughout Spain.
	Socialist and Communist youth movements merge in unified Socialist youth group, the JSU.*
	General Emilio Mola* continues with his plans for a military uprising.
May	Azaña named president of the Republic.
June	Socialist Léon Blum heads the Popular Front in France.
	The Italian conquest of Abyssinia completed.
12 June	Lieutenant José Castillo, an officer in the Republican Assault Guards,* is assassinated by Falangists. The Monarchist leader José Calvo Sotelo* is murdered in revenge.
17–20 July	Military risings in Morocco and Spain.
18 July	Insurgents successful in Morocco and Seville.
19–20 July	The military rising defeated in Madrid and Barcelona.
	Hitler agrees to support the insurgents (later known as the Nationalists).
	Anti-Fascist militias formed in Barcelona.
	Committee of National Defense established by the Nationalists in Burgos.
20 July	General Sanjurjo killed in air crash.
	The British Labor party expresses its support for the Republic, while the Conservative government under Stanley Baldwin remains uncommitted.
21 July	The siege of the Alcazar in Toledo begins.
	The rebel rising in Almeria is crushed.
25 July	The first shipment of French planes reaches Spain.
26 July	The Comintern agrees to seek volunteers and funds to aid the Republic.
	Hitler agrees to Franco's request for military aid.
30 July	The airlift of the Army of Africa to mainland Spain begins.
2 Aug.	Blum's cabinet splits and France announces a policy of nonintervention in the Spanish war.
8 Aug.	France closes its border with Spain.
9 Aug.	Merida falls to the rebels.
12 Aug.	The first International Brigade volunteers reach Spain.
14 Aug.	The Nationalists capture Badajoz and massacre the Republicans. Terror and counterterror within the country.
15 Aug.	Britain bans the export of arms to Spain.
19 Aug.	Murder of poet Federico García Lorca.
24 Aug.	Soviet Union's first ambassador to Spain arrives in Madrid.
	Germany, Portugal, and Italy agree "in principle" to a proposal for nonintervention.
28 Aug.	First aerial bombardment of Madrid.

4 Sep.	Francisco Largo Caballero* forms a government of Republicans, Socialists, and Communists.
	The Stalin purge trials begin. Recruiting for the International Brigades approved.
5 Sep.	The Nationalists take Irun and close the border with France.
7 Sep.	First autonomous Basque government formed under the Republic.
9 Sep.	First meeting of Non-Intervention Committee in London.
13 Sep.	San Sebastian falls.
27 Sep.	The Nationalists take Toledo and end the siege of the Alcazar.
29 Sep.	Franco named head of state and commander in chief of the Nationalist forces.
30 Sep.	The Republican government creates the Popular Army.
1 Oct.	The Republican government approves Basque autonomy.
	The British Labor party rejects the Communist party's application to affiliate.
	Sir Oswald Mosley, leader of the British Union of Fascists, stirs up anti-Semitic feeling in London.
12 Oct.	The first Soviet aid for the Republic arrives.
6 Nov.	Republican government flees from Madrid to Valencia.
7–8 Nov.	All-out assault on Madrid, but the city is saved by the peoples' militias and the International Brigades.
	Roosevelt reelected president of U.S.
15–17 Nov.	The Condor Legion, a squadron of the German airforce, in action.
18 Nov.	Germany and Italy recognize Franco's regime.
20 Nov.	The Falangist leader, José Antonio Primo de Rivera, executed in Alicante.
23 Nov.	The battle for Madrid ends in stalemate.
17 Dec.	The POUM ousted from the Catalan government at Communist insistence.
22–23 Dec.	Italian "volunteers" arrive in Spain to help the Nationalists.
1937	
6 Jan.	U.S. forbids the export of arms to Spain.
5–24 Feb.	Jarama battle: renewed Nationalist assault on Madrid is thwarted.
7–8 Feb.	Malaga captured by Italian-aided Nationalists.
14 Feb.	The POUM and a militant Anarchist group, the FAI,* demonstrate in Barcelona in favor of social revolution before victory in the war.
20 Feb.	The Non-Intervention Committee forbids the enlistment of volunteers to serve in Spain.
8–18 Mar.	Battle of Guadalajara. The Popular Army, with the International Brigades, routs the Italian Corps.

24 July	The Popular Army launches an offensive along the river Ebro.
22 Sep.	International Brigades are withdrawn from Spain.
30 Sep.	The Munich Pact ends the Republic's hopes of Anglo-French aid.
28 Oct.	Trial of POUM leaders in Barcelona.
29 Oct.	Farewell parade of the International Brigades in Barcelona.
16 Nov.	The Ebro battle ends with the retreat of the Popular Army.
19 Nov.	Franco grants mining concessions to Germany in return for military aid.
23 Dec.	Nationalist offensive in Catalonia opens, and meets with only sporadic resistance.
1939	
25 Jan.	Negrín government abandons Barcelona and sets up in Figueras.
26 Jan.	Barcelona falls. Mass flight of refugees to the French frontier.
1 Feb.	The Cortes meets for the last time, in Figueras.
27 Feb.	Britain and France recognize the Franco regime.
4–12 Mar.	Negrín's attempts at Communist dictatorship to ensure continued resistance provoke a second Republican civil war. Heavy fighting in Madrid. Communist forces defeated. Negrín, his cabinet, and Soviet advisers fly out of Spain. The Defense Council in Madrid unsuccessfully attempts to negotiate with Franco.
15 Mar.	German troops enter Prague.
27 Mar.	Nationalist forces enter Madrid. Refugees trapped in Alicante, Valencia.
1 Apr.	Franco announces the end of the war. U.S. recognizes Franco's government.
23 Aug.	The Nazi-Soviet Pact signed.
1939–43	Severe repression of Republicans. An estimated 150,000 to 200,000 executions.
1942	During World War II, Spain declares herself neutral, but sends the 47,000-strong Blue Division of Spanish volunteers to fight alongside Germany on the Russian front.
1945	At the Potsdam Conference, "fascist" Spain is declared unfit for membership in the United Nations.
1947	Franco declares Spain a kingdom, with himself as regent.
1953	Franco signs a military and economic agreement with U.S. in return for NATO bases.
1955	Spain admitted to membership of the United Nations.
1969	Franco nominates Juan Carlos de Borbón, grandson of Alfonso XIII, as heir to the throne.
1975	Death of Franco.
June 1977	The first democratic elections in Spain since February 1936.

Introduction to the Spanish Civil War

The Historical Background

DAVID GARRIOCH

We have largely forgotten the Spanish Civil War of 1936–1939. Open a textbook of European history, and you will find scant mention of it, often no more than a couple of pages in a chapter on the lead-up to the Second World War. Lost are the emotions, the sense of crusade, the passions that stirred a generation. They are gone, partly because they were swallowed up in the turmoil and the disillusionment of the great conflict that was to follow, but also because they now seem very foreign. We can perhaps understand the policy of appeasement or the appeal of fascism to many people in Europe in the 1920s and 1930s. But that thousands of young men and women were moved to leave their own countries and risk their lives in a war that, to our eyes, had nothing to do with them, is incomprehensible to a post-Vietnam generation. Their idealism often seems naive, their prior understanding of events in Spain undoubtedly very limited. And how could Spain – subsequently largely absent from world affairs for nearly forty years, and even in the nineteenth and early twentieth centuries clearly marching to a different rhythm from the rest of Western Europe – occupy such a central place in the preoccupations of world leaders and politically conscious Europeans, Americans, and even Australians?

For the Spanish Civil War was a very Spanish affair, incomprehensible without some familiarity with the broad themes of Spanish history since the nineteenth century. The key to an understanding of this war is undoubtedly the place of the army, arbiter of Spanish political life for more than a hundred years. Emerging with honor from the Napoleonic Wars of 1808–1814, the army played a central role in the attempts to create a liberal Spain under a centralized monarchy. The *pronunciamiento*, a coup by a general or a group of army officers to replace one government with another, became a Spanish tradition: between 1814 and 1874 there were thirty-seven attempted *pronunciamientos*, of which

3

twelve were successful.[1] The monarchy that ruled Spain until 1931 owed its existence to such a coup, and as recently as 1923 the army, in the person of General Miguel Primo de Rivera, had intervened to abolish the Spanish Constitution. Although King Alfonso XIII remained in office, General Primo de Rivera became effective ruler of Spain until 1929.

The army's tradition of intervention in politics was born in the nineteenth-century struggles between Liberals and Conservatives, but by the 1920s many generals and officers had come to see the army not as a player defending a particular political position, but as an institution that stood *above* politics. For some of them, like General Franco, the army had an almost sacred mission to defend Spain, not only against external aggressors but against the divisive elements within: against the Catalans and the Basques who wanted greater independence from the central government, and against the Socialists and Anarchists, who, in their eyes, represented foreign interests. This belief was central in the minds of those who led the coup that began the war. It was rendered more urgent for them by the continuing war in Morocco, an area that the Spanish had been struggling to conquer since the late nineteenth century. Repeated setbacks in that war created a chronic sense of crisis within the army, with many officers tending to blame defeats on those they saw as Spain's internal enemies.

Among the issues that divided Spain most deeply, and that made its civil war particularly bloody, none was more important than religion. The conflict between the supporters of the Catholic church and their anticlerical opponents had its origins deep in Spain's past, and the passions it aroused were correspondingly deep. Here again, the nineteenth-century experience was crucial, for Spain had been one of the very few places in Europe where the Inquisition had been reestablished after the Napoleonic Wars, and it had been used ruthlessly by the Monarchy to root out political opponents, principally Liberals. In response, during the brief periods when Liberals gained power in Spain, they tried to reduce clerical power by confiscating Church lands, by placing limitations on the activities of religious orders, and by loosening the Church's hold on education. This conflict continued into the twentieth century, the main spokesmen of the Spanish Church remaining implacably opposed to democratic and Liberal ideas. In 1923

1. A. Beevor, *The Spanish Civil War* (London: Orbis, 1982), 15.

Church leaders had welcomed the military coup that had over-thrown the democratic system and, as they were to do again after 1936, had called for a campaign of moral regeneration. As a result of pressure from churchmen and religious associations, teachers in state schools were forbidden to teach anything "offensive towards religion," and a small number were dismissed for so doing.[2] As late as 1927, the catechism that all children in religious schools had to learn by heart taught that voting for a Liberal was a mortal sin.[3]

Had the economic and political influence of the Spanish Church declined, as happened in France, where anticlericalism was also strong in the nineteenth century, opposition to it no doubt would have been less violent. Although Church attendance was dropping (perhaps one-third of Spaniards remained practicing Catholics in the 1930s, and in working-class areas there were far fewer), the Church remained extraordinarily powerful. It has been estimated that in the early twentieth century the Church owned about one-third of the total wealth of the country, and its huge investments in factories and industry gave it very close ties to big business.[4] It also retained a strong hold over education, providing schools particularly for the upper and middle classes. Spain had an enormous number of convents and clergy, as well as innumerable lay organizations that campaigned on behalf of the Church against what they saw as "moral decay" in the form of obscene literature, provocative women's fashions, blasphemy, prostitution, alcoholism, and games of chance.[5]

The Church also set up its own trade unions and youth organizations to combat socialism, which, since the successful Bolshevik revolution in Russia, had come to be seen by Conservatives as a serious threat. The Catholic unions quickly earned the hatred of the Socialists and Anarchists, not only because they were rival organizations, but because they actively encouraged strikebreaking by their members. Bodies like the National Catholic Agrarian Confederation (Confederación Nacional Católica-Agraria), which was dominated by rich landlords and which thwarted attempts at much-needed agrarian reform, actively supported the dictatorship

---

2. S. Ben-Ami, *Fascism from Above* (Oxford: Clarendon Press, 1983), 104–105.

3. H. Thomas, *The Spanish Civil War* (Harmondsworth: Penguin, 1965), 54.

4. G. Brenan, *The Spanish Labyrinth* (Cambridge: Cambridge University Press, 1960 [1943]), 47–48.

5. Ben-Ami, *Fascism from Above*, 106–108.

in the mid-1920s.[6] The government-sponsored Patriotic Union* (Unión Patriótica), with a much wider social range among its members, nevertheless was controlled largely by employers in the industrial areas, and by big landowners in the rural south.[7]

Not surprisingly, therefore, the Church was perceived, not only by committed Socialists and Anarchists but also by many Spanish workers, as totally opposed to their interests. In urban and rural areas alike, Catholicism frequently was viewed as a tool of the bosses, bourgeois and hypocritical in its teachings. Church schools were frequently looked upon with hostility.[8] Committed Socialists and Anarchists amply reciprocated the hatred the Church had for them: the sentiments they expressed were not mere rhetoric. The more extreme Left, largely driven underground by successive Conservative regimes, met repression with violence, and anticlerical riots were a widespread phenomenon at times of political crisis, accompanied by the burning of churches, the desecration of altars and relics, and attacks on nuns and priests, which often involved rape and torture. The active assistance given by the main body of the Spanish Church to the Nationalist forces under General Franco, and the equally fervent support for the Republic provided by the various left-wing militias, thus arose from antagonisms established long before the creation of the Second Republic in 1931.

But the roots of this conflict were not entirely political and ideological. The character of both clericalism and anticlericalism in Spain and the allegiances formed during the Civil War were shaped by the profound social and economic inequalities within the country. Most serious of all were the agrarian problems. Spain remained a predominantly agricultural economy, with half its national wealth coming from the land and the greater part of the work force engaged in agriculture.[9] Much of this rural population was desperately poor, and the problems were exacerbated by high birth rates. Perhaps a million peasant farmers, mostly in northwestern Spain (Galicia) and in parts of central Spain, struggled to make ends meet on plots that were far too small. Even worse off, however, were the rural laborers of Andalusia, Extremadura, and La Mancha, in southern and south central Spain. In these areas up

6. F. Lannon, "The Church's Crusade against the Republic," in P. Preston (ed.), *Revolution and War in Spain, 1931–1939* (London: Methuen, 1984), 44–45.

7. Ben-Ami, *Fascism from Above*, 126–160.

8. Lannon, "The Church's Crusade against the Republic," 49–50.

9. R. Carr, *The Spanish Tragedy* (London: Weidenfeld & Nicolson, 1977), 2; Brenan, *The Spanish Labyrinth*, 90. Brenan's survey of the agrarian question in Spain (Chapter VI) is still one of the best.

to half the land, often the most fertile, was occupied by large estates called *latifundia*. These estates were owned by a few thousand wealthy landlords, who often lived elsewhere and had no connection with the local inhabitants. The bulk of the population, some two million, had virtually no land and was employed at extremely low wages. Unemployment was very high, with many men out of work for up to half the year. Not surprisingly, living conditions were appalling, and one visitor to Andalusia in 1935 reported that the pigs were better accommodated than the workers.[10] In northern and western Spain, landholdings were larger and the soil was often richer. Industrial areas and demand for exports created markets for agricultural produce, so the rural population was much more prosperous and wealth was more evenly distributed (see Map 1).

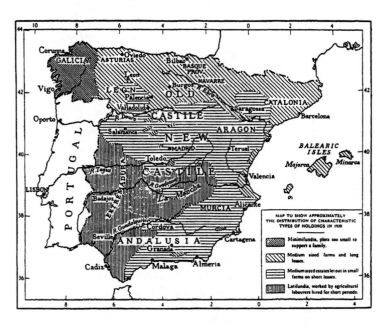

Map 1: The Distribution of Characteristic Types of Landholdings in 1930
Source: G. Brenan, *The Spanish Labyrinth* (Cambridge, 1960 [1943]), 334.

In northern and western Spain, however, it was in the cities that social and economic inequality flourished. In the heavily industri-

10. E. H. G. Dobby, "Agrarian Problems in Spain," *Geographical Review of the American Geographical Society* (April 1936), quoted in Brenan, *The Spanish Labyrinth*, 121.

7

al areas around Barcelona and Bilbao, centers of metallurgy, shipping, and textiles, many of the factories were owned by a small number of wealthy families who had taken huge profits during the First World War and the boom years of the 1920s. A combination of rapid urban growth, periodically high unemployment, and wages that lagged behind prices left the industrial workers worse off at a time when the industrialists were flaunting their growing wealth.

Divisions between employers and workers were further deepened by the extreme violence used by both sides, especially in Barcelona. The growth of Socialism and Anarchism in Spain in the late nineteenth century frightened police and employers to such an extent that they were prepared to hire thugs to beat up and even assassinate union leaders. During the 1890s *agents provocateurs* frequently were used to create incidents that would justify the imposition of martial law and thus enable the authorities to crush the labor movement. Unions responded by hiring their own gunmen, and in the crisis years following the First World War, especially from 1918 to 1920, assassinations and gun battles were frequent occurrences in the streets of Barcelona. When the Army intervened, it was invariably in support of the employers.

The same sort of partisan violence occurred in rural areas where social and economic tension ran high. Especially in poverty-stricken Andalusia, where on a number of occasions poor laborers tried to take over land left uncultivated by wealthy landowners, the hated Civil Guards were used widely. A semimilitary police force, the Civil Guards had a nasty reputation for violence, and proved themselves ready to shoot down even unarmed demonstrators. Because it was they, along with the notoriously corrupt tax collectors, who effectively represented the central government in rural Andalusia, it is hardly surprising that Anarchism, with its aim of destroying the state entirely, should have found so many supporters among the landless laborers of the region (see Map 2).[11]

In social and economic terms, therefore, Spain was one of the most divided countries in Europe, with dramatic extremes of wealth and poverty giving rise to frequent violent conflicts. But there were other serious tensions that made the country difficult to govern, most notably regionalism. The two main industrial areas, Catalonia and the Basque Country, had traditions that dis-

11. See also Cyril Connolly's article in *New Statesman and Nation* on Anarchism (included in Anthology of Texts).

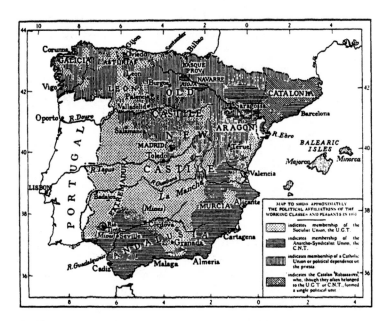

Map 2: The Political Affiliations of the Working Classes and Peasants in 1933

SOURCE: G. Brenan, *The Spanish Labyrinth* (Cambridge, 1960 [1943]), 335.

tinguished them clearly from the rest of Spain, and particularly from Castile, where the central government was located. Catalonia once had been an independent kingdom with its own laws and language, but since the fifteenth century had been under the control of the Castilians, who had imposed both the Spanish language and rule from Madrid. Catalan nationalism had revived in the late nineteenth century, and even the Catalan bourgeoisie had supported demands for some degree of regional autonomy. By the mid-1920s, however, the success of the Bolsheviks in Russia and the widespread strikes and agitation within Spain had led most wealthy Catalonians to support the central government against working-class demands. For the most part, these Catalonians supported the dictatorship in 1923, despite its abolition of even limited self-government for Catalonia. The Nationalist movement went underground, but resurfaced in the early 1930s when the Republic's promise of limited autonomy for the region won it widespread support.

The situation in the Basque region was different, for it was a

9

very Catholic area, dominated by Conservatives. But the half-million Basques also had their own language and traditions, and until 1840 had had their own parliament and law courts. Following the Carlist wars, however, the central government removed this autonomy, a loss that was still resented in the early twentieth century. As a result, there was considerable hostility in the Basque region toward the monarchy, and this provided initial support for the Republic.

The major significance of the Catalan and Basque demands for autonomy lay in their negative influence on many Conservatives. To the Conservatives, regionalism threatened the fragile unity of Spain. In particular, many army officers saw Catalan nationalism, along with communism, as the major threat facing their country, a sentiment emphasized in General Franco's manifesto of 17 July 1936. Such fears generated support for the 1936 uprising against the Spanish Republic, and Conservative opposition to regional autonomy in the end impelled the Catalans and the Basques to support the Republicans in Spain's civil war.

A range of serious and deep-rooted tensions, many of them inherited from Spain's turbulent nineteenth-century history, resurfaced in the early 1930s. But even so, it did not appear inevitable that there would be a civil war. The departure of King Alfonso XIII on 14 April 1931, following the overwhelming success of anti-Monarchist candidates in the municipal elections, offered new hope to all those who had suffered under the dictatorship over the last few years. Even many Conservatives, landowners, businessmen, and army officers had become disillusioned with the government and the king, and were quite prepared to support a Republic, provided that their interests were protected. They did not get quite the kind of Republic they wanted, however, and the next few years witnessed an increasing polarization that eventually led to war.

That polarization developed largely along predictable lines. The new government included several known anticlericals and two Socialists, and almost immediately came under attack from the primate of the Spanish Church, Cardinal Segura. A few days later a verbal dispute between Monarchists and Republicans in Madrid provoked riots, in the course of which several churches were burned down. If these incidents were not enough to inflame the long-standing hatred between the Church and Spanish anticlericals, the governmental measures that followed certainly were. The government not only proclaimed complete freedom of religion and the end of compulsory religious instruction in schools, but adopted a new Constitution, under which Catholicism was no longer recognized as the official religion of Spain, and according to which Spain no longer would pay the salaries of the priests. Other articles restricted or regulated the Church's landholdings, placed limitations on its schools, obliged religious orders to register with the state, and effectively outlawed some of them. It also introduced both civil marriage and divorce. Had these measures been passed as laws, Spanish Catholics might have worked to change them while remaining faithful to the Republic. But their inclusion in the constitution forced most Catholics to oppose the Republic itself.

Many Conservatives, including many in the army, were prepared to accept even these anticlerical measures. But they were concerned by the generally democratic and – for the time – even socialist orientation of the new regime. Laws were enacted forbidding forced labor, setting minimum wages, and establishing arbitration boards composed of both workers and employers to settle wage disputes. One result of these measures was a rapid improvement in wages and in working conditions for urban and rural workers alike. A public works program was introduced to combat the effects of the Great Depression, although Spain was not as badly affected as many other countries. Currency controls were applied, and there was a huge increase in the number of strikes, which were no longer met with armed repression. The vote had been extended not only to all men over twenty-three, but also to women. Conservatives felt that many of these laws smacked of socialism. The legislation that aroused the greatest storm was the Catalan Statute of 1932. It granted home rule to Catalonia, where candidates supporting autonomy for the region had won overwhelmingly in the elections. This law was debated vigorously in the Cortes, the Spanish Parliament, because many members of the Left were just as worried about the possible disintegration of Spain as were the Conservatives, particularly because a Basque Statute was also proposed, providing similar autonomy for the Basque provinces, and a separatist movement was developing in Galicia. Most angered by the Catalan Statute, however, were many army officers who not only feared the precedent it set, but saw it as a slap in the face for the military, which had spent years combating the Catalan autonomy movement under the monarchy and the dictatorship.

All of these measures helped create a strong alliance between various Conservative forces, which, while not necessarily opposed

11

to the Republic as such, were profoundly disillusioned with the moderate, liberal government that had come to power in 1931. They were not strong enough to overthrow it as long as it retained center and left-wing support, as was demonstrated late in 1932 when a number of Monarchist army officers attempted to carry out a coup and were rapidly defeated. By mid-1933, however, the government had lost much of its early support on the Left. Despite the many reforms, few satisfied the aspirations and hopes that had been aroused by the end of the monarchy. The greatest disillusionment was created by the slowness and ultimate ineffectiveness of land reform. Many Spaniards expected, particularly in impoverished Andalusia, that the new regime would confiscate the property of the large landowners immediately and redistribute it to the poor. Not until late 1932, however, was an Agrarian Statute passed by the Cortes. It allowed for the expropriation of large estates that were not worked by their owners, and the confiscated land was to be made available to individual farmers or to peasant cooperatives, although compensation had to be paid to the former owners. Even then, however, the implementation of the law was delayed, and in practice very little land was redistributed.

In addition, the government made only feeble attempts to reform the taxation system. Most revenue came from indirect taxes, which were paid in greatest proportion by the poor. Relatively little government income came from income tax, and even that was paid largely by small farmers; most of the rich managed to evade it.

These failures were seized upon by the Anarchists, the strongest left-wing party and the one with greatest rural support, who never had supported the new government. By the beginning of 1933 there was such a high level of discontent that the Anarchists were able to lead a number of risings against the regime, principally in Catalonia and Andalusia. The government reacted strongly, sending in troops who did not hesitate to shoot to kill. In one well-publicized instance, in the village of Casas Viejas in southern Andalusia, these troops even shot unarmed prisoners, claiming to be acting on the orders of the minister of the Interior. This incident, so similar to the methods used under the monarchy, did much to discredit the government.

The elections of November 1933 produced a big swing to the Right, fueled by the combination of disillusionment on the Left and a newfound unity among the Catholic and Conservative forces. The Socialist party was discredited by its strong backing for the previous government. The Anarchists called on their massive working-class support to boycott the elections, and this cost the Left many seats. The Right, in contrast, was much more united, particularly in the newly formed Confederation of Autonomous Right Parties, the CEDA, a predominantly Catholic grouping financed primarily by the large landowners. The CEDA became the largest party in the Cortes, followed by the Radicals,* who, despite their name, were a very moderate pro-Republican group.

The new government, a Center-Right coalition, immediately repealed or suspended most of the legislation that had improved wages and conditions for the workers and the peasantry, as well as some of the anticlerical laws. Thousands of rural laborers who had received land under the agrarian reform law were expelled by the Civil Guards. Wages fell rapidly, and many workers who had supported the previous government actively found themselves unemployed. The left-wing parties and their supporters watched with dismay and growing alarm. Labor unrest became widespread, and the government was quick to use troops to dispel it. Paramilitary squads trained openly: Anarchists, Socialists, and Communists on the Left, and Monarchists and the semi-Fascist Falange on the Right. Clashes between the two sides became increasingly common. The situation was already tense in the middle of 1934, as news from other parts of Europe began to cast Spanish affairs in a new light for Spaniards and foreign observers alike.

For it was during 1934 that fascism began to assume threatening proportions throughout Europe. What originally had seemed to be a peculiarly Italian phenomenon was spreading rapidly, threatening democracy and civil liberty, and leading to the persecution of left-wing parties and sympathizers across Europe. Hitler had come to power in January 1933 and immediately had closed down left-wing newspapers, arrested hundreds of Communists and Socialists, and suspended civil liberties. By June the Nazi party was the only legal political grouping in the country. At the same time, Nazi sympathizers in Austria were using similar violence against their political opponents, and in response Austrian Chancellor Dollfuss had taken up emergency powers but had used them against the Left, seizing the opportunity to impose his right-wing Catholic policies. Like Hitler and Mussolini, he had banned the Socialist party, and in February 1934 a rising in Vienna was crushed with much bloodshed. The 6 February 1934 riots in Paris, in which a range of right-wing groups was prominent, also alarmed the European Left.

13

Against this background, the success of the CEDA in the 1933 elections and their subsequent activities appeared much more sinister. The leader of the CEDA, José María Gil Robles, was a self-confessed admirer of Dollfuss's dictatorial, clerical regime. He had said openly that his party's goal was to win power and to rewrite the constitution, using democracy only as a means to that end, and his talk of the "New State" was strongly reminiscent of Hitler or Mussolini.

Given the already tense circumstances of early October 1934, when the Center-Right government collapsed, the assumption of power by the CEDA inspired widespread fear. Although the new government included only three CEDA ministers, this was enough to provoke left-wing revolts around Spain. The Catalan nationalists, fearing the loss of their regional autonomy, revolted against the central government. In Madrid and in other parts of the country the Socialists proclaimed a general strike and there was some fighting. But the most serious rising took place in the northern province of Asturias, and was led by militant miners. The other revolts lasted only a day or two, but in Asturias it took the army, aided by the air force and by the Moorish troops of the Spanish Foreign Legion, two weeks to defeat the rebels, inflicting torture and carrying out summary executions as they went. Both the aims of the rebels and the brutality of the repression, particularly by the Foreign Legion, made this revolt a true forerunner of the civil war.

Tensions continued throughout 1935. The coalition government was unable to operate effectively and new elections were called for February 1936. The fear of fascism and the experience of the 1934 revolts, many of which had failed due to the disunity of the Left, had convinced the left-wing parties (except the Anarchists) of the need to join forces. The Communists, the Socialists, the POUM, the Catalan separatists, and a number of small Center-Left parties formed a Popular Front with a common platform. Opposing them was a right-wing bloc calling itself the National Front, composed of the CEDA, the Monarchists, and some smaller parties. The polarization that was to result in civil war was almost complete, therefore, by the beginning of 1936. The only missing elements were the army, which remained divided, and the Anarchists and the Falange, both of which chose to stay outside the political system altogether. The election results testified to this polarization. The Popular Front won just over four million votes, the National Front nearly four million, and the Center received only a half-million votes.

As the new Popular Front government set about reversing the trend of the previous two years, their supporters celebrated wildly. Churches were burned once again, and accounts were settled for the preceding two years of right-wing repression. Violence erupted between left- and right-wing militias, and both the Anarchists and the Falange engaged in a series of political assassinations. The contrast with the previous changes of government is striking. In 1931 the Right had accepted the Republic, although without enthusiasm. In 1933 the Left had accepted the victory of their opponents, if fearfully. In February 1936, however, the level of violence and mutual hatred was so great, having been exacerbated by the tensions and struggles of the intervening years, that cohabitation of Left and Right was no longer possible.

The aftermath of the Popular Front victory at last persuaded most army officers, already hostile to the Left, that the situation could not be allowed to continue. The new government was able to control neither the militias nor, apparently, its own supporters. The Socialists, who had become considerably more radical since 1933, were now proclaiming that the Popular Front would not last and that a proletarian revolution would follow.[12] Comparisons with the 1917 Russian Revolution were widely made, suggesting that the government would be overthrown by a Bolshevik-style coup, an impression reinforced by the huge May Day parades, in which portraits of Lenin and Stalin were carried alongside those of the Spanish Socialist leader Largo Caballero.

Plots against the Republic, often involving army officers, were common. But the plot of 1936 was organized by General Mola, a prominent general who had not been involved previously. Mola succeeded in winning support from both monarchist and previously prorepublican officers, as well as from the Falange and from the Carlists. He found collaborators not only throughout mainland Spain but also in Spain's colonial possessions in North Africa. The assassination on 13 July of right-wing opposition leader Calvo Sotelo convinced even the most skeptical that the government was either deliberately eliminating its opponents or totally incompetent.

The rising began in Morocco on 17 July and met little resistance there. On 18 July coordinated revolts took place all around Spain, achieving immediate success in Conservative areas but encountering stiff resistance in places where the Left was strong. Thanks to assistance from German troop planes, which ferried soldiers from

12. See also the Socialist Manifesto (included in Anthology of Texts).

Morocco to the mainland, within a few days the country was divided into two zones, with the Nationalists (as the rebels termed themselves) holding most of the north and west and a toehold in the very south, and the government or Republican forces retaining the rest of the south and the center, Catalonia, and a strip along the northern coast that included Asturias and much of the Basque region. Over the next two-and-a-half years of bitter fighting, the Nationalists gradually gained control of Andalusia and Extremadura, and then of the entire north.

In the immediate aftermath of the rising, events on both sides of the war front followed a strangely parallel pattern. Amid the initial confusion, local groups and authorities took control, and the character of each region largely determined the course of events. In the Nationalist zone it was usually local army officers who took over, and their relations with the local population generally governed the enthusiasm with which they rounded up and sometimes executed Popular Front supporters, Anarchists, and union leaders. Many gave the Civil Guards or the Falange a free hand in carrying out reprisals. In the Government zone the local councils generally remained in place, and here the unsuccessful rebels were often shot. Here, too, the ferocity of reprisals depended on the preceding level of conflict in each locality. In many areas churches were attacked, priests and nuns were killed, and in the already violent cities of Madrid and Barcelona there were indiscriminate attacks on the rich. Where the Anarchists were strong, and in some Socialist areas too, the onset of war sparked the takeover of factories and large estates by workers' committees. The Revolution had come.

The following two years saw, on both sides of the front, the growing centralization and consolidation of power. General Franco gradually emerged as the dominant figure on the Nationalist side, particularly after the death of General Mola in a plane crash in 1937. On the Republican side the previously small Communist party, acting mainly under orders from Moscow, set about eliminating its rivals, notably the POUM and the Anarchists. Among the most bitter recriminations following an exceptionally bitter war were those levelled against the Communists for their cold-blooded elimination, by any means available, of those who were allied with them in the fight against the Nationalists.

The Spanish Civil War ended in March 1939 with the total victory of the Nationalist forces, firmly under Franco's control. Although its origins were purely and peculiarly Spanish, it had

16

become an international war with the active intervention of Nazi Germany and Fascist Italy. Their contribution of massive supplies of equipment and substantial numbers of troops seemed to confirm the widely held view of the war as a struggle between the forces of fascism and democracy, or between fascism and communism, depending on the observer's political views. Support for the Republican side came from the Soviet Union, and from the roughly 40,000 volunteers – men and women – from all around the world who joined the International Brigades. Britain and France pursued a policy of active nonintervention, which, for the most part, hindered the Republic from procuring the supplies it desperately needed, while Germany and Italy openly flouted the Non-Intervention Treaty by supplying materiel to the Republic's opponents.[13]

No one ever will know the human cost of the Spanish Civil War. Estimates of casualties vary widely, but perhaps between 100,000 and 200,000 people died in the actual fighting, and maybe as many or more died after the end of the war in mass executions or in concentration camps. Spain was to experience thirty-six years of authoritarian rule and was to remain a divided country, with the victors reaping the rewards of success, and the vanquished suffering continuing repression and discrimination. The impact on the rest of Europe was no less significant. The Spanish Civil War, which, perhaps more than any other event in the twentieth century, created a sense of Europe being divided into two great blocs, one fascist and the other liberal or socialist, convinced much of the European Left to abandon pacifism and support rearmament. It helped persuade Hitler that Britain and France were not prepared to go to war in defense of democratic regimes. Ironically, Spain at the same time helped convince many in those countries that they would have to go to war against Nazi Germany.

13. See the Appeal by the Spanish Government to the League of Nations (included in the Anthology of Texts).

"Between the bullet and the lie"[1]: Intellectuals and the War

KEVIN FOSTER

T he dominant political trend of the 1930s was the increasingly stark polarization between the forces of Left and Right. Hitler came to power in 1933, reoccupying the demilitarized Rhineland three years later. In 1934 Austria's democratically elected government was overthrown in a fascist *putsch*, and two months before Franco's *pronunciamiento*, as Haile Selassie fled the Italian armies advancing on Addis Ababa, Mussolini heralded the inception of a new Roman Empire. For many, the military rebellion in Spain on 18 July 1936 laid bare the essential principles of the modern crisis. Cyril Connolly, the editor of *Horizon*, noted: "Today the forces of life and progress are raging on one side, those of reaction and death on the other. We are having to choose between democracy and fascism."[2]

Franco's *coup d'état* moved Auden, Neruda, and Spender, among others, to address "the question" to "the Writers and Poets of England, Scotland, Ireland and Wales":

> It is clear to many of us throughout the whole world that now, as certainly never before, we are determined or compelled, to take sides. The equivocal attitude, the Ivory Tower, the paradoxical, the ironic detachment, will no longer do. [...]
> This is the question we are asking you:
> *Are you for, or against, the legal Government and the People of Republican Spain?*
> *Are you for, or against, Franco and Fascism?*
> For it is impossible any longer to take no side.[3]

1. The title of this chapter is a quotation from a poem written by George Orwell, "The Italian soldier shook my hand," in *Homage to Catalonia and Looking Back on the Spanish War* (Harmondsworth: Penguin, 1966), 246. (Abbreviated hereafter as *HC*.)
2. C. Connolly, *Enemies of Promise*, rev. ed. (Harmondsworth: Penguin, 1949), 110.
3. V. Cunningham, ed., *The Penguin Book of Spanish Civil War Verse* (London: Penguin, 1980), 49–50. (Abbreviated hereafter as *SCWV*.)

The unequivocal response that the preamble solicits and the questions demand, apparently justified by the conflict's polarities, says as much about the intellectual and psychological inheritance of the thirties as it does about the political background to the Spanish Civil War itself. It can be attributed, in part, to one of the First World War's most enduring legacies, what Paul Fussell in *The Great War and Modern Memory* calls the *"versus* habit." Gross dichotomies, physically experienced in the prolonged trench warfare of the western front, established "a model of modern political, social, artistic and psychological polarisation [...]what we can call the modern *versus* habit: one thing opposed to another, not with some Hegelian hope of synthesis involving a dissolution of both extremes[...]but with a sense that one of the poles embodies so wicked a deficiency or flaw or perversion that its total submission is called for."[4] The physical and psychological experience of the First World War redefined modernist discourse and crucially shaped the syntax of the Spanish Civil War. It conditioned the editorial policies of some of the most influential journals and series of the 1930s. *New Writing,* edited by John Lehmann, pursued "a kind of literary equivalent of the Popular Front against Fascism."[5] In its first edition, in spring 1936, it declared itself "independent of any political party," yet signalled that it did "not intend to open its pages to writers of reactionary or Fascist sentiments."[6] This encouraged the establishment of yet more entrenched polarities, which influenced resulting perceptions of the Spanish conflict and culminated in the kind of adversarial myopia memorialized by "the question." With its gross dichotomies, its simple Manichaean conception of the moral and political options, its demand for total alliance or opposition, "the question" is a testament to the potency of the *"versus* habit,*"* and a vindication of the claim made by Valentine Cunningham, in his monumental study *British Writers of the Thirties,* that throughout the thirties, the First World War "was in every writer's mental luggage".[7]

For writers of the period, the conflict's apparently straightforward oppositions and the choices with which it confronted them imposed attendant responsibilities. One's declaration of political

4. P. Fussell, *The Great War and Modern Memory* (Oxford: Oxford University Press, 1975), 75–76, 79.

5. V. Cunningham, *SCWV,* 28.

6. V. Cunningham, ed., *British Writers of the Thirties* (Oxford: Oxford University Press, 1989), 31. (Abbreviated hereafter as *BWT.)*

7. V. Cunningham, *BWT,* 50.

loyalty to either democracy or fascism committed one to a corresponding catalog of moral and aesthetic doctrines. The semiotic of the Spanish Civil War, in line with the *"versus* habit" and its binary reasoning, firmly locked together systems of political, moral, and aesthetic signification. The mutual substitution of discourses expedited the transformation of a political cause into a moral and aesthetic crusade, as novelist and editor Naomi Mitchison's response to "the question" indicates: "There is no question for any decent, kindly man or woman, let alone a poet or writer, who *must* be more sensitive. We have to be against Franco and Fascism and for the people of Spain, and the future of gentleness and brotherhood which ordinary men and women want all over the world."[8] Though not an invention of Spain's Civil War, the interpenetration of political, moral, and aesthetic discourses attained a new sophistication as a result of it. Only months after Franco's final victory, the Left's diatribes against fascism provided the propagandists of the Second World War with a ready supply of ammunition for their campaigns against Hitler.

To some extent, the fervor of the European intellectuals' commitment to Spain was a reaction against their governments' response to the crisis. The policy of nonintervention generated a proportionately committed, interventionist backlash from literary and artistic communities. Of the 149 authors whose responses to "the question" were published in *Authors Take Sides on the Spanish Civil War*, 16 pleaded neutrality, 5 professed themselves "against" and 127 declared themselves "for" the Republic. Yet the compilers of the pamphlet drafted several vacillators into the Republican camp. Poet and editor of the influential 1930s journal *New Verse*, Geoffrey Grigson: "I am equivocal enough to be *against* politically, and not *for*, to fear and distrust any mass in its own control; but for me Hitler, Mussolini and Franco are man-eating mass-giants issuing from mediocrity and obscenity."[9] Others were silenced. Orwell's bitter denunciation of the questionnaire and its assumptions remained unpublished. There was no record of unpublished replies, nor was there any list of those who failed to respond to the questionnaire. The implied simplicity of the war's moral terrain demanded a correspondingly united front against fascism from the Left's literary arm. It thereby legitimated the kind of regimen-

---

8. V. Cunningham, *Spanish Front: Writers on the Civil War* (Oxford/New York: Oxford University Press, 1986), 227. (Abbreviated hereafter as *SF*.)
9. Quoted in V. Cunningham, *SF*, 53.

tation of private and public expression, which the Left had identified as one of the hallmarks of fascist barbarity, but which it was not above practicing itself.

Some writers, it should be noted, welcomed, and indeed actively pursued, the subordination of the personal by the collective voice. John Cornford, Cambridge University student and committed Communist and poet who was killed fighting in Spain, located in the tremulous first-person singular pronouns the source of the weakness that threatened his commitment to the common cause. In his overtly political verse, the bourgeois weak link and its representative pronouns are subsumed by the first-person plural and the collective confidence that it denotes: "Then let my private battle with my nerves,/ The fear of pain whose pain survives,/ The love that tears me by the roots,/ The loneliness that claws my guts,/ Fuse in the welded front our fight preserves."[10]

Yet the compulsion of unity as a political end in itself and the related effacement of the personal voice all but abolished individual liberty and legitimated a culture of repression. It politicized and outlawed dissent, transforming it from a bourgeois indulgence into a counterrevolutionary crime punishable by death. Supervised by the censor and enforced by the assassin, the sanctification of unity ushered in a Stalinist reign of terror. This put to rest any last vestiges of a genuinely popular front and unleashed a wave of bitter fighting in Catalonia between POUM, Anarchist, Republican, and Communist militias. As a member of the POUM, Orwell spent as much time evading Communist shock troops and secret police in Barcelona as he did dodging fascist bullets in the line. Little wonder that he regarded "the question's" simple assumptions about the nature of the fight in Spain as "bloody rot."[11] The Left proved itself no more tolerant of opposition from

10. V. Cunningham, SCWV, 132. Perhaps the most extreme response to this quest for a unified voice, in poetic terms at least, was mass declamation. Though predating the outbreak of the war in Spain, mass declamation attained its greatest popularity through its association with the conflict. A group recitation of poetry "performed as a massed chant with stylised movements," mass declamation "was one of the characteristic (and more successful) attempts by left-wing poets and sponsors of socialist commitment in art to achieve forms of a 'non-bourgeois' kind. It at once reflected the new and growing anti-bourgeois consciousness of writers and, since it was a group activity, it made a step at least towards the dearly wished-for 'mass' art of Marxist literary theory" (V. Cunningham, SCWV, 44). In political terms, however, most of the mass declamations were a sham because, although they were performed by a group, they were almost invariably the work of a single writer.

11. G. Orwell, The Collected Essays, Journalism and Letters of George Orwell, edited by Sonia Orwell and Ian Angus (London: Penguin, 1970), vol. 1, 346.

within its own ranks than it was of Fascism, and, as such, surrendered any lingering claims it might have had to moral superiority. Many intellectuals could not bring themselves to fully accept the betrayal of a cause in which they had invested so much, and they located in their narratives the personal and political affirmations that the circumstances and prosecution of the conflict had denied them. Gustav Regler, the German novelist who fled Nazi Germany and fought on the Republican side in Spain, found in the celebration of individual heroism the personal honor and political principle conspicuously absent from so much of the political conduct of the Republican cause. His first-person account, at the same time, limited his dejection to a mainly personal sense of betrayal. In *Spanish Testament* (Arthur Koestler's eyewitness account of the fall of Malaga and his subsequent capture and imprisonment by the Nationalists) and *Homage to Catalonia*, Koestler and Orwell wrote about their experiences in Spain with overtly sacramental rhetoric, with an almost evangelical fervor. Both discover, in brief encounters with almost total strangers, the instinctive, almost spiritual communion that "momentarily succeeded in bridging the gulf of language and tradition and meeting in utter intimacy";[12] the ideal of comradeship that motivated so many to go to Spain and was betrayed there by the ruthless political intrigues that characterized the conflict.

The Spanish Civil War's most enduring literature is that which retains its integrity in the face of personal and political disillusionment. For anybody with the least political or moral principle, the war was a profoundly disillusioning experience. To tell the disheartening truth about it, as Orwell, the poet Stephen Spender, sociologist Franz Borkenau, and a few others sought to do, was to invite critical asperity and political exile. None of Spender's poems from Spain, claims Randall Swingler, poet and former editor of *Left Review*, "is about the Spanish War. They are all about Spender and his detachment from history," and, as such, they "mean very little" to anybody who took part in the war.[13] Swingler's political hostility conditions his aesthetic judgement. His objection to Spender's political heterodoxy demands that he unshackle the dissenting evidence of Spender's poems from the Left's historical juggernaut and dismiss his contribution to the literature of the war *in toto*. Yet Spender's poetry is no less political for its per-

12. G. Orwell, *HC*, 7.
13. V. Cunningham, BWT, 441.

sonal vision; in fact, one of the great achievements of his Spanish
Civil War verse is its assertion of the continued relevance of the
individual voice. In his revised version of "Port Bou," Spender
takes stock of the symbolic frontiers that confront him having
crossed from France into Spain: the frontiers between peace and
war, safety and danger, and private contemplation and public
action, and he determines his preparedness to make the crossing
complete. Yet his unsuitability for border crossing, in its broader
sense, is clear. What Spender likes about Port Bou is the tranquility: it is the antithesis of the crisis landscapes common in the works
of Cornford, Hemingway, and Malraux. It is a place of solitary and
self-conscious contemplation, the domain of poetry and not
action: "In the bright winter sunlight I sit on the parapet/ Of a
bridge; my circling arms rest on a newspaper/ And my mind is
empty as the glittering stone/ While I search for an image." Not
even the arrival of the militiamen disturbs his peace, as they and
their weapons are worked into the collage of tranquility that he
constructs about himself. Yet on the wrong side of the frontier
between peace and war, the solitariness in which Spender finds
personal and creative strength also exposes his vulnerability and
reaffirms his weakness. As the town empties, and the old men,
children, and women "trail over the horizon" to watch the militia's
firing practice, Spender is "left alone" at "the exact centre . . . / . . .
solitary as the bull's eye in a target." Unable to efface his private
fears, to find courage – or poetry – in the surrender of self to the
collective cause, Spender accepts his failure to pass from observation to action and retreats back over the internal frontiers to the
domain of private contemplation, poetry, and abject self-abase-
ment: "I am the coward of cowards."[14]

Spender's observation that "a poet can only write about what is
true to his own experience, not about what he would like to be
true to his experience"[15] is both an aesthetic and political credo
born of his time in the civil war, and particularly germane to its literature. It expresses the conviction that the writer who prefers
neat dogma to the perhaps unpalatable truths of personal experience, faithfully rendered, condemns him or herself to silence. In a
letter to his friend and fellow poet C. Day Lewis, Spender notes
that John Cornford's dedication to the party line had compro-
mised his duty to truth, and had killed him as a writer long before

14. All of the poetry in the foregoing paragraph was quoted from Stephen
Spender, "Port Bou," in *SCWV*, 354–355.
15. S. Spender, *The Still Centre* (London: Faber and Faber, 1939), 10.

his death in battle at Cordoba in 1936: "Doesn't it strike you that he'd been forced out of the position in which it was possible for him to create, into a position which was a complete denial of it, into a position indeed in which he denied his own creative self and attacked violently all the poets who had 'collapsed into subjectivism' – so that finally, in despair, he was driven into the life of action in which he was killed."[16] Spender's loyalty to fear, his tenacious hold on subjectivism, his stubborn refusal to sing the party line and stifle his own creative voice was his aesthetic triumph and his political testament. Ironically, it made him, like Orwell, a significant political figure, whose dedicated independence marked him out as a symbol of potential heterodoxy.

It is in this urgent discourse between the symmetries of political doctrine and the evidence of the conflict's disillusioned eyewitnesses, "between the bullet and the lie," that so many of the challenges and treasures of Spanish Civil War writing are to be found.

16. V. Cunningham, *SCWV*, 41.

Art, Propaganda, Commitment: Hispanic Literature and the War

ALUN KENWOOD

T he Spanish Civil War, fought on Spanish soil over Spanish issues, inspired more literature than any other event in Spain's history, and attracted some of Latin America's best writers to its cause. Never before had the torrent of literature and posters and the rash of documentary films, radio broadcasts, and theatrical productions produced so much propaganda. The war crystallized the issue of commitment in literature. Every artistic form became, on each side, a weapon in the struggle and contributed powerfully to the politicization of European literature.

Poetry – often quicker to produce than theater or narrative, and frequently written in the heat of the moment – led the way. It achieved an extraordinary flowering on both sides, especially among the Republicans: from 1936 to 1939 roughly 8,500 poems on the war were published in the Republican popular press. Literary periodicals, such as the Republicans' *El Mono Azul* (The Blue Overalls) – a reference to the blue overalls of the worker-soldiers who made up the majority of Republican combatants – and the Nationalists' *Vértice* (Vertex), gave generous space to unknown poets as well as to established writers. *Romancero general de la guerra de España* (General Book of Ballads of the War in Spain), published in Madrid and Valencia in 1937, was one of more than fifty collections of verse on the war to appear in Spain and elsewhere. In addition, individual poets, including the Spaniards Rafael Alberti, Miguel Hernández, José Herrera Petere, and the Latin Americans Pablo Neruda, César Vallejo, and Nicolás Guillén, published books of poetry on the same topic.

Less voluminous than poetry, theater was an equally important forum for social and political indoctrination. In 1936, following the lead of Russia and Germany, the Republic established the

27

Teatro de Arte y Propaganda (Theater of Art and Propaganda) to create new proletarian theater relevant to the times, which became known as the "theater of urgency." Agitprop theater groups, such as *Guerrillas Teatrales* (Guerrillas of the Theater), flourished and brought theater to a new, wider audience, including the soldiers at the front. Using small casts and simple scenery, these groups performed short, powerful, didactic, and often satirical plays, which communicated quickly and directly with the audience. The message of the plays was conveyed through a variety of styles, including caricature, distortion, the broad effects of the puppet theater, symbolism, and unvarnished realism. Alberti's *Radio Sevilla* (Radio Seville), a burlesque of Gonzalo Queipo de Llano's nightly broadcasts and of foreign intervention in the war, and Max Aub's *Pedro López García*, the story of a shepherd's gradual awakening to the significance of social revolution, are good examples of this type of theater. The titles themselves often underlined the message of the plays: Herrera Petere's *El rifle* (The Rifle), Hernández's *El refugiado* (The Refugee), Alberti's *Los salvadores de España* (The Saviors of Spain), and Germán Bleiberg's *Sombras de héroes* (Shadows of Heroes).

The Nationalists also saw the need for a new theater to promote the communion of collective ideas, but looked to the past for inspiration. They wanted theater based on tradition that would help maintain a sense of Spanish honor, and pride in Spain's theology and Catholicism. A university theater group, *La Tarumba*, staged Spanish classical plays. The Nationalist government set up the *Teatro Ambulante de Campaña* (Traveling Campaign Theater) and, in 1938, announced a special literary prize for the production of *autos sacramentales*: one-act plays in honor of the Eucharist that treated allegorically the central mysteries of Christianity.

Short stories and novellas proliferated during and after the war, but full-length novels about the war began to appear only after the end of the conflict, when participants found time to write of their experiences. More than nine hundred novels on the war have appeared in Spanish.[1] The few full novels written during the war were powerful propaganda weapons that revealed the passions and prejudices that divided Spain at the time. Ramón Sender's *The War in Spain*, *Seven Red Sundays*, and *Counterattack*, for example, contrast starkly with such Nationalist novels as Agustín de

---

1. See M. Bertrand de Muñoz, *La guerra civil española en la novela: Bibliografía comentada* (Madrid: J. Porrua Turanzas, 1982–1987).

Foxá's *Madrid, de corte a checa* (Madrid, from Court to Cheka) and Concha Espina's *Retaguardia* (Behind the Firing Line).

Printers turned out propaganda posters, making full use of new techniques in multicoloring, design, and photomontage to inspire a positive and immediate response. These posters were plastered on walls with amazing rapidity throughout the country, and their impact was considerable. Early posters were crucial in establishing abroad the heroic image of the Spanish Revolution (the Spanish Civil War was often interpreted as a revolution of the working classes) and inflaming the hopes and dreams of the international proletariat. They exalted the historical continuity of the people, the heroism of the working class against a foreign enemy who threatened the integrity and independence of the motherland. Later posters were used to press home the needs of the moment – appeals for volunteers, party membership, unity, relief for refugees, greater agricultural production; to warn of the enemies within; and to satirize the opposing forces.

Print was not the only medium used. The documentary film merged with propaganda movies like *Spanish Earth* (Ernest Hemingway and Joris Ivens) and *Spain in Flames* (Ernest Hemingway and Prudencia de Pereda). Painters and sculptors also played their part in the explosion that took place in the plastic arts. Joan Miró, Pablo Picasso, Xavier Bueno, Jesús Martí, and Aurelio Arteta threw their formidable talents behind the Republican cause, while Ignacio Zuloaga and Carlos Sáenz de Tejada painted powerful representations of Falangist ideals and achievements.

The press and radio also became extraordinarily powerful instruments of information and propaganda. Army units, political parties, trade unions, professional and cultural groups, and some branches of government all had their own publications, many with special sections for contributions from combatants. The broadcasts of Queipo de Llano, nicknamed the "Radio General," became notorious throughout Europe and anticipated future wartime radio and television broadcasts.

Most writers and artists simply synthesized the decrees and slogans of politics and propaganda. Hernández expressed a common view when he wrote that "all theater, all poetry and all art has to be, today more than ever, a weapon of war."[2] Alberti proclaimed: "I now have clearly and luminously before my eyes the cause of the

---

2. Miguel Hernández, Prologue to *Teatro en la guerra* (Valencia: Nuestro Pueblo, 1937).

people."[3] Ernesto Giménez Caballero was only one of many Nationalists who considered art as propaganda. Although some writers occasionally questioned the use of art for political purposes, the horrors of the war and the issues involved soon convinced them that new events called for a new art and a new commitment. The use of art as propaganda was encouraged by earlier controversies in post-Revolutionary Russia and pre-Nazi Germany over the role of the artist and the function of art. The debate centered on the relative importance of "pure" art and formal experimentation in the theater, championed by the Formalists, and the need for a literature of ideas and social commitment, advocated by the Social Realists and the Communists. In the 1930s these new ideas were imported to Spain by important writers like Alberti, Hernández, and Sender, who had travelled throughout Europe and who, on their return, were quick to advocate the creation of a "committed" literature that would arouse Republican fervor and garner support based on the needs of the people.

There was little room for balance or objectivity in the literature of the period: passions were too high and conviction too great. Novelists like Hemingway, who could assert that there were heroes and villains on both sides, were rare. Writers like Arturo Barea, Gustav Regler, and George Orwell, who reported their personal experiences with remarkable honesty, were even rarer. Convinced of the moral and political rightness of their cause, most writers on both sides never considered the opposite point of view. They oversimplified and romanticized the struggle, giving it a prevailing sense of apocalypse, and even created a set of myths. Republicans modelled themselves on Benito Pérez Galdós and the concept of a Marxist dialectic, which saw literature as a defense of progress and popular culture; Nationalists imitated the high-flown rhetoric of the Carlist novels of Ramón del Valle-Inclán and the Nietzchean concept of a superrace or "select minority."

Writers and artists, divided into two camps, transformed the war into an allegory, in which the major conflicts of the decade appeared as the principal adversaries. The war became a battleground between Democracy and Fascism, Communism and Catholicism, Innovation and Tradition, Civilization and Chaos. Sometimes, the conflict was presented more universally, as a struggle between East and West, Good and Evil, Light and Darkness, Life and Death. At other times, it became an endemic crisis of the

3. R. Alberti, *La arboleda perdida* (Buenos Aires: Fabril, 1959), 321.

human condition, threatening all times and all places. As a result, the literature of the period became characterized by a pronounced Manichaeism.

Early in the war, writers concentrated on sociopolitical polemics and the social revolution. As far as Republican artists were concerned, the war was a war waged by the people for the people. They believed that the common man would create a new society in which capitalism and social classes would disappear, and everyone would enjoy justice, equality, and liberty. This hope was best exemplified in Vallejo's *España, aparta de mí este cáliz* (Spain, Take This Chalice from Me), in which the historical events of the Spanish Civil War symbolize humanity's struggle to build a better world. The Spanish Republic becomes a symbol of the future socialist society in the process of construction. In his poem "Hymn to the Volunteers of the Republic," Vallejo uses biblical language and imagery and a prophetic tone to announce a new Jerusalem, born of the sacrifice of a modern-day Christ in the shape of the worker militiaman – a socialist paradise in which a united humanity working together deploys science and technology to transform and improve the conditions of life. "Mass," a poem modeled on the story of Lazarus, is a parable of the resurrection of the dead soldier by a humanity united in common love: evil will be conquered when men learn to live by the values of the Republican militiaman.

As part of the struggle for a new society, Republicans also took up the sword and pen to defend the cultural, sexual, and political revolution that was sweeping the country. The period marks the most extraordinary educational movement in Spanish history. Writers diligently advertised the Republic's extensive campaign to eradicate illiteracy and promote culture. "Cultural militias" taught more than one hundred thousand Spaniards to read and write; mobile libraries distributed thousands of books, papers, and periodicals in the trenches and the hospitals; sound systems brought theater, music, and poetry readings into the trenches; a multitude of publications were available to the people, and sought their contributions; reproductions of the most famous works of the Prado were made and transported to the front lines; bookstalls were flooded with cheap translations of Marx, Engels, Lenin, and Stalin; and literary competitions proliferated.[4]

4. For the importance of culture generally in Republican Spain, see H. Escolar, *La cultura durante la guerra civil* (Madrid: Alhambra, 1987) and J. M. Fernández Soria, *Educación y cultura en la guerra civil (España, 1936–1939)* (Valencia: Nau Libres, 1984).

31

Intellectuals saw themselves as instruments of the people, representatives of a new kind of culture. In Madrid, the Alliance of Spanish Intellectuals, a cultural group run by Alberti, organized public lectures, conferences, and evening classes throughout the siege of the city. Intellectuals organized the Second International Writers' Congress in Madrid, Barcelona, and Valencia in 1937 to draw world attention to the plight of Republican Spain. Intellectuals also published journals during the war, of which two, *El mono azul* (The Blue Overalls) and *La hora de España* (Spain's Hour), stand out.[5] The first, the magazine most committed to the cause of popular culture and solidarity between worker and intellectual, was the first to open its pages to all who wished to send in verses, and provided an example to other periodicals. The second appeared later – in the middle of the war – and best captures the frustration and anguish of the second phase of the conflict.

The motive behind the Republic's emphasis on culture was simple: culture would help the masses overcome the ignorance that had allowed them to be dominated in the past. It would enable all people to develop their capabilities to the fullest, and would improve their capacity to understand and transform the world. It was an ideal that allowed the masses to look to the future and to blot out the sad reality of the present. The Republican concept of popular culture, which was aimed at self-benefit and societal improvement, contrasted with that of the Nationalists, which defended the culture of the elite. It also differed markedly from European fascism, which had burned books and persecuted the intellectual and cultural elite, and from Spanish fascism, which had murdered Federico García Lorca, ridiculed intellectuals, and was to mark the end of the war with a public burning of books at the University of Madrid.

Women, who traditionally had been repressed by a strict moral and sexual code, also were demanding to develop to their full potential. The Anarchist organization *Libres mujeres* (Free Women) attracted twenty thousand members. Republican women expressed their freedom in different ways: they wore trousers in public, went about unchaperoned, fought alongside the militiamen in the trenches, and assumed important roles in government. They practiced birth control and in some circumstances obtained legal

5. For the role of the intellectual in the Spanish Civil War, see V. Marrero Suárez, *La guerra española y el trust de los cerebros* (Madrid: Punta Europa, 1961), M. Zambrano, *Los intelectuales en el drama de España* (Madrid: Hispamerica, 1977), and S. Salaün, *La poesía de la guerra de España* (Madrid: Castalia, 1985).

abortions. The Republic itself penalized prostitution and encouraged sexual freedom and equality. The poster campaigns against venereal disease, however, were graphic reminders of the dangers that went with the new freedoms. The Nationalists, in contrast, egged on by the Catholic hierarchy, sought a return to traditional Spanish womanliness and Catholic motherhood. Their women adopted a passive role in the war, staying at home, embroidering for their menfolk, patiently awaiting their return.

Republican poets often expressed their affirmation of freedom through their innovations in poetic form. They threw off the shackles of meter and rejected the traditional forms of lyric poetry as if they were the chains of oppression, as seen in León Felipe's "Insignia." A combination of revolutionary fervor, absolute conviction of the rightness of their cause, and a new sense of freedom seemed to release Republican art from the old bourgeois bonds.

But all these gains depended in large measure on Republican unity. That the mainspring of the Republic lay in its efforts to present a united front can be seen in the direct appeal of many writers, in a multitude of posters on the same theme printed in the first year of the war, and in the fact that most of the more than 3,400 contributors to the Republican presses were anonymous, their anonymity underlining the solidarity and community inspired by the Republican cause.[6]

Early Republican accounts of the war clearly echoed this collective spirit. They idealized the masses who rose up against the rebels in the first days of the struggle, assigning to them virtues like courage, nobility, and determination. That there were individual Spaniards who did not quite fit into this heroic mold was unimportant. What mattered was the collective whole, the masses of Spain considered as a single body. Later, during the siege of Madrid, writers eulogized the citizens as collectively representing the people in the struggle. Madrid became for Republicans the center of the world and the forge of a new consciousness and a new humanity: a symbol of martyrdom, heroism, and anti-Fascist struggle. This role was later attributed to other groups – the dead combatants of the conflict, the Spanish peasantry, the Basques, regional groups in general, women, and the International Brigades.

It was inevitable that the struggle would create some additional popular heroes. Dolores Ibarruri, "La Pasionaria"' (The Passion

---

6. See S. Salaün, *La poesía de la guerra de España*, 303–366.

Flower), whose impassioned speeches were heard throughout Spain in the early months of the war, became the subject of many writers. Other heroes included Federico García Lorca, following his murder in 1936; Pablo Picasso and Joan Miró, two stalwart supporters of the Loyalist cause; Hans Beimler,* Enrique Lister,* General José Miaja,* Lina Odena,* and Buenaventura Durruti.

Republican writers also celebrated important events of the war, such as the creation of the Fifth Regiment, the participation of the International Brigades, the battles, and the heroes. They attacked the enemy and questioned the role and scale of foreign intervention. They inveighed against the perfidious policy of nonintervention by a majority of the international community and commented on the physical and moral effects of the devastating aerial bombings by both sides, the most brutally effective of which were the celebrated raids by the Germans on Barcelona, Madrid, and Guernica. Appalled and disgusted by the barbarity of such mass killings, writers and intellectuals expressed their feelings in poems and prose that often rose above conventional statements of protest and achieved a synthesis of outraged sensibility and tragedy.

As the war approached its end, elegies on the fate of Spain, the sufferings and hardship of civil strife, doubts and uncertainties, disillusionment and despair in the face of factionalism, and on devastation and disaster become more prominent. The intensity of personal involvement had long since superseded political sloganeering, increasing the universal impact of these works. The American artist Robert Motherwell provides insight into the mood of despair of the time in a series of black and white abstractions entitled *Elegy to the Spanish Republic,* canvases filled with symbols of repression, constriction, and rigidity. More widely known and more accessible in its symbolism is Picasso's *Guernica,* which stands as the heartbreak house of Republican hopes.

Although writers increasingly reflected on the destruction of their hopes and on death, a principal motif in this final stage was death as a source of new life. With defeat staring him in the face, Hernández claimed ultimate invincibility and victory for the brave youth of Spain, who are in perpetual and vigorous motion, communicating their dynamic qualities to everything they touch. Alberti linked the theme of death and resurrection to the role of the common man in the present and future of Spain. Even if he were to die, his death was a preparation for a new, different life in the future. Writers also expressed a belief in the regeneration of

34

the dead through the recurrent process of nature. Man and land were one since the peasant was bonded to the earth he had tilled all his life. Manuel Altolaguirre, accepting the prospect of personal annihilation and a country overwhelmed by hate and death, saw hope for rebirth and a new future through the continuing existence of the land itself. In Vallejo, the treatment of the same motif was different. In "Mass" the militiaman transcended death, not through the regenerative powers of nature, but through the collective love of mankind. While the Republic was associated with the fertility and abundance of the natural world, the Nationalists were linked to ideas of sterility, captivity, and destruction. For Neruda, the forces of privilege and authority stifled growth in the earth. Vallejo likened Fascist authority to a padlock that imprisoned life in the earth itself.

Nationalist writings also heralded a new age, an age of fascism that was structured and styled on the geometric principles of classical architecture, as suggested in some of the titles of the Falangist publications of the day – *Vértice* (Vertex), *Jerarquía* (Hierarchy), and *El Escorial* (Escorial). Geometry symbolized the rational, purposeful, and orderly structure of the mind, spirit, and society that the Falangists sought to inculcate. The symmetrical properties of classical models provided the basis of a new social edifice that was designed to convey an image of unity, totality, order, discipline, and grandeur. Above all, the emphasis was on order – a social hierarchy in which every member's place and responsibilities were clear, and in which the masses served and the elite ruled.

Falangist poets even established a hierarchy of poetic forms, favoring the more difficult and elaborate sonnets and odes over the common *romance* or ballad, which was the preferred form of Republican poets. The fragmentation of aesthetic unity espoused by such artists as Joyce and Picasso was rejected along with artistic nihilism, liberal democratic institutions, and individual freedom, all of which were replaced with discipline, hierarchy, and paternalistic authority.

Religion helped unify this hierarchical structure of Spanish fascism. A constant in Nationalist writings was the symbiosis between the military and religion, reflected in inscriptions in churches: "Caídos por Dios y por Patria" (Fallen for God and the Fatherland). The war became a crusade to restore the authority and power of the Church that had been broken under the Republic; a crusade to drive the infidels (Jews and Russians) from Spain; and a crusade to destroy materialism, which had subverted the country's spiritual values. The war was assimilated to an ecstatic and mystical vision: God, the Virgin, and the Saints rescued the Nationalist cause; José Antonio Primo de Rivera became a martyr to the cause, a second Redeemer, transmitting and revealing to the Spanish people his political and military vision; Franco was God's chosen Savior of the Spanish nation – an apotheosis maximized in Falangist propaganda; and the ordinary soldier became a crusader and martyr to God's cause who did not "die" in battle but "fell," and went to the starry firmament to stand guard over the stars on the right-hand side of José Antonio. Falangists found it difficult to define the role of the Moors, Germans, and Italians in this crusade because this rigid mythology did not allow them a part.

Republicans countered this religious emphasis by attacking the power, exploitation, and hypocrisy of the Church; by exalting the Christian values of love, equality, and brotherhood, a key part of their own ideology; and by using religious imagery and dogma to ironic effect. In his poem "Insignia," León Felipe uses the teachings of the Bible to expose the hypocrisy of the Church in its dealings with the people. In the poem "The Tower of El Carpio," Altolaguirre uses religious imagery ironically to underline the violence of the Church. Marxist and Christian imagery coexist in Neruda and Vallejo, offering examples of Christian brotherhood rarely found in the Falangist literature of the time. Consider, for example, José María Pemán's Manichaean "Poema de la bestia y el ángel" (Poem of the Beast and the Angel), in which the dead of both sides appear at first to be equal, until we are told that God knows their names and will separate them at heaven's gate according to their political allegiance.

Catholicism formed an integral part of another key concept of Falange literature: tradition – that is, nobility, property, hierarchy, authority, and other values of the past, all of which had been threatened by the advent of the Republic. The Republic was concerned with the present and the future, but Nationalist ideology looked back, seeking to restore the myth of an idealized past. The future the Nationalists envisaged was, in fact, the past.

Nostalgia for a new empire and a new age of greatness were further elements drawn from the past. Although never fully defined as a concept, empire was often an attempt to establish a Spanish mystique, a Spanish way of being. It promoted the ideal of national unity by sublimating class struggle into a great, common goal: the restoration of Spain to a new Golden Age, with Franco as its architect. If Republicans dismissed Franco as a fascist and military dictator, his own supporters compared him to the legendary El Cid, who had fought against the Moors and had helped the Christian kings reconquer Spain from the infidels. He became a cult figure, in contradistinction to the Republican emphasis on the masses of the people and the common man. José Antonio was converted into another such hero, idealized as the martyr, the poet, the transcendent reference, and the perfect symbol.

The poetic arsenal of the Right also included constant allusions to the Reconquest, the Crusades, the *conquistadores*, and the Escorial. To bolster further the righteousness of their position, the Nationalists described themselves as direct heirs to the Catholic kings and enlisted great figures of the past to their cause: Velázquez, Cortés, Pizarro, Santa Teresa, and San Juan de la Cruz. Indeed, such names, shouted in an intoxicating manner, served for a time as a substitute for ideology.

The Nationalists regarded war and violence as a natural corollary of empire and national unity. A cult of violence in their literature stood opposed to the Republican portrayal of the war as a painful necessity and as a stubborn defense of man's right to equality, justice, and dignity. War was essential to gain empire and impose the Nationalist ideology at home; violence was necessary to eradicate their enemies within the nation. Violence, both physical and verbal, was directed at all those who opposed Nationalist ideology. Preaching a "dialectic of fists and pistols," Fascist writers were aggressively antidemocratic, anti-*pueblo*, anti-Marxist, anti-Semitic, and anti-intellectual. They purged the universities and schools. They excoriated the Free Institute of Learning, writers of the Generation of 1898, and Republican intellectuals for gnawing away at the spiritual greatness of Spain, for advocating the Europeanization of Spain, for proclaiming Spain's backwardness, for decrying the emphasis on her past, and for bringing about the advent of the Second Republic. They dismissed their opponents as unpatriotic descendants of the Encyclopaedists, as enemies of Spain's traditions, as disciples of Marx and Engels, as creators of the detested vanguard movements in art and literature, and as founders of the Second Republic. Their rabid hatred was more psychotic fantasy than objective criticism. Insisting on *hispanidad*, tradition, and Catholicism, they brought into sharp focus the age-old struggle in Spain between the real and the ideal, the traditional and the progressive, the native and the foreign.

War and violence were not enough, however, to secure national unity and imperial grandeur. A strong leader, authoritarian rule, a cultured elite, and a youth committed to and eager for action were also necessary. Nationalist writers were convinced that Franco and the traditional establishment of Spain provided all these requirements.

Nationalist literature was pervaded by an aura of romance. War was a sport, a game to be enjoyed. Their heroes were all young, all prepared to die, and all guided by the light, constantly on the alert and surrounded by astral bodies and pathways through the stars. Their heroines were in the hyper-Romantic tradition – ideal representations, passive, beautiful, elegant, virginal, loyal, and patient – in complete contrast to the Republican militiawomen, whom they regarded as immoral and shameless. It was a literature of propaganda pitched at the emotions: rhetoric won over style, words distorted and falsified, images were substitutes for concepts, and emotion replaced logic. Emphasizing ritual and rhetoric, repetition and affirmation, pageant and spectacle, writers conjured up the spirit of nationalism and nurtured racial pride. They instilled a respect for tradition and created a mood for war, glorifying such concepts as heroism, grandeur, and destiny. It was a literature limited in language, form, and message, which offered less nuances than the writings of the other side, where there was much greater diversity of political and social opinion. However, few works, on either side, achieved a balanced appraisal of the event.

The Republic fell in 1939, crushing the hopes and illusions of countless Spaniards. Workers were left to face the grim reality of Franco's repression and vengeance, and intellectuals were left to roam the earth with their dreams, their ideals, and their hopes. What kind of writing did so heartstirring an event produce? Not surprisingly, much of it was amateurish and bad, even by journalistic standards, no more than propaganda. Nevertheless, the writings on the Spanish Civil War are of great historical significance. They constitute an essential and authentic revolutionary corpus that can be analyzed and appreciated only in the context of this process. Even if the historical value of this literature often overrides its intrinsic literary worth, this does not lessen its importance as a repository – at once exciting, hopeful, and sad – of the social and political attitudes of a generation of writers.

Anthology of Texts

Historical Documents

Guidelines of the Falange; the 26 points
NATION. UNITY. EMPIRE.

I. We believe in the supreme reality of Spain. The urgent collective task of all Spaniards is to strengthen, elevate, and aggrandize the nation. All individual, group, or class interests must be subordinated without question to the accomplishment of this task.

II. Spain is an indivisible destiny in universal terms. Any conspiracy against this indivisible whole is repulsive. All separatism is a crime we shall not forgive.

    The prevailing Constitution, insofar as it encourages disintegration, offends against the indivisible nature of Spain's destiny. We therefore demand its immediate repeal.

III. We are committed to Empire. We declare that Spain's historical fulfillment is the Empire. We demand for Spain a prominent position in Europe. We shall not tolerate international isolation or foreign interference.

    Regarding the countries of Spanish America, our aim is the unification of culture, economic interests, and power. Spain claims that its role as the spiritual axis of the Spanish-speaking world entitles it to a position of preeminence in world affairs.

IV. Our armed forces – on land, at sea, and in the air – must be sufficiently strong and efficient to ensure at all times for Spain total independence and a world status that befits the nation. We shall give back to the land, sea, and air forces all the public dignity they merit, and we shall see to it that a similar martial outlook pervades the whole of Spanish life.

V. Spain will look again to the sea routes for her glory and her wealth. Spain will aim to become a great seafaring power, for times of danger and for the sake of trade.

    We demand for the Fatherland equal status among navies and on the air routes.

THE STATE. THE INDIVIDUAL. FREEDOM.

VI. Ours will be a totalitarian State in the service of the Fatherland's integrity. All Spaniards will play a part therein through their membership in families, municipalities and trade unions. No one shall play a part therein through a political party. The system of political parties will be resolutely abolished, together with all its corollaries: inorganic suffrage, representation by conflicting factions, and the Cortes as we know it.

VII.   Human dignity, the integrity of the individual, and individual freedom are eternal and intangible values.

But the only way to be really free is to be part of a strong and free nation.

No one will be permitted to use his freedom against the unity, the strength, and the freedom of the Fatherland. A rigorous discipline will prevent any attempt to poison or split the Spanish people, or to incite them to go against the destiny of the Fatherland.

VIII.   The National-Syndicalist State will permit any private initiative that is compatible with the collective interest and, indeed, will protect and stimulate those that are beneficial.

THE ECONOMY. WORK. THE CLASS STRUGGLE.

IX.   In the economic sphere, we think of Spain as one huge syndicate of all those engaged in production. In order to serve national economic integrity we shall organize Spanish society along corporative lines by creating a system of vertical unions that will represent the various branches of production.

X.   We reject the capitalist system, which disregards the needs of the people, dehumanizes private property, and transforms the workers into shapeless masses that are prone to misery and despair. Our spiritual and national awareness likewise repudiates Marxism. We shall channel the drive of the working classes, that are nowadays led astray by Marxism, by demanding their direct participation in the formidable task of the national State.

XI.   The National-Syndicalist State will not stand cruelly aloof from economic conflicts between men, nor will it look on impassively as the strongest class subjugates the weakest. Our regime will make class struggle totally impossible, since all those cooperating in production will constitute an organic whole therein.

We deplore and shall prevent at all costs the abuses of partial vested interests, as well as anarchy in the workforce.

XII.   The primary purpose of wealth is to improve the standard of living of all the people – and this will be the declared policy of our State. It is intolerable that great masses of people live in poverty while a few enjoy every luxury.

XIII. The State will recognize private property as a legitimate means of attaining individual, family, and social ends, and will protect it against being abused by high finance, speculators, and moneylenders.

XIV. We shall defend the move toward nationalization of banking and the takeover of the major public services by corporations.

XV. All Spanish citizens have the right to work. The public institutions will provide adequate maintenance for those who are involuntarily out of work.

While we are moving toward the new overall structure, we shall retain and increase all the advantages the workers derive from current social legislation.

XVI. Every Spaniard who is not an invalid is duty bound to work. The National-Syndicalist State will not have the slightest regard for those who do not fulfill any function but who expect to live like guests at the expense of other people's efforts.

THE LAND

XVII. As a matter of urgency we must raise the standard of living in the rural areas, on which Spain will always depend for her food. For this reason, we commit ourselves to the strict implementation of an economic and social reform of agriculture.

XVIII. As part of our economic reform, we shall strengthen agricultural production by means of the following measures:

By guaranteeing all farmers an adequate minimum price for their produce.

By seeing to it that much of what is nowadays absorbed by the cities in payment for their intellectual and commercial services is returned to the land, in order to endow rural areas sufficiently.

By organizing a real system of national agricultural credit that will lend farmers money at low rates of interest, thereby guaranteeing their possessions and harvests and freeing them from usury and patronage.

By spreading education pertaining to matters of agriculture and animal husbandry.

By rationalizing production according to the suitability of the land and the outlets available for its products.

By promoting a protectionist tariff policy covering agriculture and the raising of cattle.

By speeding up the construction of a hydraulic network.

By rationalizing landholdings in order to eliminate both vast estates that are not fully exploited and smallholdings that are uneconomic by reason of their low yield.

XIX. We shall achieve a social organization of agriculture by means of the following measures:

By redistributing once again all the arable land to promote family holdings and by giving farmers every encouragement to join the union.

By rescuing from their present poverty the masses of people who are exhausting themselves scratching on barren soil, and by transferring them to new holdings of arable land.

XX. We shall launch a tireless campaign of reforestation and stockbreeding, imposing severe sanctions on whomever obstructs it, and even resorting temporarily to the enforced mobilization of all Spanish youth for the historic task of rebuilding our country's wealth.

XXI. The State will have powers to confiscate without compensation any land, the ownership of which has been acquired or enjoyed illicitly.

XXII. A priority of the National-Syndicalist State will be to return to villages their communal property.

NATIONAL EDUCATION. RELIGION.

XXIII. It is a fundamental mission of the State to impose a rigorous discipline on education that will produce a strong, united, national spirit and fill the souls of future generations with joy and pride in their Fatherland.

All men will receive preliminary training to prepare them for the honor of admission to Spain's national forces.

XXIV. Culture will be organized in such a way that no talent will be lost for lack of finance. All those who are deserving will have easy access even to higher education.

XXV. Our Movement* integrates the Catholic spirit, which has been traditionally glorious and predominant in Spain, into the reconstruction of the nation.

Church and State will come to an agreement on the areas of their respective powers, but any interference from the

Church or any activity likely to undermine the dignity of the State or the integrity of the nation will not be tolerated.

THE NATIONAL REVOLUTION

XXVI. The Spanish Falange of the JONS wants the establishment of a new order based on the foregoing principles. To overcome the resistance of the present regime, the Spanish Falange aims at a national revolution.

Its style will be trenchant, ardent, and militant. Life is a militia and must be lived in a spirit purified by service and sacrifice.

— José Antonio Primo de Rivera
November 1934

[In José Antonio Primo de Rivera, *Obras completas*. Translated here by Alun Kenwood.]

Manifesto of the Bloque Nacional, 1935

An unavoidable sense of national duty compels the *Bloque Nacional* to seek the support of public opinion in its deep desire to awaken a trusting Spanish society to the real dangers that surround and threaten her.

The magnificent effort made in this country by the conservative classes in 1933 has not met with the success that was expected. This is not the time to engage in a retrospective analysis, even though it would expose easily the repeated tactic of bargaining and compromises that resulted in the evident frustration of their hopes. The truth remains that, in the end, we shall have to face up to the central problem confronting Spain, in all its enormous gravity, and perhaps in conditions even worse than those of 1933. This simple statement reveals the transcendant importance of the historic hour in which we are living.

In the aftermath of last April's crisis we stated: "Some have dreamt of steering the Republic closer to the principles of a genuine Right. Yet, as recent experience confirms, although the Republic opens up for the Left an ever-expanding horizon, for the Right it is an endless barrier. For the Republic is not a system of government, but a doctrine. An old, decadent and anti-Spanish doctrine."

46

Today, we can add that revolution, inseparable from the regime that inevitably spawned it and that will destroy it, has shown its true antipatriotic and virulent colors in the course of the coup d'état attempted by communist and separatist forces last October. As yet, full responsibility for the consequences of this coup has not been determined by the courts. But there are some judges and public prosecutors who currently are demanding or favoring the dissolution of those political parties and organizations involved in the revolution. In spite of this, the central Government, paralyzed by its own weakness, shrugs its shoulders and abandons the resolute defense of the important national interests entrusted to it. In 1935 revolution triumphed, achieving one of the goals it set for itself in 1934, namely, to sweep CEDA out of ministerial office. And it has succeeded [deleted by censor] in artificially dismembering the true counterrevolutionary forces that are represented in parliament. We are not at all surprised by this. We foresaw it, although we could not prevent it. Others were in a position to prevent it, but could not foresee it, because they were caught up in a notorious immobilizing political deadlock.

Today, revolution is menacing and roaring through Spain. Never is the risk greater than when it hypocritically assumes an appearance of legality. When it is out in the open, revolutionary Marxism is less dangerous than when it adopts a guise of reason and democracy. While the former aspires to destroy the fortress from without, the latter does the same from within with no less fury, and with no less destructive power. It would be sheer madness to provide it with the means necessary to carry out such a criminal design. But, by its very nature, the State as we know it lacks the necessary strength to save us from this disease. For this reason the *Bloque Nacional* once again calls the attention of the country to the imperative need for the creation of a new kind of State, a State that, out of respect for human freedom in its most noble form, will nip in the bud the shame and destruction that separatism and Marxism will bring. The present type of State, even if it were to be headed by a monarch, would be powerless and no better able to resist the enemy than the Republic, despite the obvious advantages of unity and continuity that a monarchy enjoys. The periodical call for elections will bring us to a state of total disarray if, every time they are held, the country has to resolve, in the space of eight hours of feverish electoral tension, the problem of its own existence – not simply insubstantial, procedural questions over which disagreements would have less serious implications.

47

Therefore, it is crucial for us to ensure that the next struggle is the definitive one, on the assumption that the Right will win. The Left has already set itself the same goal, in unequivocal slogans and crystal-clear announcements.

In the recent past, there has been no dearth of opportunities for a full implementation of counterrevolutionary principles. Sadly, these opportunities have been squandered. The reason for this has been the failure of many to grasp fully the political situation; they think that they are engaged in a series of minor skirmishes, when in reality the present political conflict is nothing less than visceral. A section of Spanish public opinion remains unmoved by the imminent danger. It cannot imagine the full extent of the terrible consequences that a victory of the extreme Left would bring. Therefore, it fails to see the imperative need to take immediate action, and to prevent a similar situation from developing in the future. An effective counterrevolution cannot be forged through street fighting, but only through parliamentary and governmental action. It is high time to stop admiring the principles while declaring the conclusions abhorrent. [. . .] We must be consistent and repudiate the causes just as we repudiate their effects.

The *Bloque Nacional* has defined its policies with vigor. It wants a new State, although it is new only to those who follow the rusty principles of Rousseau. In fact, what we want is an old, time-honored State with roots in the history of Spain. This State, which will respect all differences between individuals and provinces, must have the strength to extirpate the anti-national forces that, like a disease, threaten to sap the life of the Fatherland. Therefore, it must be an authoritarian, corporatist, and unifying State. The free-for-all of party politics, which we all view with loathing, never can produce effective institutions or bring honor into the life of its people. More than twenty parliamentary crises and more than eighty government ministers in the last four-and-a-half years – the Agriculture portfolio changed hands five times in 1935 – [deleted by censor] No contrast is more demoralizing than the one between the productive classes of this country, laboring to improve the national economy, and the political parties that spend their time in a perverse struggle for the precarious positions of power, not in order to realize great national ideals, but to divide up sinecures and create fateful oligarchies.

There is no light along this path. On the contrary, only darkness looms on the horizon. A determined effort is required to clear away these shadows and usher in a brilliant and happy tomorrow. The new State will destroy forever old myths and unhealthy prejudices, restoring to all Spaniards peace and order. This task demands, as a first step, the formation of a wide coalition of counterrevolutionary forces, acting on a well-defined platform, with goals reaching beyond election day, that will enable those elected to pursue with total unanimity the full implementation of its policies in parliament.

Such a platform must have as its foundation the replacement of the 1931 Constitution, whose legal status has already been undermined [deleted by censor], as well as the extirpation of Marxism, separatism, and laicism [the exclusion of ecclesiastical influence] from national life [. . .] It will require determination, so that Spain can be saved by decisive action based on her immortal traditions.

The *Bloque Nacional* Committee, Madrid
25 December 1935

[Reprinted in F. Díaz-Plaja, *La guerra de España en sus documentos.* Translated here by Alun Kenwood]

The Manifesto of Revolutionary Socialism
General Observations

In the light of the profound changes that have been taking place in recent years in the economic structures of almost every country, and the equally extraordinary social and political mutations that Spain has undergone as a result of the restoration of the Republic in 1931 and its vicissitudes, it is necessary to review the program of the Workers' Socialist party, both in its theoretical fundamentals and the methods required to achieve them.

Paragraph four of the old program stated: "Necessity, reason, and justice demand that inequality and antagonism between classes should disappear, be it through reform or through the destruction of the social conditions responsible for them." We must put an end to the illusion that the proletarian socialist revolution can be brought about through the reform of present social conditions, i.e., that the transformation of private and corporate ownership of the means of production into common ownership by the whole society will result in the abolition of all classes and their fusion into a single community of workers. There is no other alternative but to destroy and rebuild society from its foundations.

The illusion of reformism, the hope that a capitalist society

49

might be transformed into a socialist society through gradual reform, can be explained, though not justified, by the expansion of capitalism, especially during its imperialist phase. The huge benefits obtained through the exploitation of the colonies and protectorates enabled the proletariat to snatch increasing economic benefits from the ruling class and, in general, more favorable living conditions. As a result, the working class was led to believe in the possibility of constant consolidation and improvement of its own position, and in the eventual prospect of depriving the bourgeoisie of its privileges while remaining within and working through the bourgeois legal system.

Today, this illusion appears to be a complete chimera. Capitalism is on the decline. From a phase of expansion it has shifted to one of contraction and defensiveness, for two main reasons. One is the progressive industrialization of the colonies and semicolonial countries, as a result of which the importation of products manufactured abroad has decreased, thus paralyzing a considerable part of the economy of the most developed capitalist countries and creating a pool of permanently unemployed, which is irredeemable within the capitalist system.

The second cause is technological progress. On the one hand, this eliminates labor, replacing it with machines and condemning huge numbers of workers to forced unemployment. On the other, it floods the market with excess products, which, because of unemployment and the consequent decrease in purchasing power throughout the world, results in unrealistic prices, the bankruptcy of many capitalist industries, and a corresponding increase in the number of unemployed workers. The current economic crisis is not a passing or cyclical one, as in the past, but appears with permanent features and tends to worsen by the day rather than stabilize.

This crisis allows only two solutions: one, which is provisional and goes against history and the nature of things, namely fascism; and the other, which is the natural, definitive, historically determined solution, namely socialism. In essence, fascism entails the annihilation of bourgeois democracy to deprive the working class more easily of its material gains and the political and trade union rights that it won within the framework of that democracy. In other words, the subjection of the working class once again to the conditions of servitude that prevailed in precapitalist times.

Fascism represents a regression of several centuries in human history. It is naked dictatorship, stripped of any democratic and parliamentary facade, by which the higher forms of capitalism seek to cover their own losses and avoid final bankruptcy by simply enslaving the working class. It is the brutal and unequivocal answer given by the bourgeoisie to those gullible enough to believe in the radical transformation of society through gradual reform. In fascism, there is no room for freedom or reform. There are only working days as long and salaries as low as the capitalist class wishes to make them. There is only poverty or misery. No rights, just obligations. No freedom, just political and social despotism.

In addition, fascism inevitably leads to war, which it uses to avoid or delay internal social revolution in the hope of an external victory that will divert the attention of the local proletariat away from its own problems and, at the same time, shift onto the workers of the defeated nations a part of the burden of serfdom, which is now the lot of its own proletariat. Fascist war is a political and economic necessity, whereby the bourgeoisie, after enslaving and almost exhausting the resources of its own working class, seeks to transfer to the workers of other countries the losses and burdens of its own state of bankruptcy.

The alternative solution to the current economic crisis is revolutionary socialism. In some countries bourgeois democracy already has fulfilled its historic mission. In other countries where this has not been so, it will be difficult for the bourgeoisie to hold its own, unassisted, against the capitalist forces that aim to destroy and replace it with a totalitarian fascist State. The proletariat is the only class in a position to stop fascism. However, wherever this struggle may take place – and it is already happening in all countries, either openly or covertly – the proletariat must not content itself with defending bourgeois democracy. Instead, it must seek to take over political power by whatever means possible, with a view to achieving its own socialist revolution, a full and humane democracy: a classless democracy.

In order to repress any resistance of the exploiting class, prevent all attempts to restore private capitalism, and destroy both the infrastructure and superstructure of the existing social order, the system of government that will prevail during the period of transition from a capitalist society to a socialist one will be the dictatorship of the proletariat.

Dictatorship, however, does not necessarily mean, as many believe, arbitrariness and lawless violence. Just as bourgeois democracy will be the legal dictatorship of the bourgeoisie against the other classes (the aristocracy in the past, and now the proletariat), the workers' democracy is the legal dictatorship of the proletariat against the remnants of the aristocracy and against the bourgeoisie. In other words, even if it be a dictatorship, the dictatorship of the proletariat will be at the same time the most perfect and extensive democratic system ever implemented in History because, for the first time, the largest class, the working class, will be in command, and the rights of workers will be not a formality, as is now the case in bourgeois democracies. Rather, the proletarian State will provide the material means for the realization of those rights: buildings for the holding of cultural and political meetings; newspapers and other means that might serve to spread knowledge and culture; economic freedom in order to elect freely and revoke at any time public office, ranging from the head of State to public officials, judges, military officers, etc.

Equality for all, regardless of race, sex, religion, or nationality, will be unrestricted. All colonies, as well as provinces, will be granted the right to political self-determination, even the right to secede. Step by step, the dictatorship of the proletariat (that is, the workers' democracy) will become a fully developed, classless democracy, in which State coercion gradually will disappear. The Socialist party will be the organ of such a dictatorship and will remain so for as long as the transition from one society to another may last, and for as long as the threats from the surrounding capitalist States may warrant the existence of a strong proletarian State. [. . .]

In order to accomplish this, it is essential to achieve the immediate unification of all revolutionary forces through the fusion, on the political and trade union fronts, of all workers' groups, and the complete divorce of the Socialist party from any reformist or centrist tendency. [. . .]

For all these reasons, and considering:

that this society is unjust, because it divides its members into two unequal and antagonistic classes, one, the bourgeoisie, which, by possessing the instruments of work, dominates the other;
that the economic subjection of the proletariat is the primary cause of exploitation in all its forms: social poverty, intellectual degradation, and political dependence;
that the privileges of the bourgeoisie are guaranteed by the government in power, which it uses to dominate the proletariat;
that necessity, reason, and justice demand that inequality and antagonism between classes must disappear through the destruction of the

social state that produces them;

that this can be achieved only by transforming individual or corporate ownership of the means of production into common ownership by society as a whole;

that political power, which the bourgeoisie uses to prevent the restoration of our rights, must be the means by which the proletariat destroys the obstacles that prevent the transformation of ownership;

the Socialist party therefore states as its immediate objectives:

1. The conquest of political power by the working class by any means at its disposal.
2. The transfer of individual or corporate ownership of the means of production to collective, social, or common ownership.

    In the period of transition from a capitalist to a socialist society, the form of government will be the dictatorship of the proletariat, organized as a workers' democracy.

    (By the term "means of production," we mean land, mines, transport, factories, machines, cash, banks, and large capitalist organizations – unions, trusts, cartels, etc.)
3. The organization of society based on an economic federation, the collectivization of the means of production, the guarantee to satisfy the needs of all its members as far as the resources of the society allow, and the access of every individual of both sexes to all general, scientific, and professional education. [...]

In short, the ideal of the Workers' Socialist party is the complete emancipation of the working class; that is to say, the abolition of all social classes and the creation of a single class of workers, all of whom are free, equal, educated, and useful to society.

The Workers' Socialist party considers the following political and economic measures necessary for the achievement of its aims:

POLITICAL

Freedom of the press. The right to demonstrate, petition, hold meetings, and form associations. The right to form unions and political parties.

The formation of a confederation of Iberian nations, including the present protectorate of Morocco, and the recognition of the right of all nationalities to political self-determination at any time, including independence. The abolition of the official, obligatory State language[1] and equality of rights for all languages spoken within the Iberian confederation.

1. The official language was Castilian Spanish.

Individual security. The inviolability of correspondence and the home. The impossibility of suspending Constitutional guarantees.

Universal suffrage for both sexes from the age of twenty-one, and after only six months of residence; guarantees of secret ballots; the removal of obstacles to the nomination of candidates by making a notary's[2] authorization a free official service.

All political posts to be salaried.

The suppression of all provincial councils.

The abolition of permanent armies and the general arming of the people.

The exclusive right of civilians to hold ministerial office.

The prohibition of civil and political posts being held by the military.

The abolition of the clergy's budget, the confiscation of all their goods, and the dissolution of all religious orders.

Free legal aid. A jury for all offenses. The abolition of the death penalty. Tenure for members of the judiciary until the nomination of judges by election is established.

A revision of the Code of Military Justice. The application of military justice only in times of war and only for military crimes committed by military personnel.

Effective criminal liability by employers for breaches of social legislation.

Free, technical, and lay education at all levels.

ECONOMIC

A legal maximum of forty hours per working week for adults. The prohibition of work for those younger than the age of sixteen, and the reduction of the working day to six hours for those aged sixteen to eighteen. Two days off per week and three weeks' paid annual leave.

A minimum legal wage. Equal wages for workers of both sexes.

The prohibition of work for women that is morally or physically harmful.

Work inspections to be carried out by State-paid delegates at the request of workers' societies.

The establishment of obligatory insurance against work accidents, sickness, disability, old age, and retrenchment.

Laws ensuring hygiene and security at work.

2. A notary is a public official who draws up and witnesses legal documents of all kinds.

Laws protecting children.

The total reform of the penitentiary system and the regulation of prison work.

The abolition of piecework. The reform of tenancy and eviction laws. Houses for workers.

Worker control in all industrial and commercial establishments.

FINANCIAL

The nationalization of the banking system. The abolition of all indirect taxes. A progressive tax on unearned income over six thousand pesetas. The taxation of land, not according to what it produces but according to what it is capable of producing. Abolition of the public debt. Nationalization of mines, water, weapons production, transport, and land, except for those small plots cultivated by the owners or their families. The reversion of all monopolies to the State.

MUNICIPAL PROGRAM

A minimum wage and maximum working day for all municipal workers and employees, full-time and casual.

The abolition of indirect taxation. Taxes on the increased value of property due to urbanization.

Political and administrative self-government. Free washing facilities and public toilets. The provision of school canteens, summer camps, and free school clothing.

Free medical assistance and pharmaceutical services.

Lodging and food for temporary workers. Houses for the aged and invalids, with an obligation to provide everything necessary for the professional education of invalids. Child centers for the children of workers during working hours.

The creation of meeting halls.

General services to be taken over by city councils.

Each and every one of the above measures represents a partial victory, a minor success that will enable us to realize our fundamental objective: the conquest of political power and the conversion of property to collective and common ownership.

— Reform project of the Spanish Worker's Socialist party
March 1936

[Originally published in the Spanish Socialist newspaper *Claridad*, 19 March 1936. Reprinted in F. Díaz-Plaja, *La guerra de España en sus documentos*. Translated here by Alun Kenwood.]

Manifesto by General Francisco Franco, 17 July 1936

Spaniards! The nation calls to her defense all those of you who hear the holy name of Spain, those in the ranks of the Army and Navy who have made a profession of faith in the service of the Motherland, all those who swore to defend her to the death against her enemies. The situation in Spain grows more critical every day; anarchy reigns in most of the countryside and towns; government-appointed authorities encourage revolts, when they do not actually lead them; murderers use pistols and machine guns to settle their differences and to treacherously assassinate innocent people, while the public authorities fail to impose law and order. Revolutionary strikes of all kinds paralyze the life of the nation, destroying its sources of wealth and creating hunger, forcing working men to the point of desperation. The most savage attacks are made upon national monuments and artistic treasures by revolutionary hordes who obey the orders of foreign governments, with the complicity and negligence of local authorities. The most serious crimes are committed in the cities and countryside, while the forces that should defend public order remain in their barracks, bound by blind obedience to those governing authorities that are intent on dishonoring them. The Army, Navy, and other armed forces are the target of the most obscene and slanderous attacks, which are carried out by the very people who should be protecting their prestige. Meanwhile, martial law is imposed to gag the nation, to hide what is happening in its towns and cities, and to imprison alleged political opponents.

The Constitution, effectively violated and disregarded by all, is in total eclipse; there is neither equality before the law, nor liberty unfettered by tyranny; there is no fraternity when hatred and violence have taken the place of mutual respect; nor is there unity in our Fatherland, which is threatened with territorial disintegration even more than by the regionalism that has been encouraged by public government; nor is the integrity of our borders being defended, when in the heart of Spain foreign radio broadcasts are heard announcing the destruction and division of our land. The judiciary, whose independence is guaranteed by the Constitution, is the object of persecution, and serious attacks are being made on its independence. Electoral pacts, made at the expense of the integrity of our own Nation, together with assaults on civil governments and strong boxes in order to falsify electoral documents, make up the mask of legality that presided over us.

[. . .]

All kinds of authorities, whose slackness and negligence are protected by a bungling central government, lack the authority and standing to impose order upon the domain of freedom and justice, and contribute to the rebellious and unthinking attitude of the masses, who have been tricked and exploited by Soviet agents who hide from them the bloody realities of a regime that sacrificed twenty-five million people for its own survival.

Can we permit one more day of this shameful spectacle we are presenting to the world? Can we abandon Spain to the enemies of the Motherland and, in an act of cowardice and treachery, surrender her without so much as a struggle?

No! Let traitors do so, but not we who have sworn to defend her.

We offer: justice and equality before the law.

Peace and love among Spaniards; liberty and fraternity, free from licentiousness and tyranny.

Work for all, social justice, brought about without rancor or violence, and an equitable and progressive distribution of wealth, without destroying or endangering the health of the national economy.

But, against this, we shall wage a war without quarter upon political manipulators who deceive the honest worker, and against foreigners and foreign sympathizers who, either openly or by deceit, are trying to destroy Spain.

Today the whole of Spain is rising up to demand peace, fraternity, and justice. In every province of the country, the Army, the Navy, and forces of public order are rising up to defend the Motherland.

The force that will be used to maintain order will be proportionate to the magnitude of the resistance encountered.

Our action is not motivated by the defense of illegitimate interests, nor by any desire to turn back the clock of History, because each and every one of our institutions must guarantee a minimum of cooperation among the citizens who, in spite of the illusions of so many and in spite of the compromises and understanding of all national organizations, have tasted anarchy and, seeing its fraudulence, know that it cannot be tolerated.

Just as the purity of our intentions prevents us from reversing those gains that represent a real advance in the political and social area, so a spirit of hatred and vengeance has no home in our breasts. From the inevitable shipwreck that some legislative experiments will suffer, we shall know how to save whatever is compatible with the internal peace of Spain and its longed-for greatness. For the first time in the history of our Motherland we will create a reality of the trilogy – and in this order: fraternity, liberty, and equality.

Spaniards: Long live Spain! Long live the honorable Spanish people!

— General Francisco Franco
Tetuán, 17 July 1936

[Originally published in *ABC*, Seville edition, 23 July 1936. Reprinted in F. Díaz-Plaja, *La guerra de España en sus documentos*. Translated here by Alun Kenwood.]

Speech by the Monarchist Poet José María Pemán*

Sevillians, Spaniards [. . .] . The severe Lent of our Homeland has finally passed. Today the purple veil that was thrown over its true face has been torn away. Today is the Easter of Spain's resurrection. Because today you, our old flag, have returned. You have arrived with the timeliness of a nurse, at a time of sorrow and solace; with a bride's punctuality, just as we grew too impatient to wait any longer. You have arrived just when you were supposed to arrive: neither early nor late. Not early, because it would have been a sacrilege for you to preside over Spain's ignominy. Not late, because it would have been cruelty for you to miss the glorious moment of her resurrection. [. . .] Your arrival was legislated by God, like the dawn. Furthermore, you did not arrive unexpectedly . . . We could feel you coming, just as one feels spring coming. You were preceded by a renewal of the old Spanish virtues that seemed to be lying dormant. Amid the snow of that cold, anticlerical, and antinational winter that had afflicted us, all the birds of long ago suddenly began to sing again. All those members of true Spain stood up, fired by a strong desire for salvation. The whole of Spain was shaken by waves that told of the heroic feats of yore. Here three soldiers defended themselves alone, starving in a turret; over there was a Civil Guard who, repeating the exploits of Guzmán the Good,[3] preferred his son to be killed rather than sur-

3. Guzmán the Good is the name by which the thirteenth-century patriotic hero Alonso Pérez Guzmán is popularly known. He allowed his own son to be killed by the besieging forces rather than cede the town of Tarifa he was defending. His action symbolized the Spanish ideal of boundless loyalty to one's Monarch, and it inspired a number of poems and plays in succeeding centuries.

58

render; here a general was laughing through a microphone, while his heart was weeping. Everywhere there are tales of heroism. The telephone lines trembled with them like the strings of a harp. Telegrams and official communiqués were full of chronicles of bravery. All the airwaves heard of our History. There was a sense that something was about to happen . . . And that something was your return, my beloved flag, and your coming could be felt just like the coming of spring can be felt [. . .]. How welcome you are! Now our heroes have a worthy ensign! Now our martyrs have a worthy shroud! Because this change of colors is not simply an imposing ceremony but an accurate reflection of a deeper truth. Official Spain which persecuted us – the burner of churches, reaper of crosses, assassin of her best men – that was not true Spain. That was an invading army which had camped in our official institutions. We already knew this. But now, suddenly, in the crude reality of war, how much more glaring this shamelessness has become. Once unmasked, the antinational nature of those who governed us, who had sold their souls to foreign powers, can be seen plainly in all its nakedness. They were transients of History, temporary workers and scabs outside real Spain, totally lacking in responsibility and national sentiment, who, when confronted with a blunt choice, did not hesitate to surrender Spain before surrendering themselves. They bombed the Pilar of Saragossa and the Alhambra of Granada with the same coldness a Turk or Ukrainian would display, because they were totally unmoved by all that those great lyrical stones signify and represent. [. . .] This is why the war we are fighting against them is not a contest between two factions: it is a new War of Independence,[4] a new Reconquest, a new expulsion of the Moors.[5] [. . .] We are not fighting for something trivial; we are fighting at one and the same time for Spain and for civilization. Nor are we fighting alone: twenty centuries of Western Christian civilization are mobilized behind us. We are fighting for God, for our land, and for our dead. We are fighting for our women, for our children, for our faith, and for our churches. We are fighting for love and honor, for tenderness and irony, for all the subtleties of the civilized soul that the Asian bloc[6] now wants to crush with its purely economic system. We are

4. The War of Independence refers to the Spanish war against French occupation. Napoleon invaded Spain in 1808 and was expelled in 1814.
5. The Moors, who brought Islam to Spain in the eighth century, were driven out in the twelfth century.
6. The Asian bloc refers to Soviet Communism.

fighting for the paintings of Velazquez and the plays of Lope,[7] for Don Quixote and the Escorial; for all the achievements and values of twenty centuries, which, at our backs, inspire us to defend a future that foreign forces with colonial pretensions want to snatch away from us. Not only this, brother Spaniards: we are also fighting for the Parthenon, for St. Peter's in Rome; we are fighting for Europe and the world. The cause of civilization that we are defending is not ours alone, but belongs to the whole world. Spain's providential and historical mission has always been this: to redeem the civilized world from all its perils: to expel Arabs, arrest Turks, baptize Indians, turn its energies toward East and West, towards Lepanto[8] or the New World, and offer itself, crucified and bled white, to the generous duty of human redemption. Now new Turks and new Red, cruel Asiatics are threatening Europe again. A five-pointed star is again disturbing the quiet nights of the West, which were disturbed yesterday by the crescent.[9] In the East, Russia – like a new Constantinople – gives in and makes way for them. But to the West, Spain, the second door of Europe, again stands up to them and saves and redeems civilization. One day the world will understand this and thank Spain for it. Once again Spain has become a Golgotha and Calvary; once again Spanish soil is steeped in blood for everyone; and once again Spain marches along the harsh roads of Extremadura and through the passes of the Guadarrama and Somosierra, cross held high, carrying out its historical mission of redeemer through its love of mankind. Therefore, because this is a holy war and a crusade for civilization, the call goes out to everyone. Because we need everyone. [...] Therefore let us not think of ourselves and our individual problems. Let each one of you march to the front, because the rifle is now the hoe and pen, paintbrush and chisel.

[...]

And you, women of Spain, you have a place too: nurse the injured, the children and the needy; encourage your menfolk, smile at the heroes, pour scorn on those who are slow to act. Be the beauty and the light of the epic. And finally you, the workers,

7. Lope de Vega Carpio (1562–1635) was one of Spain's most important and prolific dramatists, and one of the world's leading writers for the stage.
8. The battle of Lepanto occurred in 1571: Spanish, Papal, and Venetian ships defeated a Turkish fleet.
9. The five-pointed star and the crescent moon were supposed to be the emblems of the infidels: the Jews and the Moors. (The Star of David actually has six points.)

men in overalls and men of labor, victims of the most tragic deception ever recorded by History. I know that they are still saying on the street corners that this Movement is against the people. Against the people! As if the army were not made up of the people, too; as if the Falange and the Carlist loyalists were not filled with the courage of the people! I tell you, workers, that this Movement is for you above all else; that it is you who will reap the richest harvest from the seeds that are now being sown. Open your eyes! Don't you see that you were trying to cut down the very branch that supported you, that you were making holes in the very boat in which you were sailing? You shouted "Death to Spain!" without understanding that at the same time you would die, too, for you yourself are no more than Spain's human content and its living expression. Don't be afraid, for this is a moment of love, not hatred . . . [Join the delirious crowds outside the town hall who] raised their arms, not with a closed fist in a sign of aggressiveness, but with an open hand in a sign of welcoming, and raised aloft into the clear sky a flag of fresh and vivid colors. [. . .]

This is the profound historical perspective of our time, which, summed up and stated in the old true flag, has been returned to Sevillians today, thanks to the Blessed Virgin. Because it was She who did it. On the stroke of eight o'clock this morning, She came out through the door of Los Palos,[10] fresh in the August sun, tall and slender like a young gypsy girl, on a platform of love and religious zeal. As the Virgin cast Her protective glance over the Sevillians, and they cast their faithful eyes on Her, it seemed to me that [. . .] She was murmuring softly words that, echoing Seville's ancient motto, explained the miracle of what we now see: "Seville, you have not forsaken me . . . and therefore I have not forsaken Seville." And it is true: You have not forsaken Seville. [. . .] Yes, events bear the stamp of Providence. Some days ago God decided that the man seen by many as a leader, Calvo Sotelo, should become a martyr and symbol to us. Generals Balmes* and Sanjurjo died in unforeseen accidents. Sea routes were unexpectedly closed to us, but new ones opened up in the air.[11] God wanted to set aside careful plans and calculations to remain alone, face to face with History, and to teach us that anything is possible for one who makes a tree out of a seed, a condor out of an egg, and a

10. Los Palos is a church in Seville.
11. At the start of the Spanish Civil War the Republic controlled the seaways. However, Hitler provided Franco with transport planes to lift his forces in Morocco to the mainland.

redeemed world out of a crib and a manger. And in truth, seeing the wonders of these last few days, and still acknowledging in good measure the courage and genius of our glorious leaders, I continue to be amazed when I look at the Virgin [. . .]. Blessed Virgin, on behalf of those who are suffering and fighting at this time, for the mothers who weep, for the widows and orphans, for the yoke and the arrows – the sheaves of a new harvest for Spain, for the rivers of red berets[12] that flow down through the mountains and plains like a transfusion of historic and traditional blood [. . .], see to it that the banner that we have raised today in Seville soon will be raised on the Alcazar in Madrid and preside over a Spain that is free, great, and imperial.

— José María Pemán
July 1936

[Originally published in *ABC*, Seville edition, 23 July 1936; broadcast over *Radio Sevilla*, 15 August 1936. Reprinted in *Enciclopedia ilustrada universal*, 1936–1939. Translated here by Alun Kenwood.]

Barcelona

It is in Barcelona that the full force of the anarchist revolution becomes apparent. Their initials, CNT and FAI, are everywhere. They have taken over all the hotels, restaurants, cafés, trains, taxis, and means of communication, as well as all theatres, cinemas, and places of amusement. Their first act was to abolish the tip as being incompatible with the dignity of those who receive it, and to attempt to give one is the only act, short of making the Fascist salute, that a foreigner can be disliked for.

Spanish anarchism is a doctrine which has gone through three stages. The first was the conception of pure anarchy which grew out of the writings of Rousseau, Proudhon, Godwin, and to a lesser extent, Diderot and Tolstoy. The essence of this anarchist faith is that there exists in mankind a natural trend towards nobility and dignity; human relations based on a love of liberty combined with a desire to help each other (as shown for instance in the mutual generosity of the poor in slum districts in cases of sickness and distress) should in themselves be enough, given education and the right economic conditions, to provide a working basis for people to live on; State interference, armies, property, would be as super-

---

12. This is an allusion to the "red berets" of the Carlist *requetés*.

fluous as they were to the early christians. The anarchist paradise would be one in which the instincts towards freedom, justice, intelligence and "*bondad*" in the human race develop gradually to the exclusion of all thoughts of personal gain, envy, and malice. But there exist two stumbling blocks to this ideal – the desire to make money and the desire to acquire power. Everybody who makes money or acquires power, according to the anarchists, does so to the detriment of himself and at the expense of other people, and as long as these instincts are allowed free run there will always be war, tyranny, and exploitation. Power and money must therefore be abolished altogether. At this point the second stage of anarchism begins, that which arises from the thought of Bakunin, the contemporary of Marx. He added the rider that the only way to abolish power and money was by direct action on the bourgeoisie in whom these instincts were incurably ingrained, and who took advantage of all liberal legislation, all concessions from the workers, to get more power and more money for themselves. "The rich will do everything for the poor but get off their backs," Tolstoy has said. "Then they must be blown off," might have been Bakunin's corollary. From this time (the Eighties) dates militant anarchism with its crimes of violence and assassination. In most of its strongholds, Italy, Germany, Russia, it was either destroyed by Fascism or absorbed by Communism, which has usually seemed more practical, realisable, and adaptable to industrial countries; but in Spain the innate love of individual freedom, a personal dignity of the people, made them prefer it to Russian Communism, and the persecution which it underwent was never sufficient to blot it out. Finally, in the last few years it has gone through a third transformation; in spite of its mystical appeal to the heart anarchism has always been an elastic and adaptable faith, and looking round for a suitable machinery to replace State centralisation it found syndicalism, to which it is now united. Syndicalism is a system of vertical rather than horizontal Trade Unions, by which, for instance, all the workers on this paper, editors, reviewers, printers and distributors, would delegate members to a syndicate which would negotiate with other syndicates for the housing, feeding, amusements, etc., of all the body. This anarcho-syndicalism through its organ, the CNT, has been able to get control of all the industries and agriculture of Catalonia and much of that in Andalusia, Valencia and Murcia, forming a more or less solid block from Malaga to the French frontier with considerable power also in the Asturias and Madrid. The executive militant spearhead of the body is the *Fed-*

eración Anarquística (sic) Ibérica, usually pronounced as one word, FAI, which partly owing to acts of terrorism, partly to its former illegality, is clothed in mystery today. It is almost impossible to find out who and how many belong to it.

The ideal of the CNT and the FAI is libertarian Communism, a Spain in which the work and wealth is shared by all, about three hours' work a day being enough to entitle anyone to sufficient food, clothing, education, amusement, transport, and medical attention. It differs from Communism because there must be no centralisation, no bureaucracy, and no leaders; if somebody does not want to do something, the anarchists argue, no good will come of making them do it. They point to Stalin's dictatorship as an example of the evils inherent in Communism. The danger of anarchism, one might argue, is that it has become such a revolutionary weapon that it may never know what to do with the golden age when it has it, and may exhaust itself in a perpetual series of counter-revolutions. Yet it should be an ideal not unsympathetic to the English, who have always honoured freedom and individual eccentricity and whose liberalism and whiggery might well have turned to something very similar had they been harassed for centuries, like the Spanish proletariat, by absolute monarchs, militant clergy, army dictatorships and absentee landlords.

— Cyril Connolly
21 November 1936

[In *New Statesman and Nation,* vol. XII, no. 300.]

Appeal by the Spanish Government to the League of Nations, 11 December 1936

M. Alvarez Del Vayo.* – I had the honour of drawing the attention of the Assembly last September[13] to the danger to peace arising out of a new form of aggression, which consisted in a State making war to all intents and purposes, but without declaring war, by first provoking a rebellion within another State and then giving military assistance to the rebels. I fully realised, in making this statement, how strongly the demand was pressed from different quarters to supply irrefutable proof of my allegations. They were contained in the notes addressed to the members of the Non-Inter-

13. See *League of Nations Official Journal,* Special Supplement, no. 155, 47.

vention Committee in London, which were reprinted in our White Book.

To-day, these proofs have become such that no one can any longer entertain any serious doubts as to the facts of the situation.

Last September, I alluded to the tragic proof supplied by the youth of Spain, who fall in thousands in the trenches of freedom as the victims of Fascist aeroplanes and of the foreign war material delivered month after month, despite the non-intervention agreement, by those who base their international policy on the systematic breaking of treaties and of their international undertakings. To-day, Madrid has become one more irrefutable proof. No one can doubt the validity of this evidence. Every foreign mission which has visited Spain has brought back fresh accusations against this monstrosity: that the capital of a State Member of the League has been reduced to ruins, and that the women and children of this capital have been butchered in hundreds by bombing planes under the orders of rebel generals and supplied by States which have, in fact, begun a war, and which are continuing to make war, while statesmen talk of preserving peace.

The war is there; an international war is raging on Spanish soil. We have seen how, in the last few days, the rebels, after the failure of their Moroccan troops, are now preparing to receive the assistance of fresh forces which they themselves call "blond Moors." Moreover, we must expect that poison gas, which has already been employed these last days, will continue to be used in the attacks against Madrid, and that the parts of the city in which the workers live will be bombed more and more violently in order to try to obtain by panic what the rebels have failed to obtain by other means. It would be both useless and dangerous to continue to ignore the situation. The worst thing that could happen to the League of Nations would be to contribute by its own silence and inaction, to the spread of this war.

It is, of course, possible to conceive of a European peace which would result from a policy of successive surrenders to the aggression of the forces of destruction and of war. After Germany and Italy had succeeded in getting the upper hand in Spain and in using the occasion to retain for themselves the Balearic Islands and perhaps other naval bases in key positions either in the Mediterranean or the Atlantic, the same game might be started again elsewhere. Other democratic countries, which are also looked upon as dangerous centres of international trouble and discord, might also be reduced to impotence. As the final result of this process, it is possible to conceive of a Europe wholly pacified because all problems and all difficulties would have been settled, thanks to the decisive action of international Fascism.

Such a peace, it is true, would have cost the lives of millions of men, women and children and would have meant that many capitals would have suffered the fate of Madrid, that hundreds of towns would have known the fate of Cartagena and of Alicante. But, from a formal point of view, peace would not have been disturbed. When the Spanish Government decided that it was its duty to assume the grave responsibility of requesting a meeting of the Council of the League, it did so precisely because it wished, so far as it was concerned, to declare in the most solemn fashion its firm decision to oppose any such paradoxical and murderous "peace policy."

Allow me to recall just what were the reasons that made the Spanish Government feel it was necessary to demand a meeting of the Council. In the first place, the Spanish rebels have just been recognised as a legitimate Government by two great European Powers – Germany and Italy. The moment the rebels had received this recognition their chief threatened to start a blockade of the Government ports in the Mediterranean. At the same time, naval attacks took place at different points on the Spanish coast by warships whose nationality it was impossible to establish. Two Government warships have been attacked by two submarines also of unknown nationality at the entry to the port of Cartagena.

All these facts together have led the Spanish Government to fear that the international consequence of the Spanish military insurrection may become particularly threatening for the peace of Europe. The Spanish Government therefore considered it to be its duty to do all that lay in its power to enable the Covenant of the League to be applied at least for the maintenance of general peace. Since the power of the Covenant to prevent the outbreak of hostilities, about which so much has been heard of late, has been unable to stop the aggression of which Spain is the victim it is to be hoped that the Covenant may at least be used to prevent the outbreak of the general conflagration which now appears to be daily more probable.

If the Spanish Government has now asked for a meeting of the Council, it did so solely for the reason that an international war exists in fact, and that this war, if it is still ignored, may, when it is least expected, produce a situation which can no longer be controlled. This view of the situation is not ours alone and cannot therefore be attributed to excessive apprehensions on our part. On the contrary, this view is finally confirmed by the Anglo-French *démarche* of 4 December, of which the whole world learned in the *communiqué*, which reads as follows:

"The British and French Governments proceeded last week to exchange views on the situation created by the prolongation of the civil war in Spain and the resulting dangers for the peace of Europe." [...]

There is no question therefore of submitting to the Council any request on behalf of the Spanish Government or of the Spanish people. We are not prompted by any selfish interests. We are not asking the Council to do anything to assist the Spanish people to solve their own problems. If our initiative had been due solely to consideration of our national interests we should have acted long ago. We are convinced that, even before the insurrection, the rebels were able to count on moral and material assistance from abroad. The importance and effectiveness of this assistance and co-operation, as regards aerial and land warfare, can hardly be doubted by anyone. But this assistance, although it was just as harmful to the Spanish people and just as much a violation of international law, was not such an immediate danger from the point of view of general peace. [...]

The Spanish Government has faith in the efficacy of the Council and of the technical and political apparatus of the League of Nations. We are convinced that the Council can find means of avoiding or of reducing to reasonable limits the dangers of the present situation. [...]

During all this time, the Spanish people, who when setting up the Republic, were the first to incorporate the fundamental principles of the Covenant in their Constitution – not because they could foresee the military rebellion of July and the armed assistance from abroad, but because the cause of peace is dear to their hearts – have been disappointed to see how the institution that was created to preserve the peace of the world is repeating, in the case of Spain, the indecision it has displayed in the past. It would be vain and dangerous to overlook the fact that this feeling of disappointment has been shared in the last few months by the great bulk of world opinion, even outside the State Members of the League. It has been shared by millions who cannot resign themselves to the policy of successive surrenders to the forces of war and aggression. Those who want peace are conscious of the fact that they represent the will of the majority, and, in spite of constant disappointment, they are always ready generously to overlook the errors of the past. [...]

At this grave hour, when all feel how close the danger of war has come, and when every sane European who has not fallen a victim to the aggressive contagion of Fascism is haunted by the prospect of the place where he lives and works going up in smoke and flames, as is the case in Madrid to-day, those who want peace in the world demand, and are right in demanding, a firmer and more resolute attitude than would be required in the case of a mere controversy between rival doctrines.

But I do not want this meeting of the Council to be purely negative, or even, as has been suggested, recriminatory in character. The interests of the League and those of peace demand that our discussions should end in constructive decisions. I realise fully, and I am the first to regret, that certain absences at this table make it more difficult for the Council to take constructive action. But I am convinced that there is no one here who thinks that these absences should be a reason for the Council declaring in advance that it is powerless.

And now allow me to add a few words on certain more general aspects of the question. From the first moment of the Spanish military insurrection, certain European Powers have been chiefly concerned to prevent the extension to the rest of Europe of the conflict that is drowning Spain in blood. The non-intervention policy and its executive organ, the London Committee, have been the means employed to attain this end. The Spanish Government has made its view clear on this question. It maintains its point of view in all respects, and the reservations that its view implies. The cynical and open violations of the non-intervention agreement by certain Powers, and the fact that the Committee has been powerless to prevent or to stop these violations, have had as their natural consequence the declaration by other Powers that they considered themselves bound by the non-intervention agreement only to the extent that the agreement was respected by its other signatories. It is, at any rate, clear that no one can have any doubts as to the complete ineffectiveness of the system, as it has been conceived and applied hitherto. There is certainly no doubt on that point amongst the heroic population of Madrid, victims of the cruellest and most barbarous aerial bombardments ever suffered by a civilian population, carried out by aeroplanes and by bombs which have certainly not been manufactured in Spain and by airmen who have certainly not been born on Spanish territory. [...]

The question now raised is how to make good these shortcomings by setting up a system of control which will render the agreement effective. [. . .]

Spain has done everything that could be required of it as a Member of the League in order to serve the cause of peace. But peace cannot be attained at the instance of only one nation: it must be the result of the collective endeavour of all who feel equally bound by the obligations of the Covenant.

Before I conclude, allow me to put before you certain considerations as to the true and profound historical significance of what is called the "Spanish question."

If, in the course of these considerations, I touch upon aspects of the matter which might be regarded as an internal affair of Spain, that does not mean that the Spanish Government asks the League to intervene, nor even that it would be ready, without further ado, to accept the League's intervention. But it is becoming more and more difficult to draw a clear line between what is the internal affair of a nation and what may be regarded as a matter of international concern. In any case, the Spanish Government considers it its duty to put before the League in authoritative fashion the information necessary for a clear understanding of both the domestic and international aspects of the question.

In the eyes of many, the conflict in Spain is simply a particularly acute and bloody manifestation of two rival political doctrines: Communism and Fascism. I shall not insult you by assuming that it is necessary for me to refute here this puerile and over-simplified conception of the situation. This conflict, it is true, began with a clear and indubitable case of Fascist aggression, in order to prevent the democratisation of the political regime in Spain. It is also certain that the Spanish people is firmly resolved not to let the upheaval produced by this aggression pass without eliminating finally and for all time the obstacles which have traditionally obstructed the political development of Spain towards democracy, freedom and social justice.

Finally the upheaval has been exploited, not to say instigated, by European Fascist Powers, in order to establish in Spain a Fascist political regime, which would put Spain, with all that it represents in resources and geographical position, at the service of the international policy of these Powers. That is the point which should, in the Spanish Government's view, be regarded as its central feature; that is the heart of the problem. The Government and people of Spain are sure of the final and complete victory of their cause.

Afterwards, when Spain has once more regained normal conditions of democracy, liberty and social justice, the Spanish Republic will remember that its Constitution incorporates the fundamental principles of the Covenant of the League. These principles and the international co-operation which is their essence will certainly remain the basis of the national and international policy of the Spanish Republic.

— 95th Session of the Council of the League of Nations,
Second Meeting
11 December 1936

[In *League of Nations Official Journal,* January 1937.]

Hispanic Responses to the War

Introduction

ALUN KENWOOD

The following sets of extracts primarily contain the literary record of the years 1935 to 1939, the most traumatic period in contemporary Spanish history. Variously condemned as propagandistic, or worse, unpoetic, the literature of this period deserves more careful attention than it has received to date. The fact that many of the extracts represented here originally were written to advance specific causes and to spread certain ideas does not make them automatically less literary than other works. They should be judged not simply on their effectiveness to persuade, but from the dual perspective of art and society, poetry and politics.

The extracts provide a balanced representation of Nationalist and Republican writings on the war. They set out the major themes of both sides and offer the student the opportunity to compare the ideology and literary merit of writers who represented two different worlds to their respective readers and supporters.

The Roots of Tragedy

For more than a hundred years Spanish society has sought a solid footing. We haven't found it yet, and we don't even know how to go about finding it. In the nineteenth century our political confusion showed up in coups d'état, army pronunciamientos, dictatorships, civil wars, dethronements, and restorations. This present war, as an internal Spanish conflict, represents a grandiose incident in that history. It will not be the last of them. In her short lifetime the Republic hasn't created the forces that are now tearing her apart. For years we somehow ignored enormous elements of Spanish society, even pretending that they didn't exist. The Republic destroyed this fiction and brought them into the light. From the beginning these forces have belaboured the government, which has succeeded neither in dominating them nor in attracting their support. Like it or not, the Republic had to develop as a compromise solution to government. I have heard it said that, as a national system, the Republic could not be based on any extremist position. Obviously. But unfortunately no one agreed about the middle course. In their rush to destroy each other the newly exhumed elements of society have upset the balance the Republic offered, and they are pulling her to pieces.

— Manuel Azaña, *Vigil in Benicarlo*, 1939
[Translated by Josephine and Paul Stewart.]

THE PLOUGHBOY

Flesh for the yoke, he's born
More humiliated than handsome,
With his neck pursued
By the yoke for his neck.

Born like the tool
Destined for the blows
Of a discontented land
And an unsatisfied plough.

Amid the pure and living cow
Dung, he brings to life
An olive-colored soul,
Old already and calloused.

74

Beginning to live, he begins
To die, step by step,
Lifting the crust
Of his mother with his team.

Beginning to feel, he feels
This life as if it were a war,
And wearily he strikes upon
The bones of the earth.

Although he doesn't know his age
Already he knows that sweat
Is a grave crown of salt
For the farm laborer.

He works, and while he works
Masculinely serious,
He is anointed with rain
And adorned with cemetery flesh.

Strong from the heavy work
And tanned by the sun,
He rips apart, with death his ambition,
A hard-fought-for loaf of bread.

Each new day he becomes
More root, less infant,
For he hears beneath his feet
The call of the grave.

And like the root he sinks
Slowly down into the earth
So that the earth may cover
His brow with peace and bread.

This hungry child pains me
Like an enormous thorn
And his ashen-colored life
Disturbs my soul as hard as oak.

I see him plough the stubble
And devour a scrap of bread
And question with his eyes
Why he is flesh for the yoke

His plough strikes me in the heart
And his life in my throat,
And I suffer seeing the fallow land
Lie so large beneath his feet.

Who will save this little boy,
Smaller than a grain of oats?
From where will come the hammer,
The executioner of this chain?

Let it come from the hearts
Of these day-laboring men,
Who before becoming men
Are and have been ploughboys.

— Miguel Hernández, *Poetas en la España leal*, 1937

[Poem translated by Alun Kenwood.]

Heliodoro was the lord and master of the township. His position as
political boss was inherited from his father and grandfather who
had been the usurers and *caciques*[1] of the place. Half the ground
and the houses were his, and the few men who still worked on their
own land were dependent on him. At the coming of the Republic,
people had hoped for a decent way of living. A few of the independent landowners had dared to pay higher wages. Heliodoro had
proclaimed that people had to work for him at the old terms or not
at all; his own living was not dependent on the land. Two years ago,
the men had become desperate and destroyed trees and fields on
Heliodoro's property. From that time on, he employed no labor at
all, and since his latest political patrons had come to power, he gave
no peace to the other proprietors.

"He fixed us with his lorries, mainly. He has got two, and so he

1. *Cacique* is the current term for the local "boss" of the Spanish countryside, who
is often the local moneylender as well. [Original footnote.]

used to carry our grain and fruit to Madrid. Most of us sold our produce direct to him. Then he refused to buy any more and our people tried to hire his lorries from him. He said no. They hired lorries in Torrijos, but because the Deputy comes from there and needs Heliodoro, the hire of the lorries was stopped. Then they hired lorries in Madrid, which was much more expensive. They had to pay double, but still, they sold their stuff in town. Then Heliodoro went to Madrid himself." [. . .]

[On his return] Heliodoro laughed and said: "You people don't understand business. No one in Novés can sell fruit in Madrid except me." And so it was. Now, of course, people have to bring him their stuff, take what he decides to pay and dance to his tune if they want to sell anything at all. So that's why he lets his land lie fallow while the village is starving, and earns more money than he ever did from the few of us who still work. And that's why the man you saw in the Casino, and who was the father's electoral agent, has to trail round with him as a bodyguard. Because one thing is certain: Heliodoro will get it in the neck one day. Well, here you are – good night, and come and see me in my mill. It's still working." [. . .]

I have met many sane businessmen and industrialists, honest within the limits of their human search for more money and greater scope, and I never believed they were evil just because they were businessmen. But there were those others, those who hadn't names like Brown or Mueller or Durand or Pérez, but who were called the "British," the "Nederland," the "Deutsche," the "Ibérica," with the impunity of the anonymous; who destroyed countries to increase that intangible, irresponsible power of theirs. Their agents and managers, the people someone like myself would meet, had only one standard: dividends. But to the trust or combine it was important that they should appear legally honest. If it was necessary to bribe a Minister, the firm gave the money, but its agent had to know how to do it in such a form that no one would ever be able to prove where the money had come from.

— Arturo Barea, The Forging of a Rebel, 1946

[Translated by Ilsa Barea.]

THE INSIGNIA

. . . .

There are two Spains:
The one of forms

And the one of essences.

The one of forms that wear out

And the one of eternal essences.

The one of forms that die

And the one of essences that are beginning to organize them
selves anew.

In the Spain of the worn-out forms

There are obliterated symbols,

Senseless rites,

Inflated uniforms,

Legendless medals,

Hollow men,

Sawdust bodies,

A domestic and somnambulistic rhythm,

Pharisaical exegeses,

Vain verse

And the dead prayer with which they count the perforated
hazel nuts of the rosaries.

God, the creative force of the world,

Has abandoned Spain,

And everything has been left without substance.

Our national abode, therefore,

Is a cave where greed holds sway,

And the privileges of that greed.

It is the epoch of foxes.

And those nations with a History as pure as ours

Now are nothing more than lairs

Where the foxes pile up their pillage.

Spain of the essences that want to organize themselves anew

Feels the first gusts of wind that move our national entrails,

The uncontrollable hurricanes that shake the sleeping
substance,

The pristine substance from which the tree is made, and the
body of man.

And it also feels the earthquakes that tear up the ground,

That rip the flesh apart,

78

That make the rivers
And the arteries of our national anatomy overflow
In order to provide an escape for our enchained spirit
And direct it toward renovation and toward the light.

It is the epoch of heroes.
Of heroes against the foxes.
It is the epoch in which everything is deformed and stirred up;
The exegeses are turned inside out,
The omens of the great poets become reality,
New Christs appear.
And the old evangelical parables escape the naive rhetoric of
   the versicles in order to come here to change and organize
   our life.

. . . .

— León Felipe, *Poetas en la España leal,* 1937
[Poem translated by Alun Kenwood.]

I walked right in and found myself in the great hall. All was red
and yellow. I looked to see who was in charge and went to a man
who was said to be President of the Chamber. I asked him what it
was all about; he became stern, and looked at me as a woman does
when she won't have anything to do with you, and at last said that
it was the opening of Parliament. I'd have asked him a lot more,
but he was dolled up in black and white, like the dummies in a tai-
lor's shop, and it seemed that another question would have made
him stain his shirt-front. Up above in the galleries there were bishops and women; down below, rows of benches and clusters of electric lights. Photographers everywhere. [. . .] I talked again with the
President and then with one or two others, who, it appeared, were
ministers. Decent people, Sir, although no one of them seemed to
be quite sure of what he was doing. They stared at me and weren't
a bit ready to reply. Then one of them spoke up, in quite a home-
ly way, and all the rest applauded. Then another made a speech
and they all cheered, although he had hesitated over his words
and had to repeat himself. It reminded me of the "Mickey Mouse"
films, where the poor animals are in a theatre, get excited and
applaud. One of them was like a young goat, another like a rat.
Most of them were good enough chaps, but there was a yellow-

faced fish so small that he could hardly be seen. When the others cheered, he whistled, and when they protested, he cheered. They stared at him as if they'd like to eat his head off . . . And so that was Parliament! I didn't see much sense in it.

— Ramón J. Sender, *Seven Red Sundays*, 1936
[Translated by Sir Peter Chalmers Mitchell.]

Liberty [. . .] can only be the patrimony of a few select, exquisite persons; of those who know how to use it without abusing it, of those who know very well that one person's liberty stops where prejudice begins to harm that of another. Nothing is more dangerous or absurd than to preach liberty to uneducated, ignorant people. It would only occur to a madman to go and preach it to savages. [. . .]

In short, what we must preach to the great majority of people is not "liberty," but discipline and reverence for higher values; not equality, but fairness and hierarchy, not fraternity, but mutual respect and consideration.

— Manuel Machado, "Liberté, egalité, fraternité," 1937
[Originally published in *ABC*, Seville edition, 7 October 1937. Excerpt translated by Alun Kenwood.]

Revolution and Reaction

THE FIRE

Europe has been kindled, set on fire;
From Russia to Spain, to the ends of the earth,
The conflagration spreads that carries on high,
With fury, a supreme impetus.

Its conflagration rides on,
Its devastating flame dashes on,
It emits hot, floating banners
And victorious flames over the sad west.

It purifies, it penetrates the cities,
It sheds light, it gusts, it clashes with skyscrapers,

It overturns statues, it chews, it fans:
Vast numbers of putrid buildings
Burn up like fine linen;
Night ends and daylight grows.

A great storm of aeroplanes
And desires crosses the sky.

The shadow of Lenin spreads, it spreads,
And reddened it advances through the ice,
It inundates steppes, it leaps mountain ranges,
It gathers in, closes, kisses all wounds,
It overcomes misery and melancholy.

It is like a sun that eclipses lunar darkness,
It is like a heart that extends and absorbs,
That fans out like the coral of the seas
In floods of blood over the whole globe.

It is a scent that gladdens the olfactory
And a song that finds its echoes in the mines.

Spain rings out full of portraits
Of Lenin among morning blazes.

Beneath a flood of extinct men,
Spain is defended
By a soldier enraged by all corruption.
And across the offended Pyrenees
She raises her flames, her conflagration she stretches out
To embrace with Russia the circles of light.

— Miguel Hernández, *Viento del pueblo*, 1937

[Poem translated by Alun Kenwood.]

THE ANARCHISTS

Their tomorrow was a glorious tomorrow, with red banners on the
balconies and respectable matrons weeping as they were dragged
off, and wine in fine glass goblets that were then broken after the

81

toast. A tomorrow in which they would dress up their sisters in the undergarments of the young ladies and dance in the dimly-lit "clubs" to the slow music, which they sometimes heard as they went by. A tomorrow in which they would run the factories and study the books that they had been denied. In short, knowledge, the sort of knowledge possessed by those with the luck to be born rich. A tomorrow free of coughing fits and of drunkenness in which they wouldn't have to see their wives' youthfulness wither, or, worse still, hear them offer themselves to the powerful, all of them with the same smile, paid in easily-won money, beautiful, acquiescent little creatures, smelling of French perfume and committing treason with a waddle of their backsides. A tomorrow in which they would each be as good a man as the next, or even better, and in which they wouldn't watch the limousines roll by, as they stood behind a handkerchief stretched on the ground into which a few miserable coins fell, with a placard in front saying: "Out of work." A tomorrow in which to be able to sing, to shout, to bite, to die – blast it! – how and when you wanted.

— M. Pombo Angulo, *La sombra de la bandera*, 1969
[Excerpt translated by Alun Kenwood.]

The triumph of the Spanish workers therefore is now foreshadowing new political orientations. Now we are going to make democratic forms more advanced than those which the Constituent Cortes[2] established. [. . .] What forms will they be? No one can venture to prophesy, but quite easily we can all see that the communist will sacrifice some of his basic principles to reach agreement with the republican. We all see that he is accepting forms of socialization which formerly he would not have tolerated, and we see the anarchist accepting the idea of power and authority. And every day that passes, all parties see the atmosphere being impregnated a little more with syntheses made in the social experiences of the last few years. In any case, it will be a step towards solutions which will form the heart of western civilisation. It is in these solutions, inevitably democratic, that civilisation will find the force to preserve itself and make it enduring.

— Ramón J. Sender, *The War in Spain*, 1937
[Translated by Sir Peter Chalmers Mitchell.]

2. The Constituent Cortes was the democratically elected government that ruled Spain under the Second Republic from 1931 to 1936. It drew up a new constitution and passed many major reforms before the military uprising in 1936.

The Ward theatre in which our meeting is to be held is in a wide street with tramways. Beer-vendors on the pavement pour out their foaming glasses. At the corner where the street widens into a square, there are three hawkers. An old woman offers cakes of soap from a tray strapped to her neck. The theatre stands higher up, with its first floor level with the trees. No one who wasn't a member of our party worked on its construction. "That first floor," said a member of the Builders' Union, "has a beam more than a foot thick and could carry eight thousand men without noticing. A good beam! A daughter of the forges of Biscay, tempered under swift hammers, shaped by the skill of workers in metal; its fibrous strength won't flinch under the weight of thousands of workmen. The echo of our speeches and of our applause will reach its entrails and make them throb with pleasure. Even while it was still in the workshop, it heard the workmen speaking the same language – its own language. The beam knows nothing of the 'common good', of democracy or of parliaments. Its whole universe consists of work committees, of the delegates of sections, of subscriptions, of the ups and downs of the Movement, of 'tools down', of sabotage and of boycotts. In the middle of the hall it is helped by two alert round pillars, and these also speak the same language. The tall beams of the vault, the lights hidden under the moulding on each ledge, the doors, the fire-proof curtain, the wooden chairs, the orchestra pit, the straight rafters of the second story, and the oval windows, more like those of a ship than of a cathedral. All speak the same language, bolts, nuts, artificial lights, and glass; – machine, workshop, daily wages, disputes, strikes, revolts. What does it matter although on a Sunday night a magistrate goes there to gloat on the legs of the chorus girls? For such a *bourgeois* it is only a theatre. Revues, knees, and thighs. Drama – domestic tragedies within the limits of the Common Law. Comedy – pleasant adulteries in a setting of fine sheets and honeyed words. For the beams and planks, the pillars and panels, it is a co-ordinated piece of work wrought like the poop of a ship. Let the pretty girls show their thighs! If the theatre is to be kept going, the pretty girls must sometimes doff their petticoats to dance! But today, wood, iron and crystal find their soul in the sunlit morning – the Meeting. 'Against oppression! For the release of our comrades in gaol!'" The theatre laughs from its balcony with its arc of blue windows.

— Ramón J. Sender, *Seven Red Sundays*, 1936
[Translated by Sir Peter Chalmers Mitchell.]

The workers in 'Cultura Popular' also lived there [in the 'Casa del Pueblo']. Thus they saved time and also walking at night, for the work began at seven in the morning with making up parcels of printed matter for hospitals and barracks, and continued all day with arranging lectures, cinema exhibitions, plays, and the formation of travelling libraries to be sent to the fronts. The work lasted until late at night, and it was more convenient to stay on to sleep. The palace, which was arranged entirely for the gloomy and solemn idleness of Spanish aristocrats, had been changed into a hive of work. In the first month more than three hundred libraries had been organised, and 'Cultura Popular,' which had constructed two travelling exhibitions on lorries, had visited the nearest fronts in noisy caravans which announced their passage through towns by the music of loudspeakers. They also had four light cars on which they went round the barracks and hospitals daily on press service. They distributed the newspapers of the day, both the industrial ones and the political organs of the parties and syndical groups. In all their activity there was spontaneous and cheerful order. [. . .] 'Cultura Popular' was then the best cultural organisation born under the war. I felt much at home in that circle, as it corresponded closely with my interpretation of culture. For me the University, rather than the administrative machine it had come to be, was a unity of the whole life of the country, full of the vital breath of the people.

— Ramón J. Sender, *The War in Spain*, 1937
[Translated by Sir Peter Chalmers Mitchell.]

According to Julio [. . .] interest in bullfights was dying out. Perhaps this was true. The English, it was said, considered it a cruel, inhuman spectacle. As for Don Agustín Santillana, he was amazed at the new craze for jazz. Jazz was heard everywhere. It was sweeping away the polka and the like, and was even threatening the waltz. Matías could not imagine himself dancing to those new rhythms with his arm around Carmen Elgazu's waist. They were all agreed that silence was dying out along the banks of the Ter, where athletes congregated every afternoon. Sports, especially boxing, athletics and swimming, needed basic training facilities, and it was said that two old warehouses had been fitted out as gymnasiums for workers. The windows of the bookstores were full of manuals of physical culture, all by foreign authors. All this was public knowledge, and everyone interpreted it as he wished. A Choral Society had been organized – it was the end of solo singing – and a swarm of bicycle riders filled the city. The Choral Society and the Bicycle Club were two brand-new institutions whose by-laws had been approved by the Police Department, according to Julio. The Sunday stroll through the Dehesa, arm in arm with his wife, was becoming increasingly difficult for Matías and for many other couples like him and Carmen Elgazu. It was hard to find a bench to sit on to look at the trees, or watch the bowlers in their roped-off area, without men wearing eyeshades coming by, shouting: "Watch it, step back! Here come the racers." [. . .]

Julio believed that such changes were the result of an instinctive rebellion of the masses, a rebellion favored by the new political climate. In his opinion, sport was a declaration of the will to power on the part of the common people. "Note that the majority of those who go to the Ter are workingmen." Jazz was an escape mechanism, with bodies seeking postures less rigid than those adopted in religious ceremonies; the bicycle was the first outright refusal of the people to continue using their feet as a means of locomotion. And all this had come about as a result of the movies and the prestige of North America.

—J. M. Gironella, *Los cipreses creen en Dios*, 1953
[Excerpt translated by Alun Kenwood.]

Prostitution presents a moral, economic and social problem that cannot be resolved juridically. Prostitution will come to an end when sexual relations are liberalized; when Christian and bourgeois morality is transformed; when women have professions and social opportunities to secure their livelihood and that of their children; when society is set up in such a way that no one remains excluded; when society can be organized to secure life and rights for all human beings.

— Federica Montseny, one-time CNT Minister
of Health and Social Welfare, 1937
[Excerpt translated by Alun Kenwood.]

The good National-Syndicalist State depends on the family. It will be strong if the woman at home is healthy, fecund, hard-working and happy, with the windows of her home and her soul open to the sweet, imperial dawn that the sun of the Falange is bringing us.

— *Azul,* February 1938

[Excerpt translated by Alun Kenwood.]

THE MARGARITAS[3] OF TAFALLA

Solemnly promise on the Sacred Heart of Jesus:
1. To observe modesty in dress: long sleeves, high necks, skirts to the ankle, blouses full at the chest.
2. To read no novels, newspapers or magazines, to go to no cinema or theatre, without ecclesiastical licence.
3. Neither publicly nor in private to dance dances of this century but to study and learn the old dances of Navarre and Spain.
4. Not to wear make-up as long as the war lasts.
    Long live Christ the King! Long live Spain!

Quoted in R. Fraser, *Blood of Spain,* 1979

The Fatherland is a total unity, in which all individuals and classes are integrated; the nation cannot be in the hands of the strongest class or of the best organized party. The nation is a transcendent synthesis, an indivisible synthesis, with its own goals to fulfill; and we want this movement of today, and the State that it creates, to be an efficient, authoritarian instrument at the service of an indisputable unity, of that permanent unity, of that irrevocable unity that we call the fatherland.

And we already have the principles for our future acts and our present conduct. [. . .]

Here is what is required by our total sense of the nation and the state that is to serve it:

That all the people of Spain, however diverse they may be, feel in harmony with an irrevocable unity of destiny.

That political parties disappear. No one was ever born a member of a political party; on the other hand, we are all born members of a family; we are all neighbors in a municipality; we all exercise a trade or profession. [. . .]

---

3. The *Margaritas* were branches of a female Carlist association that carried out social and humanitarian activities during the war.

We want less liberal word-mongering and more respect for the deeper liberty of man. For one only respects the liberty of man when he is esteemed, as we esteem him, as the embodiment of eternal values; when he is esteemed as the physical receptacle of a soul capable of being damned and of being saved. Only when man is considered thus can it be said that his liberty is truly respected, and even more so if that liberty is integrated, as we aspire to integrate it, into a system of authority, of hierarchy, and of order.

[. . .]

Finally, if on some occasion this can only be achieved by violence, we desire that there be no shrinking from it. [. . .] It is very correct indeed that dialect is the first instrument of communication. But no other dialect is admissible save the dialectic of fists and pistols when justice or the fatherland is offended. This is what we think about the future state that we must struggle to forge.

But our movement would not be understood at all if it were believed to be only a manner of thinking. It is not a manner of thinking; it is a manner of being. We ought not merely to propose to ourselves a formal construction, a political architecture. At every moment in our life, in each one of our acts, we must adopt a complete, profound, and truly human attitude. This attitude is the spirit of service and sacrifice, the ascetic and military sense of life.

[. . .]

I believe the banner is well and truly raised. Now let us defend it gaily, poetically. There are some who think that in order to unite men's wills against the march of the revolution it is proper to offer superficially gratifying solutions; they think it is necessary to hide everything in their propaganda that could awaken an emotion or signify energetic or extreme action. What a mistake! The people have never been moved by anyone save the poets, and woe to those who do not know how to counter the poetry of destruction with the poetry of promise!

In a poetic movement we shall raise on high our zeal for Spain; we shall sacrifice ourselves; we shall do without; and the triumph will be ours, a triumph that, needless to say, we shall not win in the next elections. In those elections vote for whomever seems to you the least undesirable. But our Spain will not emerge from Parliament [the Cortes], nor is our goal there. The atmosphere there is tired and murky, like a tavern at the end of a night of dissipation. That is not our place. [. . .] Our place is out in the fresh air, beneath the cloudless heavens, weapon in our hands, with the stars high above us. Let the others go on with their merrymaking.

Outside, in tense, fervent, and confident vigilance, we already feel dawn breaking in the joy of our hearts.

— José Antonio Primo de Rivera, *Discurso de la fundación de la Falange Española*, 29 October 1933

[Reprinted in José Antonio Primo de Rivera, *Obras completas*. Excerpt translated by Alun Kenwood.]

The blue shirt, with the Roman style of salute with the arm fully extended, is the universal symbol that the Falange has contributed to the national and imperial resurrection of Spain.

The Falange Shirt is a universal symbol. Just as the *toga* was in the time of the Caesars. Just as the militant *monastic habit* was in medieval times. Just as the *frock-coat* was supposed to be later during the Enlightenment. And the *dress coat* at the time of Liberalism. And just as the *overalls* are among the Marxist socialists.

The shirt has come to represent the new Catholic universality that the Falange defends. It is not an undergarment, but rather an outer gown. Instead of being a shameful garment, it is a costume, a *whole garment*; a totalitarian garment. Affirming and aggressive.

Today the peoples of the world are differentiated not only in the way they open and close their fists, but also in whether or not they have a shirt, whether they hide it or show it off.

And the shirt has returned – with History – as a front-line, categorical symbol, just at the time when the people who need only this elemental garment in order to live and command have revived once again in the world. The peoples of the sun and blue sky against the peoples of rain and snow.

The peoples of herdsmen and farmers against the peoples of machines and materialism. Rome against London, and Spain against Moscow.

— Ernesto Giménez Caballero, "Símbolos de unidad. La camisa azul," 1937

[Originally published in *ABC*, Seville edition, 30 July 1937. Excerpt translated by Alun Kenwood.]

Seve read him pages from a strange and passionate literature. It spoke of pathways through the stars, and of an Arcadia where men were equal and just. There was always an Arcadia at the bottom of all politics. What most attracted Bernardo in the new doctrine was its idealistic manner of resolving all problems. It didn't speak of codes, but of astral bodies, and in it the terrorist attack had the poetic justification of an ancient tournament. Spain was to be rescued as one rescues a princess. Seen in this way, Spain became for Bernardo something alive, thrilling, and full of promise and future. The Falangists didn't like Spain, nor did Bernardo, for in reality Spain was a pretty poor thing, with a maimed Republic and some hungry, forgotten peasants who cut the hooves of the cattle, as if in this way they could be avenged on their landlords. The landlords invested all their money outside the country and were not particularly upset that the cattle were being mutilated, as they hadn't visited the pastures in a long time. Only the odd young country gentleman went the whole way and made an unholy fuss in the villages when it was least expected.

— M. Pombo Angulo, *La sombra de la bandera*, 1969
[Excerpt translated by Alun Kenwood.]

SONG FOR THE DESIRED SPAIN

I want a Spain the same as that Spain
That 200 years ago fell asleep on us . . .
A perfect and generous Spain, compendium
Of constant efforts and supreme conquests.
A Spain, like that one, fruitful and beneficent
And, like her, hated and attacked;
Made from dreams of virtue and from love,
And with the rigor of effort and discipline . . .

Captains of Flanders, seamen of Lepanto,
Heroes and missionaries of the Indies,
Teachers of Alcalá and Salamanca,
Painters and sculptors of Seville . . . !

Theologians of Trent, craftsmen of the Escorial,
You poets who sang to the Eucharistic God,
You saints who felt and taught
The internal laws of mysticism . . . !

All you who enjoyed that eternal toil,
All you who felt that restless life,

89

Give us your swords and your bright pens,
Your faith, your efforts, your rhymes.
And join us in the toil of combat
To know our venture and enjoy our day . . . !

Spaniards of today, Saints and Martyrs,
Heroes of independence and reconquest.
Spaniards of today. The clock of time
Has struck the hour of the immortal watchword:
Let us make a Spain like that Spain
That 200 years ago fell asleep on us . . . !

— Miguel Martínez del Cerro, *Antología poética del alzamiento,*
1936–1939, 1940

[Poem translated by Alun Kenwood.]

POEM ON THE ANTIQUITY OF SPAIN
(A RUSSIAN TANK IN CASTILE)

Russian tanks, Siberian snows,
In these noble Spanish fields,
What hope has the poppy against your cold bulk?
What can the poplar by the river oppose to your fury?

We still had oxen and wooden ploughs.
Castile is not scientific; no factories are
Raised on her soil; her clay produces, like Athens,
Theogonies and olive trees, battles, kings and gods . . .
To win Spain, you have to say, like Christ:
"My Kingdom is not of this world"; don't raise sickles
Or promise the body earthly paradises,
For in Spain voices surge forth from the sepulchres.
And there is a clear, clear destiny hanging from the heavens
Because there are genealogy, race and prayers,
Because the child who is born is already 2,000 years old
And, with the demeanor of kings, his shepherds rule.
Come, Russian chariots, ugly machines,
Animals without blood, mate or sweat.

90

With a little fire, just as someone burns a tree,
In your heavy tracks you'll be brought to a halt.
And the earth will cover you and the rain and the ants,
The lark of the skies and the flowers of the fields.
And as your rust returns to the land
Castile will again fill her horizon with Saints.

—Agustín de Foxá, *El almendro y la espada*, 1940
[Poem translated by Alun Kenwood.]

THE CARLISTS, MALE AND FEMALE

The Carlists believed in the promised land and had their prophets, their legendary heroes, their stubborn and constant faith that united fathers, sons and grandfathers in one and the same loyalty. Bernardo had been many times to the traditionalist Secretariat [. . .] and to the Youth Club. [. . .] The same confused mixture of expensive and cheap suits, of sports jackets and work shirts, of red berets, pistols, projects and commentaries was to be found in both places. It was a passionate and picturesque tumult. They understood the coming to power as nothing more than a sort of warlike revenge, with unfurled flags, the *Oriamendi*[4] deafening the air, and the King of Spain on horseback through the streets of Madrid. God, the day they took hold of their guns again! They were their fathers' and grandfathers' guns. [. . .] The old men showed off their decorations and side whiskers. [. . .] The young men of the Carlist forces always wore a protective bullet-proof vest. [. . .] In this mixture of Romanticism and reality Bernardo always felt confused, but he sensed that a great force was in movement, buried beneath that anachronistic, fantastic, and aggressive appearance, which only admitted to there being courage in the ranks of the reactionaries. [. . .] Just as the Falangists sang their hymn, they sang old mountain war songs. They also asked the women to put on their sandals for them as they were going to the front to kill the enemy, just as the Falangists asked the women to embroider their shirts, which were to serve them as lyrical shrouds. For the moment, they had the same enemy and defended the same motherland. But Bernardo knew that nothing could induce them to unite once and for all with anyone.

4. *Oriamendi* is a reference to the hymn of the Carlists.

The young girls wore white berets and their organization was called "Las Margaritas," in memory and honor of that queen. They had a sweet daydream of antique stamp, in which the men go off to war and the women stay behind to wait, and every day they go up to the hermitage to beg the Virgin to favor their own loved one. The young men showed off before them and waved their pistols about nonchalantly. [. . .] Bernardo thought that what most united the Falangists and the Carlists was the way they both dreamt of rescuing Spain, the former organizing themselves like the Romans, the latter like guerrillas. But they were both dreaming.

— M. Pombo Angulo, *La sombra de la bandera*, 1969

[Excerpt translated by Alun Kenwood.]

In order to achieve union, all you need to do is to bring together those things that are separated. To achieve Unity, you have to fuse them together.

And the Unity thus achieved is always something distinct from and superior to the sum of its parts.

From the fusion of Aragon and Castile emerged Spain.

The Spain of yesterday, the conqueror of the East and the discoverer and civilizer of the West.

From the fusion of the traditionalist spirit – which represents the basic and fundamental Spain of yesterday – and the fascist spirit – which guides us towards a just and prosperous tomorrow – Spain is again emerging. The Spain of today. The Spain that conquered Marxism, with its eastern barbarity. The Spain that is once again the Reconqueror of the Christian, civilized West.

And it is to be noted that the intimate, powerful leavening that has "precipitated" both yesterday – and today! – that life- saving fusion, has been the religious spirit, the soul of the nation.

And the man of providence, chosen by God to carry out the great work, is our unconquered Leader. The man of war and peace. The man of Spain. Franco, Franco, Franco[. . .]

— Manuel Machado, "Intenciones – ¡España! ¡Una!" 1937

[Originally published in *ABC*, Seville edition, 7 December 1937. Excerpt translated by Alun Kenwood.]

I very much admire the old democratic spirit of Spain, but . . . I do not share it.

As far as I'm concerned there are only digits. The rest are zeros, which, if they increase the value, only do so because they are found to the right of the one that counts, behind him, under his command and management.

In any case, they are a blind force that, lacking leadership, only knows how to destroy and to be destroyed.

As far as I'm concerned the masses will never be right against their betters.

All they can manage are lunacy and madness, which the logic of the very Platitude itself will immediately reduce to absurdity . . .

If all are in charge, who will obey?

If everyone governs, who will be governed?

Democracy . . . ? Anarchy, confusion, and cannibalism.

These declarations do not imply even the least spirit of class.

The modern concept of a State – which establishes the community of an entire nation – has just erased the borders that used to separate and hold back the different social classes . . .

And it opens up to everyone, whatever his origin may be – Hitler, Mussolini – the path to true aristocracy.

Aristocracy: the rule of the best.

But the best, eh? [. . . .]

For the best, the pain, the anxiety, and the responsibility of command.

For all: the pride of service.

Service. This is the only possible equality. [. . .]

— Manuel Machado, "Jerarquía," 1937

[Originally published in *ABC*, Seville edition, 11 May 1937. Excerpt translated by Alun Kenwood.]

THE EAR OF WHEAT

. . . .

Never, under the pretext of a millennial hunger,

Will we give you Christ, asleep, at his post.

Grace, the rhythm of the waltz, courtesy,

The winged fan, sea spray, pure love,

Our theological sky, prayer and ermine,

The sword, the flag and monarchical Versailles,

Never will we cast off, trembling, before the clenched fist.

To defend these ineffable treasures

We grasp the gun and raise the flag.

It is not bread the Falange will give you but rather the ear of
wheat,

That is the bread of miraculous goldsmithing.

—Agustín de Foxá, *El almendro y la espada*, 1940
[Poem translated by Alun Kenwood.]

Everything was conspiring against the old culture. Picasso was
breaking the intangible lines of painting with his anarchy of volume and color. Blacks in dinner jackets were on the stage, and
intellectuals were supporting Josephine Baker[5] in her banana
dress in the struggle against Vienna's sweet waltz. Any exotic art,
whether black, Indian or Malayan, was accepted gladly, with the
aim of shattering the classical and Catholic clarity of the ancient
artistic norms.

—Agustín de Foxá, *Madrid, de corte a checa*, 1938
[Excerpt translated by Alun Kenwood.]

The Call to Arms

THE NATIONAL ANTHEM

To the struggle, Spaniards,
Legionaries, let's vanquish
The Popular Front,
Let's advance, let's pursue
That indomitable enemy
Whom we are going to annihilate.
Long live Spain!

. . . .

Come on, quick, militiamen,
And wipe out the enemy, come on.
The germ that has risen up,
We are going to crush it

5. Josephine Baker (1906–1975) was a dancer and singer who symbolized the
vitality and beauty of Black American culture, which took Paris by storm in the
1920s.

And burn to ashes
The poison that it has injected,
Robber of the national treasure,
U-sur-per.

— Constantino Gómez Pardal, *Expaña gloriosa y culta, única,*
patriótica y poética, 1936
[Excerpt translated by Alun Kenwood.]

It is a Revolution – unique in History – carried out by youthful
arms and intellect against an abject view of life. It is a holocaust of
impatient youth dedicated to redeem the guilt of their elders and
even the guilt of their own executioners. It is a Christian, apostolic
revolution against the revolution of Lucifer. It is a war of
Archangels against the powers of darkness. It is an Army of Salvation under the command of a young, pure Leader and his great
captains.

— Ricardo León, quoted in Carlos Fernández,
Antología de cuarenta años, 1936–75, 1983
[Excerpt translated by Alun Kenwood.]

Above all this is a religious war, the most religious of all Spanish
wars, that is to say, every war there has ever been and every war to
come, because the enemies we are fighting now are the greatest
the Church has had or can ever have, for, when all is said and
done, the Turks, the Moors, the Jews, and the Protestants, whom
we had to fight against in former times, all had their religions. [. . .]
But today's enemies are worse than the demons themselves
because not only do they have no religion, but they are trying to
destroy all our foundations and those of moral and religious order
by denying the existence of God.

— Félix G. Olmedo, *El sentide de la guerra española,* 1938
[Excerpt translated by Alun Kenwood.]

HANDKERCHIEF IN THE AIR

The chain has been broken, my beloved,
And I separate from you; the fire calls me;
I do not run to it discouraged and blindly,

95

But with eyes full of happiness.

The war for the Fatherland is a pilgrimage,

Combat is a sport, an honorable game,

So that you may pray and I die — and then

Await your company in the blue of the sky.

The sound of the bugles is stronger

Than your crystalline voice, and death is

The most faithful and jealous lover.

> — Esteban Calle Iturrino, *Antología poética del alzamiento,*
> *1936–1939,* 1940

[Poem translated by Alun Kenwood.]

DAWN

There is no Empire that has not rocked its cradle

In a lake of blood and tears.

Struggle is the motto of virile peoples,

War is the crucible of races;

Without struggle there are no days of blue skies,

Nor golden, triumphant plenitude,

Nor unanimous toil for ecumenical dominion.

Without wars there are no fatherlands.

> — Esteban Calle Iturrino, *Selección de poesías: Juegos florales,* 1938

[Poem translated by Alun Kenwood.]

A National-Syndicalist Spain will form with a Fascist Italy and a Nazi Germany, not a military nor a political but rather an ideological triangle, which is to say much more. It will impose on Europe the rhythm of the new era in an irresistible manner. If that Spain is also a strong, heroic, renewed, youthful nation, if it ascends in status to the supreme hierarchy of Empire, if it has once again the implacable will to power, the face of Europe will be profoundly changed, as has always been the case when Spain has given her vital impulse to the world.

> — José María de Areilza, *Diario vasco,* 22 May 1937

[Excerpt translated by Alun Kenwood.]

REMEMBER

Remember well: it was July
And it was a summer night.
Through the streets asphalted
With tarts and sleepwalkers,
Men were coming and going
In their work suits,
Their gazes feverish,
With racing steps.
With what destination so late
Those who rise so early?
Remember well: it was July . . .
And it was a summer night.
Through the Lower Corredor,
Tudescos and Desengaños Street,
To Luna Street,
To where the Unions were,
With the violence of a torrent,
A human river flowed.
Give us arms! they begged impatiently,
Give us arms! they begged angrily,
Give us arms to subject
The fascist rabble!
As they didn't give them arms
They threw themselves into the struggle,
Half of them half naked,
Half of them shoeless,
And at daybreak
The assault began.
The Montaña Barracks
Surrendered to the Unions![6]
Remember well: it was July

6. The Montaña Barracks was an army barracks in Madrid that was stormed by the militias and working class on 20 July 1936 in search of arms to defend the revolution.

And it was a summer night.

Free men struggled.

Free men won.

— Antonio Agraz, *Romancero general de la guerra de España,* 1937
[Poem translated by Alun Kenwood.]

We are fighting in self-defense, defending the life of our people and its highest moral values, all the moral values of Spain, absolutely all – the past, the present, and those that you will know how to create in time to come.

We, the innovators of Spanish policy, we, the restorers of the Republic, the workmen of the Republic, who labored to make it an instrument to bring civilization and progress to our community, we have denied nothing of all that is noble and great in the history of Spain – absolutely nothing.

— Manuel Azaña, *Discurso en el Ayuntamiento de Valencia,*
13 November 1937.

[Excerpt translated by Alun Kenwood.]

Many artistic, cultural, and intellectual tendencies which were part of the current of growth of artisans and peasants attracted some of the Spanish lower middle-class youth. They were all agreed on the fundamental need of preserving at any cost the conquests made by the workers, as upon them the impetus Spanish life had gained depended in every sense. It was necessary to secure political liberty, to unwind the tentacles of the Church from the people's organs of power, to preserve once and for all the right and civic duty of discussion – on the practical side liberty of speech and of printing, to secure it, compelling the obedience of the feudal landowners who had always considered themselves outside and above the State, and wished to retain their privileges even after the coming of the Republic.

— Ramón J. Sender, *The War in Spain,* 1937
[Translated by Sir Peter Chalmers Mitchell.]

SPANISH FOLK SONG OF THE WAR

Frontiers that divide the people,
Soon we'll tear apart.

The masses speak a thousand tongues —
But have one heart.

For the workers no boasting Fatherlands,
Only freedom and peace,
So that through peace and freedom
All may find release.

The men sing as they work.
The women sing at their tasks.
All the World is singing
When the people are free at last.

But silent now the guitar
And the jota aragonesa.
First comes the International,
Then the Marseillaise.

But with the people's blood
From the bombs of the enemy's raids,
Our flags are blooming like flowers
On freedom's barricades.

Girl of the People's Army,
Do not be jealous of me
If to my heart I take
Both you and liberty.

— Anonymous

[Translated by Langston Hughes for *Daily Worker*, 16 July 1938.]

WHY THE STRUGGLE, COMRADE?

Why do you struggle, comrade?
I fight for our Spain,
The Spain we are already forging;
For the Spain we never had,
For the Spain they want to take away from us.
Liberty, Love, and Happiness!
For these we are struggling.

— Anonymous, *Adelante*, 18 July 1937

[Poem translated by Alun Kenwood.]

99

STRUGGLE, PEASANT, STRUGGLE

Struggle for your great nation,

For a Spain freed

From all infamous scum!

For your children, for your wife,

For your fellow brothers,

Who with their very soul beg you

Not to give up the struggle.

— Antonio Muñoz, *Stajanov*, 9 August 1937

[Poem translated by Alun Kenwood.]

I knew that there existed Fascists who had good faith, admirers of the "better" past, or dreamers of bygone empires and conquerors, who saw themselves as crusaders; but they were the cannon fodder of Fascism. There were the others, the heirs of the corrupt ruling caste of Spain, the same people who had manoeuvered the Moroccan war with its stupendous corruption and humiliating retreats to their own greater glory. We had to fight them. It was not a question of political theories. It was life against death. We had to fight against the death-bringers, the Francos, the Sanjurjos, the Molas, the Millán Astrays,* who crowned their blood-drenched record, selling their country so as to be the masters of slaves and in their turn the slaves of other masters.

We had to fight them. This meant we would have to shell or bomb Burgos and its towers. Cordova and its flowered courtyards, Seville and its gardens. We would have to kill so as to purchase the right to live.

I wanted to scream.

—Arturo Barea, *The Forging of a Rebel*, 1946

[Translated by Ilsa Barea.]

I believe in the creations that will emerge from this tremendous upheaval in Spain. [. . .] The regime that I desire is one where all the rights of conscience and of the human person are defended and secured by all the political machinery of the State, where the moral and political liberty of man is guaranteed, where work shall be, as the Republic intended it to be in Spain, the one qualifica-

100

tion of Spanish citizenship, and where the free disposal of their country's destiny by the people in their entirety and in their total representation is assured. [. . .] No regime will be possible in Spain unless its based on what I have just said. [. . .]

Peace will come, and the victory will come; but it will be an impersonal victory: the victory of the law, of the people, the victory of the Republic. It will not be a triumph of a leader, for the Republic has no chiefs, and because we are not going to substitute for the old oligarchic and authoritarian militarism a demagogic and tumultuous militarism, more fatal still and even more ineffective in the professional sphere. Victory will be impersonal, for it will not be the triumph of any one of us, or of our parties, or of our organizations. It will be the triumph of Republican liberty, the triumph of the rights of the people, of the moral entities before which we bow.

— Manuel Azaña, *Discurso en el Ayuntamiento de Valencia,*
21 January 1937

[Excerpt translated by Alun Kenwood.]

The Enemy

From these two contradictory halves into which Spain is divided, it would be interesting to extract some statistics of the enemy groups. Of course, almost all the professionals in the liberal careers, artists, academics, doctors, are with the army.

Whilst with the reds live the hairdressers, the clerks, shop assistants and waiters, along with various types of illiterates and loafers, those devoid of merit and value, people of doubtful lives, the spiteful and the envious.

On the right, too, almost in their totality, are the religious orders, the diplomatic corps, the navy, and all sorts of aristocrats.

On the left, the great majority of railworkers, the school teachers, and miners, always discounting exceptions.

— Concha Espina, *Retaguardia,* 1937

[Excerpt translated by Alun Kenwood.]

Tonight there won't be a *bourgeois* left in the world. Someone asks: "Whose is the machine?"

Four or five reply: "It belongs to the revolution."

Graco comes up to me:

"Look at it, grandmother! How clean and swelling with youth. It is one of the first that have come to our side. But there are others, whores, bitches, handled by the Civil Guard. Comrades," he went on, addressing them all, "here you have it! A machine-gun Hotchkiss, American model! It is the best weapon –"

An old man interrupts:

"Forgive me, comrade Graco. There is another weapon, still more effective – culture."

They all laugh. The machine is packed up. Graco says:

"Culture is a trick of the *bourgeois*, because there is nothing like *bourgeois* culture to enslave us."

"We don't want culture! To hell with culture! The machine-gun will help us sink culture."

The communists cry out:

"Culture began with Marx."

The old man with the white whiskers said:

"And Greece? and Rome? Does not Demosthenes stand for something? And Plato?"

The youngest of them shout him down:

"Bloody nonsense! *bourgeois* dirt!" [. . .]

Graco calls out:

"All machines enslave us except our Virgin Hotchkiss."

The crowd replies like an angry sea:

"The Virgin Hotchkiss is our Holy Mother."

The old man with the whiskers calls out:

"Our Mother will tell us that anarchy is the best."

No one takes any notice. Graco speaks again:

"With our own hands we have wrought the machine-gun."

"The Virgin Hotchkiss," they all reply, "is our daughter."

Graco stands up, holding out his revolver:

"Let us put our trust and our hope in the machine of the revolution."

"The Virgin Hotchkiss is our soul. Hurrah! Hurrah!"

Then Graco begins to pray as if he were reciting a litany:

"Ministers, Director-Generals, Archbishops, Duchess-bitches."

"You shall die at our hands!"

"Elegant highbrows! servile journalists! pimps of luxury!"

"You shall die at our hands!"

"Members of Parliament, Governors, Priests!"

"You shall till the land, harnessed to our plough!"

"Nuns!"

"For the first time you shall smile, pumping milk from your dry breasts!"

"Saints of the Church!"

"Splintered into chips they shall warm the soup of our cohorts."

"The Holy Vessels!"

"We shall use them to celebrate our great day of blasphemy."

"Certificates of Government stock, patents of nobility, wills and armorial bearings!"

"They shall blaze in the streets, and our children shall singe their shoes leaping over them!"

"The Holy Virgin!"

"She shall bring forth in sorrow!"

"Jesus, the Son of God!"

"We shall send him to a school for defectives!"

"God, One in Three and Three in One, the Almighty!"

"There is no God! We have done with God!"

"We shall use the holy napkins of His ritual as swaddling clothes for our new-born babes!"

"There is nothing but the revolution!"

"The revolution!"

"Nothing else?"

"Nothing else! And as its symbol we accept only one kind of machine: the Virgin Hotchkiss!"

— Ramón J. Sender, *Seven Red Sundays*, 1936
[Translated by Sir Peter Chalmers Mitchell.]

Those who, like the Communists, today are burning down the Catholic temples of Spain will tomorrow, if you let them, burn down everything from the Mosque at Mecca with its holy stone to St. Paul's Cathedral in London. Their shots are also aimed at the pagodas and their Brahmin, at the Chinese bonze and the Shinto priests, at everything human and divine that has around it that holy halo of religious adoration.

— Vicente Gay, *Charla radiofónica: Radio Salamanca*, 4 April 1937
[Excerpt translated by Alun Kenwood.]

[S]ocialism acquired a horrifying blackness when the figure of that Jew, Karl Marx, appeared on the scene; and it acquired this blackness because he considered as false all types of sentiment,

103

even love, religion, and the Fatherland. For him nothing existed except the preponderance of economic factors. [. . .]

When Marxism culminates in an organization such as the one in Russia, children are told in school that religion is the opiate of the people, that the Fatherland is a word invented in order to oppress, and that even modesty and filial love are bourgeois prejudices that must be rooted out at all costs. That's what socialism has turned into. Do you think that, if the workers knew this, they would feel any attraction to an ideal like this, the fearful, frightening, inhuman ideal that was conceived in the head of that Jew called Karl Marx?

—José Antonio Primo de Rivera, *Obras completas*, 1942
[Excerpt translated by Alun Kenwood.]

The Masons – who are they? Those who put possessions before duty; those who desert the militia and live in luxury; those who behave toward the State as if the State had to provide its udders for them and not demand of them their efforts. The Masons – what do they do? They make fun of Spain, they deride the Movement, they jeer at the Law, they are overflowing in vices and in little daily betrayals that spread to the popular consciousness and agitate, distress, and embitter it.

—Juan Tusquets, *Discurso (Burgos)*, 1 November 1936
[Reprinted in J. Rodríguez Puértolas, *Literatura fascista española.*Translated here by Alun Kenwood.]

[The Free Institute of Learning[7]] was a ghetto, a Jewish district and refuge. [. . .] Going by his surname, its founder was a Jew. [. . .] (Ríos. Have you ever heard a more Jewish name?). His face and manners gave him away too. The family was Jewish, and it turned up such rare figures as don Fernando and his ilk. [. . .] Those who

---

7. The Free Institute of Learning was a free university, later expanded to include younger pupils, founded by Francisco Giner de los Ríos (1839–1915) in Madrid in 1876, where liberal professors expelled from the universities could carry on their teaching. It quickly established a reputation for progressive teaching methods and an emphasis on intellectual honesty and open enquiry. Many of its students came to be associated with the writers of the Generation of 1898 (see note 9 below).

Fernando de los Ríos (1879–1949), a nephew of Francisco, was a distinguished professor of international law from Granada University, and a Socialist minister of justice under the Republic. He was a Freemason, a humanist, and an ardent and articulate opponent of the Church's role in Spanish life.

lived in the ghetto had the same unity as is usually established in Hebrew communities. They even grew their beards at a time when the fashion in personal hygiene was the American clean-shaven, crew-cut look.

— Vicente Gay, *Estampas rojas y caballeros blancos*, 1937

[Excerpt translated by Alun Kenwood.]

[The young of the 1930s] have been born in the century of the automobile and of the dehumanization of the arts, and they have had to abandon God in the squalor of the Athenaeum, their girl-friends in the zoological books of Freud, and the Fatherland in the statutes of Geneva. [. . .]

[Republican intellectuals are] square-eyed students and FUE* pedants, Krausist[8] professors, essay-scribbling doctors, taciturn writers of the mood of '98,[9] and a whole gaggle of great, failed, sickly intellectuals of ill-defined sexuality [. . .]; officers who have been thrown out of the Army, journalists from The Voice and The Herald, and students who have failed to get university positions.

— Agustín de Foxá, *Madrid, de corte a checa*, 1938

[Excerpt translated by Alun Kenwood.]

I want to be your canticle, Madrid, because I feel your grief! My heart weeps for you with the roar of the seas! I want to be the arrow of your pain and fly through the air towards God! And I want to beg him: "Mercy!" "mercy!" "mercy!" Quieten your wrath! Have mercy upon the accursed sins of your Madrid! [. . .] And it is sweeter to be dead and beneath the earth than to suffer the name-less iniquity of looking on you, Madrid, Madrid, cursed by God, cursed seven times seven. [. . .]

8. Karl Krause (1781–1832) was a German philosopher whose ideas were adapted and brought to Spain by Julián Sanz del Río. Krausism in Spain promised a harmonious synthesis between faith and reason and a pacifist ideal of the brotherhood of man, which revolutionized intellectual life there from 1860 until the end of the nineteenth century.

9. The Generation of 1898 was the name of a group of writers who saw that a radical readjustment in political conditions would be necessary following Spain's defeat in the 1898 war against the United States. The group included Miguel de Unamuno, Antonio Machado, Azorín, Pío Baroja, and Ramón del Valle-Inclán. Two strong but opposing currents dominate the thinking of this group. On the one hand they were inspired by Spain's glorious past and set out to decipher her literary and intellectual traditions. On the other hand, they turned toward the ideas and culture of Europe with the aim of Europeanizing or modernizing their nation.

Madrid! Contaminated with the plague, oblivion, scorpions, insults, vulgarities, democracy, abominations, repulsive warts, food slops, bourgeois tea-drinkers and Saxon swaggers, intellectual, pedantic, academic, Geneva-inspired, you have the sensitivity of a monkey. [. . .] Abominable Madrid, full of the masses in slippers and office backsides resting on imperial seats. And finally the Escorial, the Escorial! The origin and dream of an august Madrid, whose tombs have been profaned by Red worms.

[. . .]

Go on, weep, Babylonian city, traitor, biblical city of the wilderness! Expiate your sins! Weep blood! Gird your loins with sackcloth! Sit before your devastated gates, devour your evil and gnaw on your foul ways. And destroy your vanity with its monstrous, pale, Satanic head, you house of active sodomy. May your locks be serpents and your eyes squinting. Clear your sterile lap of scorpions, and weep for your infidelities.

— Ernesto Giménez Caballero, *Nuestro Madrid*, 1937

[Excerpt translated by Alun Kenwood.]

The sickness of the translations of foreign works [. . .] deformed our taste and disoriented our character. This was no less than to graft on to the healthy and holy tree of Tradition all that verminous liberal creed that was to end up in communism and war! But right here at home we have the antidote: served up perfectly well in the imperial goblet of the Inquisition. We are still ashamed at the mention of its name, but fail to remember that the whole Black Legend was born out of having abandoned the task and mission of the Holy Office, when it was a legitimate legal institution, a healthy frontier for the Faith and customs, and a vigilant custodian of Spanish spirit and thought. Never did Spain radiate with such a universal fire and light as in the days of the Holy Tribunal. For this reason, within the limits of National-Syndicalist orthodoxy, we champion the cause of an Inquisition adjusted to current conditions. A sacred, austere, and strict Tribunal. Let the world laugh at us. . .but may we know again the ever sunny days of the Catholic Monarchs and of Philip the Second![10]

— Editorial, *Arriba España*, 23 April 1938

[Excerpt translated by Alun Kenwood.]

10. The Catholic Monarchs were Ferdinand II of Aragon (1452–1516) and Isabel I of Castile (1451–1504) who after marriage in 1469 united the kingdoms in 1479.

Literature, Art, Music – they are nothing to us. We couldn't care less if we passed through this life leaving only the imprint of our hob-nailed boots, of the cross in the corner and of the occasional trace of a disinterred tomb. We have no aspirations to consecrate ourselves to a masterpiece, to the poems we feel but have no time to write, to the pictures we see but cannot paint, to the beautiful, naked statues our imagination outlines in the stone that serves us as a parapet. The only mission of those now under the Spanish flag is to bring about a century that will serve the Fatherland.

— Rafael García Serrano, "Episodios nacionales o historia de la ocasión perdida," *Arriba*, 27 July 1943

[Excerpt translated by Alun Kenwood.]

The Leaders

A PRAYER TO JOSÉ ANTONIO

José Antonio, Master! . . . On what astral body,
On what sun, on what wandering star
Do you stand guard? When I gaze towards
The divine vault, I await your answer.

Your bright life was all beauty;
Sublime understanding, strong spirit . . .
And at the height of your triumphant ardor, an early death,
So you would never lose your youth.

Speak to us . . . The lesson to us of your perfect glory
Is today darkened by weeping. But now
You are accompanied by a sacred halo.

Their common policy was fundamental to Spain. They organized the Holy Brotherhood (1476), established the Inquisition (1480), conquered Granada and expelled the Jews (1492), and annexed Navarre (1512). Their support of Columbus led to the exploration of Latin America (1492).

Philip the Second (1527–1598) became king of Spain in 1556 after the abdication of his father. He was a champion of Catholicism and pursued unsuccessfully the projects of his father for world domination. He sent the Armada against England, lost the Low Countries, and built El Escorial.

And, on the cover of its New History,
The Fatherland inscribes your holy name.
José Antonio! Present! Long live Spain!

— Manuel Machado, *Horas de oro: Devocionario poético*, 1940
[Poem translated by Alun Kenwood.]

It's not by mere chance that when our leaders are compared physically with the Red leaders, the latter appear a collection of obese, effeminate monsters, zoologically deformed. Sometimes I think that if our era had the imagination of the medieval age, Franco would be represented as Saint Michael killing the devil, a dragon with the hooves of a pig and seven heads – one for each of the cardinal sins (those of Azaña, Casares,* Indalecio Prieto,* Ossorio y Gallardo,* Alvarez del Vayo, the Nelken* woman, Marcelino Domingo*) – and the tongue of a viper, which could well be that of Dolores Ibarruri.* If we see them face to face, these leaders of ours really have about them something of the champions of chivalric poems, not only in their physical excellence but also in their moral purity, which makes of them true likenesses of the heroes of the Crusades.[...]

Franco has that personal seductive power that emanates from his physical and physiological poise, and from his inner serenity and restraint, which are his major characteristics. When the years have gone by, and his personality has passed into History and may be studied free from the authority and presence that are so difficult to ignore when censuring or eulogizing him, it will be seen that he was the man predestined for this hour. I remember the first time I saw him – after the national uprising was under way. He was leaving Burgos cathedral. I saw him against the background of age-old stones, of crenellations and pinnacles that looked as if they were silverplated, beneath the sky one victorious Sunday, surrounded by a cheering crowd, as he went down the stone steps leading into Laín Calvo street. Bells were ringing and trumpets sounding, as standards of glory fluttered in the blue air. Through the heart of that fervent multitude there passed a current not just of admiration and trust but also of love toward the young hero. He was wearing a sober campaign uniform, but upon his smiling face the radiance of an imaginary silver helmet seemed to project itself, as if through him the memories of the legendary Lohengrin and

Parsifal[11] were being unconsciously evoked, or the memory of that Cid whose sacred bones rested below the vaults of that very temple, but this time a beardless, almost adolescent Cid, resurrected in order to command both Moors and Christians. That capacity to smile at his people, at all of life, in prosperity and in adversity, seemed to me to be the best promise he could make us. That smile of his – the expression of a man who enjoys the confidence of others as well as being confident in himself – dissipated, as if belonging to a terrible nightmare, the vision of the monsters of Red Spain, the ferocious, cruel, sarcastic and bestial grimaces of those who, sick with envy and hate, had placed Spain in chains. [. . .]

Even so, he was far removed from all that demagogic attention-seeking, because his whole life had been seclusion and discipline. [. . .] Books are his favorite pastime. He finds entertainment in studying anything to do with his military profession. He doesn't smoke, nor does he drink. No one has ever heard gossip about easy affairs that, for many reasons, must have come his way without his looking for them. In the disorderly world in which we live, he exemplified humbly that ideal of the brave and austere Christian soldier, intelligent and modest, who, while not sharing in the misconduct or even in the everyday vices of others, does not censure them either. Rather, he's full of understanding and indulgence, and free of hypocrisy and sanctimoniousness. His honesty is so much an integral part of him that he doesn't exhibit it, much as nobody shows his or her skeleton. It seems as natural in him as do excusable weaknesses in others. And so, little by little, without wanting it or seeking it, that pure, brilliant life had gradually attracted to itself every dream and every hope of every patriot, and, above all, of the soldiers themselves. Many times during these dreadful years I have heard youthful captains and lieutenants say:

"If Franco wanted. . ."

—Juan Pujol, "Cruzados," *Domingo*, 21 February 1937
[Excerpt translated by Alun Kenwood.]

11. Lohengrin, Knight of the Swan, was the son of Percival and a hero of German versions of a legend that circulated widely in variant forms in Europe during the Middle Ages. The basic story tells of a mysterious knight who arrives in a boat drawn by a swan to help a noble lady in distress. He marries her on the sole condition that she not ask him his name or lineage. When she forgets this promise, he leaves her, never to return.

Parsifal was Percival, a knight of King Arthur's Round Table. He was distinguished by his quality of child-like innocence and his quest for the Holy Grail – the cup or chalice traditionally used by Christ at the Last Supper, which was the subject of a great amount of medieval legend. In his quest for the Grail, Percival gradually learned the true meaning of chivalry and its close connection with the teachings of the Church.

Once upon a time in a country full of happiness and contentment,
a Dragon with seven heads was born. [. . .] Oh unhappy inhabitants of that beautiful country! No one could go out into the street
without fear of being devoured. The Dragon attacked properties
and set fire to churches; it trampled on crucifixes and insulted the
Virgin Mary. The children could neither pray nor laugh. [. . .] And
one burning hot day in July, like rain from the sky, a brave, determined hero came down to earth on a metal bird and went out with
his sword unsheathed to confront the Dragon. [. . .] And one day,
as spring began to laugh about us, the Dragon was killed forever,
and the beautiful country laughed and sang once more. It was
happy again. [. . .]

> — Quoted in R. Lezcano, "La política en la escuela," *El País*,
> 25 December 1981

[Excerpt translated by Alun Kenwood.]

The Reds thought that Spain was like Cinderella, who, misunder-
stood by everyone, only trusted in the prince of her dreams. For
Spain, Mussolini was that prince, because he understood her and
gave her his hand while others did not hesitate to support the
Reds, and so manifested their lack of understanding.

> — Quoted in Carlos Fernández, *Antología de cuarenta años,
> 1936–75*, 1983

[Excerpt translated by Alun Kenwood.]

RADIO SEVILLE

Attention. Radio Seville.

This is Queipo de Llano barking,

Bellowing and spitting,

And braying on four legs.

Radio Seville.

(Coughs and then with a drunken voice.)

Ladies and gentlemen!

Here you have a savior of Spain.

Long live wine! Long live vomit!

Tonight I'll take Malaga.

110

(He drinks a glass.)

On Monday I took Jerez;

(He takes another drink.)

On Tuesday, Montilla and Cazalla;

(He takes another glass.)

On Wednesday, Chinchon; and on Thursday,

Drunk and in the morning,

All the coach houses of Madrid

And all the stables,

Fluffing up their horse dung,

Will provide me with a soft bed.

(Enter Catite, the bullfighter.)

Oh, how delightful it is to sleep,

Having as a pillow

And within easy reach of my snout

Two mangers full of hay!

What an honor to be led to the farrier

By the halter! What a notable favor

To receive on my hooves,

Nailed in with spikes,

The horseshoes that Franco

Boldly won in Africa!

(Imitating the movements of a horse.)

Already my back is tightening,

Now my haunches are rearing up,

Now my ears are growing on me

And now my teeth are lengthening,

The girdle is too short for me,

The reins can't hold me.

I gallop and gallop. . .slowly.

Tomorrow I'll be in Madrid.

Close the schools,

And open the taverns.

I'll have nothing of universities

Or colleges, nothing, nothing.

Let wine run out to greet

111

A liberator of Spain.

Attention!

— Rafael Alberti, *Romancero de la guerra civil*, 1936
[Excerpt translated by Alun Kenwood.]

TO LISTER, COMMANDER OF THE ARMY OF THE EBRO

Your letter – oh noble heart on vigil,
Indomitable Spaniard, strong fist –
Your letter, heroic Lister, consoles me
In this my death-laden flesh.

The din of a holy struggle on Iberian fields
Has come to me in your letter;
My heart too has awoken
Surrounded by aromas of gunpowder and rosemary.

Where a marine spiral announces
The arrival of the Ebro, and on the cold crag
Where that Spanish river rises,

From mountain to sea, this my word be:
"If my pen were worth your captain's pistol,
I would die content."

— Antonio Machado, *Hora de España*, May 1938
[Poem translated by Alun Kenwood.]

WE WILL FOLLOW YOUR EXAMPLE!

(Union of Revolutionary Writers and Artists, Valencia)
Blind, blind;
We were blind.
We were looking with the eyes of God
And we could not see the moss surrounding the temples of the
    children of the out-of-work laborers.

Hunger was before our eyes.
We wept, we wept
With the song of frogs in a poplar pond.

But you

Broke the backbone of the Earth

And created a world, our World;

The world of workers, students, peasants, and Red soldiers.

And you discovered a new sky over our earth.

With guns at our shoulders

We mounted the chargers of expectation.

Your flag set our eyes on fire!

— Pla y Beltrán, *Poetas en la España leal*, 1937

[Poem translated by Alun Kenwood.]

Foreign Ideologies and Intervention

SINGLE FRONT

Anarchist and brother, wasn't there a time

When argument on argument parted you from me?

Don't you agree?

Sure, you agree!

We had each our ways to heaven, not at all the same:

Marx said, Bakunin said . . . Hell, but we were dumb!

Your sweat and my sweat

Made the same earth wet;

Your girl went barefoot, famished;

Always ill my little son;

And the old folks of both of us,

Those who taught us everything,

From the cradle onwards

Always stretching, always searching

For shade and rest and shelter, shelter from the sun —

And you and I arguing

Whether Marx or Bakunin . . .

Hell, but we were dumb!

Now in field of fighting

Our companions
Pierced by the same shrapnel
Their broken bodies mingling
Cry out in their death-rattle
The crime of our disputes.

Anarchist and brother: we know their cry is true.

When the enemy pours out
His barrage on our parapet
Shoulder close to shoulder,
Courage beside courage too,
We grip hands with nothing said.

And Marx and Bakunin. . .hug each other warmly
As brothers swearing loyalty
There where lie our dead.

—Pedro Garfías, *Poems for Spain (1939)*, 1939
[Translated by Tom Wintringham.]

THE SOVIET UNION

There are in the Soviet Union
Millions of men who work
Millions of men who burn brightly just like the tongue of a flame

There are in the Soviet Union
Millions of men who smile
Millions of men who sleep in trust
When the youth of the world is becoming lost in darkness

There are in the Soviet Union
Millions and millions of men in the foundry of a dream
Of bodies transfused by the light of a blood
That is already beginning to flow freely in their veins

There are in the Soviet Union
Millions of men who have sown the vigor of their muscles and
    their wills
And who smiling pure and fortunate are now germinating
Beneath a sky fashioned with a new understanding

There are in the Soviet Union
Millions and millions of men who greet us
Of beings who call to us
Of faces that look on us

There are in the Soviet Union
Millions of men who work

They know that one day
From their hands life will spring on wings
They know that one day
The equality of their arms will be eternal
That only the hungry enslaved mouths of
Machines will chomp steel and wind
Whilst free they will show off their naked bodies
The human rose of their essence

They know that one day
A fuller world will spin free of frontiers
That a hand in the south will cast the same shadow as in the
seas of the north

They know that one day
The Earth will know the mission of their flesh
The value of their strength

They know that one day
Just as they work
All men will sleep in trust
Without the youth being lost in the darkness of the world

There are in the Soviet Union
Millions of men who know
What their eyes believe
And what their hands direct

There is love there
Not just as a shadowless word
Friendship is an arm that offers its smile
The bird and the tree grow equally free beneath the sky

There are no bosses
Only one master who resides in the conscience of each
Like the light to give himself solely to being

There if a man is born
One truth bows before his cradle
One sure path is prepared
And one star lights up on the wind

In Russia the city marches hand in hand with the countryside
Pursuing dreamlessly the socialist rose
In Russia every farm is
Like a nest that is born
A flower that springs up amidst the birds

There every factory is
Like a tree that grows
The heart of Lenin that is raised up singing
Illuminating the Universe
There are in the Soviet Union
A nation that forges hope in silence
A man who even as he sleeps keeps vigil looks out and watches
over the pulse of this people
And a date still recent that cuts through Time
Which bleeds onto the World its teaching
And waves like a cry over the sky

—Emilio Prados, *Octubre*, 1933–34

[Poem translated by Alun Kenwood.]

The plague has always come from Asia like an inexorable, barbaric and physical punishment. It had frightening, repugnant characteristics, and brought with it the certainty of contagion and the sure danger of an unavoidable spread. [. . .]

Such was the plague that devastated Europe the first few times, a medieval scourge that figures among the most terrible and notorious plagues in the world. [. . .]

And one day the Asiatic plague is transmitted to the spirit and becomes intellectual matter, acquiring the same pathological characteristics as when it only sunk its sting into the clay of the flesh. But now it has a much greater evolutionary power, having a much more fertile prospect before it.

Then it emigrates, spreads, and becomes more cruel, if that's possible, than it was in its first phase, and it is no longer called the **black death** but the **red death**. But it still comes from Russia with the same miasmatic symptoms, and now affects the soul the same way as the body.

With its double visage of virulence and terror, the **red death** has found its most propitious growth in the historic soil of Spain, hitherto clean of the corrupting seed and free of foreign slaveries.

Evil became endemic here through the very fertility of our valleys, and, with a face of infernal malevolence, claimed a harvest of victims without any known precedent.

And as consciences twitched in the sadism of hydrophobia – a frenzy of mauling and killing – the tons of rubbish in Barcelona and Madrid especially were composed of tumors full of pus, the morbid imprint of swelling. Rags in the wind, tattered buildings, debris and ashes stunk like a stormy, intestinal main.

Streets, squares, and avenues were tumors and carbuncles, like those whose rankness, according to science, can only be cured with boiling water and the sun.

That's the truth, because in Spain that astral body rose with the morning resplendence, bringing with it the restoration of health. And wherever its golden light touched, the Russian plague disappeared, like a radiant exorcism of the devil.

The shining water of faith was boiling, crosses and towers were raised amid the heat of swords and rifles. Virile youth was a torrent of clarity and example.

In this way, in the midst of the struggle against the **red death**, majesty and delicacy established certain boundaries inside the Fatherland, which are also called trenches. From these one breathes in life as in the best years of urban culture, at the same time as morale is built up to the apex of heroism.

> — Concha Espina, "La pesta roja," *ABC*, Seville edition,
> 13 December 1938

[Excerpt translated by Alun Kenwood.]

POEM OF THE BEAST AND THE ANGEL

I curse you [Lenin] in the name of every twilight
And every rose; I

117

Curse you in the name of Venice and its gondolas,
Of Vienna and its violins,
Of Seville and its sun!
I curse you in your failure, because
You are the anti-Spirit and the Spirit is God!
You are dried up, in the snow, there in Red Square. . .
But in Granada the Nightingale goes on singing!
— José María Pemán, *Poema de la bestia y el ángel*, 1938
[Excerpt translated by Alun Kenwood.]

GERMANY

Beneath the blue curve of the firmament
The rattling of your spurs is heard again;
Over the courses that your ships have sailed
Your flowering propellers tear the wind.
The notes of your bugles vibrate
With the desire of your arms for victory,
And your triumphant story is the noble lesson
That adapts and gives vigor to thought.
We quarter your shield under ours,
And your mottoes have been sculpted
In marble by Hispanic chisels,
For not in vain did your mighty eagles,
On alighting from imperial flights,
On Spanish peaks make their nests.
—Esteban Calle Iturrino, *Arriba España*, 25 October 1936
[Poem translated by Alun Kenwood.]

BALLAD TO THE RUMANIAN KNIGHTS

They came from Rumania.
From Rumania they came.
He was a knight and Prince
Without any cohort of courtiers
But with rather an escort

Of military knights.

Seven knights, seven,

Composed his entourage.

. . . .

They came from Rumania,

From Rumania they came.

Colony on the route to Asia,

Founded by the Roman Empire

And an Andalusian,

The most talented Trajan.[12]

. . . .

Their origin, you could say,

Is Andalusian and so

They neither appear strange to us

Nor feel themselves strangers here.

— José Simón Valdivielso, *La ametralladora*, 25 January 1937
[Excerpt translated by Alun Kenwood.]

HYMN TO THE VOLUNTEERS OF THE REPUBLIC
_____

. . . .

Italian volunteer, among whose campaign animals

Limps an Abyssinian lion!

Soviet volunteer, marching at the head of your universal breast!

Volunteers from the south, from the north, from the east

And you, the westerner, bringing up the rear of the dawn's

    funeral chant!

Known soldier, whose name

Parades in the sound of an embrace!

Combatant whom the earth raised, arming you

With dust,

Shoeing you with positive magnets,

You, with your personal beliefs in full force,

12. Trajan (52–117), born near Seville in Spain, became a Roman emperor in 98 and pacified Dacia and Parthia. He was renowned for his great virtues and service to the Roman empire.

Your distinct character, your intimate rod,
Your immediate complexion,
Your language walking about on your shoulders
And your soul crowned with pebbles!
Volunteer swathed in your cold,
Temperate or torrid zone,
Heroes all round
Victim in a column of victors:
In Spain, Madrid, they're calling you
To kill, volunteers of life!

Because they're killing in Spain, others kill
The child, his toy which comes to a stop,
Radiant mother Rosenda,
Old Adam who talked aloud with his horse,
And the dog which slept on the stairs.
They kill the book, they fire on its auxiliary verbs,
On its defenceless first page!
They kill the statue's exact case,
The scholar, his stick, his colleague,
The barber next door – possibly he cut me,
But a good man and, besides, unfortunate;
The beggar who yesterday was singing opposite,
The nurse who today went by weeping,
The priest burdened with the persistent height of his knees. . .

Volunteers,
For life, for good men, kill
Death, kill the wicked!
Do it for the freedom of everyone,
Of the exploited and of the exploiter,
For peace without pain – I intuit it
When I'm asleep at the foot of my forehead
And even more when I go around shouting –,
And do it, I say,
For the illiterate to whom I write,
For the barefoot genius and his lamb,

For the comrades who have fallen,

Their ashes embracing the corpse of a road!

. . . .

— César Vallejo in *César Vallejo: A Selection of His Poetry*, 1988
[Translated by James Higgins.]

It is therefore an evident truth that if the war in Spain has now lasted a year, it is no longer a movement of repression against an internal rebellion, but an act of war from without, an invasion. The war is entirely and exclusively maintained, not by the military rebels, but by the Foreign Powers that are making a clandestine invasion of the Spanish Republic.

Spain [has been] [. . .] invaded by three Powers: Portugal, Italy and Germany. [. . .]

What, then, are the motives of this three-fold invasion? [. . .] The internal political regime of Spain does not matter greatly to them, and even if it mattered, would not justify the invasion. No. They have come for our mines, they have come for our raw materials, they have come for harbours, for the Straits, for naval bases in the Atlantic and the Mediterranean. What is the purpose of all this? To check the Western Powers who are interested in maintaining this balance and in whose international political orbit Spain has moved for many decades. To check both the British Power and the French. That is the reason for the invasion of Spain.

— Manuel Azaña, *Discurso en el Ayuntamiento de Valencia*,
18 July 1937

[Excerpt translated by Alun Kenwood.]

War-Time Spain

Barcelona

A sign on the facade proclaims its transformation into the University of Catalonia. These days we are more nationalistic than ever. A committee of beadles and lower-echelon employees, under the rector's nominal presidency, had charge of purging the professo-

121

riate. I didn't want to get involved in all that. Some tenured professors who opposed the regime lost their jobs; others opposed to
science remained. In spite of a freeze on hiring administrative
staff, they increased to a hundred and thirty employees, many
more than the professors. Well, anyhow, I got away from all that.
Now they are reviving the purge. The first round didn't go far
enough, and they want me to take part in it. Accusations: "Don So-
and-So said this or that; Beadle So-and-So kept some of his tips; he
has a photograph of So-and-So in his house. . ."

Much of the population had disappeared, all of the money.
They divided provisions with traditional inequality, but now different persons got the larger shares. Great confusion, much good
will, overwhelming fear. Where before one person performed a
service mediocrely or badly, now seven, twelve, or twenty were
determined to do it very well by talk. Those who still had no reason to feel frightened seemed insolent, overbearing, proud, like
kids with new shoes. As if by magic they had their hands on the
apex of the world, and they felt inclined to change its course.

The population flaunted the new style of sloppiness, filth, and
rags. They seemed to belong to a swarthier race because young
warriors let their beards grow, and these, almost all black, darkened faces. Long hair, woolly chests, rifles slung across shoulders,
romantic lunacies after the style of a century ago, barricades.
Many people went along with the crowd from fear of appearing
well-to-do, especially if they were or had been. No hats, berets at
most. Shirts without collars; to wear a necktie would have been an
act of defiance. It seemed a deed of valour for me to keep my
usual style of dress. "They had adopted the new fashion with
greater enthusiasm here than in Barcelona," I thought, remem-
bering how the Ramblas[13] looked after the capital adopted the
beret and its people began to look as if all their clothes came from
the same warehouse. Soldiers of the old army kept some modified
vestige of regulation dress. The officers gave up their uniforms
altogether and sported a new elegance, with luxuries like leather
zippered jackets, little chains, and fancy ornaments. . .

— Manuel Azaña, *Vigil in Benicarló*, 1939

[Translated by Josephine and Paul Stewart.]

13.The *Ramblas* is a tree-lined avenue in the center of Barcelona with a central
walking area surrounded with all sorts of kiosks and vendors.

Madrid

José Félix, helped by the old maid and the porter's wife, was burning Falange newspapers and some portraits of the king in the bathroom heater.

"Your daughter had this here."

"We'll just have to burn it."

It was a photo of Calvo Sotelo dedicated a few days before his death. A small Spanish flag also burned among the kindling. The previous night they had buried an old revolver in the cellar.

He took his leave of the porter and his wife.

"Well, I'm going away from here. If anyone asks for me, I've gone to Valencia."

He went out into the street. He found Madrid desolate, different; although with the same buildings and the same people, it was now a different city. In this way he realized the great force of ideas. In spite of its geography, none of it was Spain any longer. On the Gran Via and Alcala Streets the great horde was encamped! It was a touch of Cuatro Caminos and Vallecas between the sumptuous hotels of the Castellana Parade, beneath the skyscrapers of Peñalver Avenue. The sniping had ceased, but the cars occupied by militia men passed incessantly through the streets. Trucks adorned with red flags were departing for the mountain front to the cry of "FAI, FAI," "CNT." Men and bossy women in corduroy trousers, mixed with wide-hipped militia women, all in shirtsleeves and belts, were shaking menacing clenched fists and waving their guns.

Remnants of the old world still remained: the shops and their display windows, and the open café-bars. The militia men, with their submachine guns on their hip, were going into the Granja del Henar and ordering beer and cocktails.

They were leading an amusing life. In the mornings they would take an aperitif in "Chicote." In this way they showed they didn't hate the rich kids, but rather wanted to be rich kids themselves; they weren't really Marxists, only envious.

They would march up to the mountain front, as if it were an outing, with militia women of easy virtue. Many of them didn't get past Villalba. Having fired a few shots at the "rebels," they would return to Madrid for afternoon tea at the "Aquarium."

The evenings were more amusing. At sunset the searches began. They loved going into the luxury apartments to humiliate the bourgeoisie, to make them serve them liqueurs and cigars, and make the lady of the house, who drove about in a car while they went on foot, cry for them. Moreover, they always took some souvenir, a gold cigarette-case or lighter. The systematic sacking hadn't yet begun.

That, however, wasn't enough for them. They wanted blood.

Fortunately, during those searches, they nearly always found some pale young fellow of eighteen or twenty years of age, a son of the family, whose identity card said "student."

Straight away they would claim that he was a fascist and that he had fired shots from the balcony.

They felt a sadistic pleasure listening to the cries of the mother and sisters. They would push him roughly out of the house. Sometimes the father insisted on accompanying his son.

"You come then, too."

And they looked at each other with a mocking smile.

They would shoot them at daybreak on the outskirts, in the Casa de Campo, in the Maudes Heights, or by the Tetuán bull ring. They would joke about the slaying.

"Let's see your profile. I'm going to do a portrait of you."

"Come on, let's get you a little high."

They didn't believe they should treat them as men, with blood and tears and a nervous system. They played with them as if they were dolls; they laughed at their families. A wife would be crying, and one of the more humane militiamen would intervene. The one in charge would cut in curtly:

"Let her cry. She'll sweat less that way."

Or he would say to the children:

"What shall we do with daddy? Shall we take him for a walk?"

They would tear religious pictures with their bayonets, and throw ivory and nacre crucifixes to the ground.

"Please, no! My son had it between his fingers after his death."

They would dogmatize:

"God doesn't exist. That's all finished."

Modesty, beauty, nor courage disarmed them. They were primitive or hellish forces, prehistoric dreams that had come alive again, and their hate was chemically pure.

It was the great day of revenge, of the weak on the strong, the sick on the healthy, the brutes on the intelligent. Because they hated all superiority. In the chekas[14] it was the triumph of the hunch-backs, the cross-eyed, the ricket-ridden, and the thin-

---

14. *Chekas* were Russian interrogation centers.

breasted, loveless whores, who had never known the beauty of a young body in their arms.

"We're going to give these girls what for."

They wanted to see those beautiful bodies humiliated in death, those lovely rosy breasts naked at their feet. These men were driven on by something satanic. It was as if they were all possessed by the devil. The red reflections in their blackened faces and their ferocious smiles were virtually speckled with saliva. They smelt of blood, sweat, and canvas sandals.

An instinct for evil sharpened their senses. So ignorant workers who had never set foot in the Prado knew how to destroy the best canvases, to tear up the most complex "Riberas." [. . .]

They were throwing out the entire past – the legends, the memories, the nostalgia. They had smashed miniatures and wind-up clocks, lithographs and display cabinets, and private letters from Isabella the Second, Prim, and O'Donnell,[15] ancient contracts, relics, fans from old operas, photographs of grandparents, and archives. The city was left with no history, like a new city in Australia or North America, with no link with the past, without furniture of style or swords or monks' choir stalls.

It was not simply a struggle of ideas. It was crime, hate, and sexual instinct roaming the streets.

— Agustín de Foxá, *Madrid, de corte a checa*, 1938
[Excerpt translated by Alun Kenwood.]

Political Powerlessness

Where do you see national solidarity? I don't see it anywhere. The roof of the house began to burn, and its tenants, instead of hurrying to help put out the fire, have turned to plundering each other, carrying away what they can. This general dissociation has become one of the war's most miserable aspects, this assault on the State and dispute about spoils. Class against class, party against party,

15. Isabella (1830–1904) was Queen of Spain from 1834 to 1868. Her succession to the throne over the rights of her brother, Don Carlos, led to civil conflict throughout the rest of the nineteenth century. She was expelled from Spain in 1868 for her scandalous conduct and shameless administration.

General Juan Prim (1814–1870) was one of Spain's greatest liberal Generals and the architect of Spain's First Republic, which was proclaimed in 1872 and dissolved in 1874.

General Leopoldo O'Donnell (1809–1867) was a moderate Liberal leader and founder of the Liberal Union party. His goal was government by consensus and by avoidance of ideological intransigence.

region against region, regions against state. The Spaniards' racial Bedouinism seems stronger than the rebellion itself, so strong that for many months they have forgotten their fear of the rebels and concentrated on satiating their repressed greed.

— Manuel Azaña, *Vigil in Benicarló*, 1939

[Translated by Josephine and Paul Stewart]

THE FIFTH BATTALION

Anarchists, unionists,

Socialists, communists

And also republicans –

The hour has come

For us to embrace as brothers

And to say to each other in unison:

We are all of the proletariat,

And such as we are

We must never separate.

— Rafael Alberti, *El mono azul*, 22 July 1937

[Poem translated by Alun Kenwood.]

Political Persecution

Today it can be seen that the persecution of every individual on the right, even the nonactivist at times, merely for not belonging to the opposite faction or for some casual bourgeois connection, is an implacable hunt that breaks the bounds of criminal law.

The confiscation of current accounts in the banks; the seizures of stocks and financial deposits, of properties and industrial firms; the requisition of jewelry, clothes and all types of goods, even private homes; the prohibition of religious symbols and practices; the dismissals, often accompanied by violent murders that go unpunished; taxes, prison sentences, fines, the forced extension of hospitality to Marxist refugees; manual labor obligatory for the lords of the manor; the most uncivil, savage cruelty against all that which intelligence, art, and tradition stand for — in short, the greatest social aberrations against history, culture, and the recognition of the Deity have fallen blindly on the Spain presided over by the communists. [. . .]

You have taken away from the bourgeoisie their weapons, their fortunes, their religious practices, their homes, even their over-coats in the street, and their lives. And all this in the name of equality and fraternity, in order to give pistols, powers, palaces, and art treasures to the illiterate, homicidal rabble that you insist on calling the people. You who give to nobody, not even to your adored politics, do you have the right to demand that they who abhor it give everything to it? Is that justice? Is that liberty?

— Concha Espina, *Retaguardia*, 1937

[Excerpt translated by Alun Kenwood.]

Military Incompetence

And the command? Where was the command? Why were we there without leaders? Why had the general staff not told us what they knew, given us the advantage of the technical knowledge by which the defense would have been easier and less bloody? Perhaps military technical knowledge is not granted to rank and file when these are not mechanized soldiers, soldiers of the regiments, but only masons or peasants? But after all it was war, and it ought to have had some kind of professional interest for a professional. Perhaps in these first days they all held back, expecting that events of themselves would take a definite direction, so that its accomplished fact would have to be accepted in favour of the conquerors? But in that case the accomplished fact could only be the victory of Franco. In the enemy camp not a soldier moved except under the direct orders of his officers. All that we had to oppose to that discipline were the enthusiasm and the free initiative of the working mason, the business clerk, the labourer and the out-of-work journeyman, a rifle and a cartridge-pouch not too full. No one thought of going to the front provided with a tin of food and a flagon of water. A man was a rifle and forty cartridges. Yes, but also his heart, which carried a load of generosity larger than the charge of trinitrotoluene in a shell. We looked round again.

— Ramón J. Sender, *The War in Spain*, 1937

[Translated by Sir Peter Chalmers Mitchell.]

Anticlericalism

The temples have already been destroyed, the sanctuaries blemished, the images ridiculed and profaned; everything around the faith of Christ falls silent and hides, relegated to the torment of the vilest persecutions. Works of art in wood and canvas were burnt; holy marble and alabaster sculptures, chopped up by destructive axes, were sent tumbling down. Every religious building still in existence is today scoffingly destined to service as a stable or garage or storehouse. Priests are suffering martyrdom and death by the hundreds.

— Concha Espina, *Retaguardia*, 1937

[Excerpt translated by Alun Kenwood.]

The streets round the Plaza de Antón Martín were choked with people. They were filled with an acrid, dense smoke. They smelled of burned timber. The Church of San Nicolás was on fire. The dome had a helmet of flames. I saw the glass panes of its lantern shatter and incandescent streams of molten lead run down. Then the dome was a gigantic, fiery ball with a life of its own, creaking and twisting under the impact of the flames. For an instant the fire seemed to pause, and the enormous cupola cracked open. [. . .]

"Arturo, Arturo, this is terrible, what's going to happen here? They've burned down San Nicolás and all the other churches in Madrid, San Cayetano, San Lorenzo, San Andrés, the Escuela Pía –"

"Don't worry," a customer who sported a pistol and a red-and-black scarf challenged him. "There are too many of those black beetles anyhow." [. . .]

Twenty neighbours started giving me information: Fascists had fired at the people from the churches, and so the people had stormed the churches. Everything was burning. . .

[. . .] It was impossible to applaud the violence. I was convinced that the Church of Spain was an evil which had to be eradicated. But I revolted against this stupid destruction. What had happened to the great library of the College, with its ancient illuminated books, its unique manuscripts? What had happened to the splendid collections of Physics and Natural Science? All that wealth of educational material! Had those priests and those Falangist boys really been so incredibly stupid as to expect the College to serve as a fortress against an enraged people?

— Arturo Barea, *The Forging of a Rebel*, 1946

[Translated by Ilsa Barea.]

Executions

The rebels sowed desolation during the seven days in which the village was in their hands. There was not a single peasant's house in which some relation had not been murdered. The chiefs of the syndicate were marched on foot to the cemetery, where they were forced to dig their own graves. Whilst they were digging, the gentry of the Falange taunted them: 'Don't you say that the earth is for those who labour in it? Now you see you are going to get your share. You can keep that piece of land over you until the Day of Judgement.' Others of them said: æYou needn't dig so deep; it is already deep enough for a dog's grave.' Or they would advise them to leave a little step where the head would lie, 'so that they would be more comfortable.' The peasants went on digging in silence. One of them tried to escape, but they caught him after wounding him in the leg. [. . .] They compelled the unfortunate man to open a grave, telling him that it was for someone else, and when that was done they made him lie down at full length in it, 'to see if it would hold a human body.' When he had done so, they fired on him and without seeing if he had been killed, ordered the grave-digger to fill in the grave. He said to them: `He seems to be moving still.'

The Falangists pointed their revolvers at him and warned him to take care, because 'many a man is hung by his tongue.'

— Ramón J. Sender, *The War in Spain*, 1937
[Translated by Sir Peter Chalmers Mitchell.]

A file of elegant cars battered by communist abuse, some bearing coats of arms, awaits these prisoners, and in these stolen vehicles they are driven to certain nearby lonely roads, where they are executed, having previously suffered insults and sentencing to death. Time after time the victim's own carriage serves him as his hearse, and there the dead are left at the edge of the fields or simply on the side of the road. The executioners are in a hurry. They can't waste time digging graves.

— Concha Espina, *Retaguardia*, 1937
[Excerpt translated by Alun Kenwood.]

Here now was the Law of Flight. The shadows all round proclaimed it. The four, handcuffed, were walking in file. Alongside

---

them, also in file, were the six guards with their short street carbines. One agent marched in front, the other at the rear. Here was the Law of Flight! Liberto showed what was about to happen, and Helios, who was behind too, by dragging their feet and stumbling at every pace without cause. Liberto was in front. He did not know how the others were taking it, but he would have liked to look at their faces. [. . .]

Helios was humming under his breath and marking time with his feet. He didn't understand what he was doing at first, but soon found that he was singing "The International." Liberto felt that the new certainty, the knowledge that Helios also was expecting death, confirmed all his suspicions, and the certainty was too much for him. He felt his resolution slipping away, and his feet trod the ground carelessly as if he were bare-footed and had been so all his life. Margraf and Crousell joined in Helios' song. Their voice was the voice of men who were drunk or who had not been to bed for days. They sang in a low voice. Liberto saw the darkness round him and recalled his childish fears, and wished to die in the full sun. To die in the darkness was a fate for beasts of prey, for highwaymen, for tramp criminals with garments infested by lice caught in houses of Peace and Charity. He would have wished sun, air, the wide horizon. [. . .]

Crousell directed short phrases to the others as if they were parts of a speech.

"Courage, brothers; the revolution goes marching on."

The footsteps of the four were much firmer than those of the agents and guards. It gives strength to know that one is dying without guilt. It has an unnatural beauty. To kill an innocent man is to exalt innocence, to heights inaccessible to the human mind. On the other hand the killer has lost peace, lost moral equilibrium. He in his turn will die in the darkness, and self-disgust will in the end close his eyes.

— Ramón J. Sender, *Seven Red Sundays*, 1936

[Translated by Sir Peter Chalmers Mitchell.]

"They've killed him, Victor, they've killed him!," she cried in a torn voice. [. . .]

"But do you know who did it?"

"They did it. They who have neither Fatherland nor God. Those lacking souls and light. Those black jackals of the Russian night. Those without Mother or Faith. Those against whom we of the yoke and arrows are struggling. Does it matter that we don't know their names? They don't even know their own names, and that doesn't matter to them. The most revolting monsters, those who have never been suckled by a mother, they don't know their names either. We'll crush them like insects, Carmela. I swear to you, by the children of our children who have yet to be born, that they will pray to the untarnished star from which Enrique will bless them for ever and ever!

All the tragically lyrical and proudly beautiful Poetry of the Spanish Falange, born amidst death and Glory, rocked in the cradle by gunshots and brought up amidst hate and heroism, shone out in Victor's voice as he was transfigured into a flame over the ashes of pain that lay upon the house of his dead comrade. His words shed the light of a flowing prophecy , not of an immediate tomorrow, but of an Eternity of splendid tomorrows and of generations to come who would stretch out their hands over a bridge of stars to those who were now being cut down in ignominious treachery.

— Felipe Ximénez Sandoval, *Camisa azul: Retrato de un falangista*, 1938

[Excerpt translated by Alun Kenwood.]

The Siege of Madrid

I'LL EXPLAIN A FEW THINGS

You'll ask: and where are the lilacs?
And the poppy-covered metaphysics?
And the rain repeatedly spattering
Its words, and filling them
With apertures and birds?

I'll tell you all that's happened to me.

I used to live in a suburb,
A suburb of Madrid, with bells,
And clocks and trees.

From there you could look out
Over the dry face of Castile:
An ocean of leather.

My house was called

131

The house of flowers, because in every crook and cranny
Geraniums flowered: it was
A beautiful house
With dogs and little children.
              Raúl, do you remember?
Do you remember, Rafael?
              Federico, do you remember,
Beneath the earth,[16]
Do you remember my house with balconies where
The June sunlight would smother flowers in your mouth?

              Brother, my brother.
Everywhere
Was loud with voices, the salt of the market place,
Piles of palpitating bread,
The stalls of my suburb of Argüelles with its statue
Like a pale inkwell amid a swirl of hake:
Spoons spouted with oil,
A deep pulsing
Of feet and hands swelled in the streets,
Meters, liters, the sharp
Essence of life,
              Stacked-up fish,
Rooftops woven beneath a chill sun in which
The weather vane falters,
The fine, inflamed ivory of potatoes,
And endless waves of tomatoes.

And one morning all this was burning,
One morning the bonfires
Leapt out of the earth
Devouring the living —
And from then on fire,
Gunpowder from then on,
And from then on blood.

Bandits with planes and with Moors,
Bandits with rings and duchesses,

16. Neruda is calling to his friends, the poets Raúl González Tuñón, Rafael Alberti, and Federico García Lorca.

Bandits with black friars spitting out blessings
Came out of the sky to slaughter children
And through the streets the blood of the children
Ran without fuss, like children's blood.

Jackals that the jackals would despise,
Stones that the dry thistle would bite on and spit out,
Vipers that the vipers would abominate!

Face to face with you I have seen the blood
Of Spain rise up like a tide
To drown you in a single wave
Of pride and of knives!

Treacherous
Generals:
Look at my dead house,
Look at broken Spain:
From every house burning metal flows
Instead of flowers;
From every crater in Spain
Emerges Spain.
And from every dead child sprouts a rifle with eyes,
And from every crime bullets are born
That one day will find
Their way into your hearts.

And you will ask: Why doesn't poetry
Speak of the earth and leaves,
And of the great volcanoes of his native land?

Come and see the blood in the streets.
Come and see
The blood in the streets.
Come and see the blood
In the streets!

— Pablo Neruda, *España en el corazón: Himno a las glorias del pueblo
en la guerra 1936–1939*, 1937

[Poem translated by Alun Kenwood.]

133

ODE TO THE CHILDREN OF MADRID KILLED BY MACHINE-GUNS

You can see poor women running in the streets
Like formless shadows or fright in the mist.
Things are shrunken,
Houses broken, splattered with blood,
Rooms where a scream was caught trembling,
Where nothingness exploded suddenly,
Livid dust between floating walls
Raise aloft their deathly phantom.
They are the dark houses where children died.
Look at them.

. . . .

The machine-gun searches them out,
The machine-gun, the lightning serpent,
Death bursting forth for their martyrdom.
Rivers of dead children go looking for
A final destiny, a world above.
In the moonlight one sees
The foul-smelling birds of death:
Aeroplanes, motors, dark vultures whose plumage encloses
The destruction of still-living flesh,
The horrible death of pieces that throb
And that voice of the victims,
Broken in the throat, that irrupts into the city like a groan.
We all hear it. [. . .]

— Vicente Aleixandre, A *hora, diario de la juventud,*
18 February 1938

[Excerpt translated by Alun Kenwood.]

MADRID, BATTLEFRONT

Black afternoon, rain and mire,
Trams and militiamen.
On the causeway, a tangle
Of little carts without horses,

Or donkeys with the villagers'
Wretched household effects.
Colorless faces that are fleeing
From the fields of Toledo;
Children, old people,
Women who were once fair,
The flower of their village,
Today are a flower of tatters.
No one speaks. They all are going,
We all are going
Off to war, or through the war,
Carried by the wind or tumbling
Along by thousands, like leaves
In the golden autumn.
War trucks and ranks
Of militiamen pass by
Amid these zones of silence,
Rain and mire.
Red pennants pass by,
Tattered, madly streaming
Like harbingers of victory
On the bows of cars
While the women form
"Lines" for milk and chickpeas,
Coal, lentils, and bread.
The ground is littered
With glass and the houses
No longer have bright eyes
But rather frozen caverns,
Tragic cavities.

There are tram rails
Like upraised horns;
There are cordoned-off streets
Plumed with the crest of smoke;
There are stone barricades
Where before we would sit down

135

And look at the bright sky
Of this entrusting Madrid,
Open to all the breezes
And kindly thoughts of man.

Bewildered, like a fish
In a bowl of water, I wear out
My footsteps in the streets.
Back and forth,
I visit the underground.
There, like sacks,
Sleep homeless families.
It reeks like a stable;
The air is foul.
I go up and out.
I return to the cloudy afternoon.
I feel as if I am enclosed
In a Madrid made into an island tomb,
Alone, beneath an asphalt sky
Where the crows seeking out
Children and old folks cross.
Black afternoon; rain, rain,
Trams and militiamen.

— José Moreno Villa, *Poetas en la España leal,* 1937

[Poem translated by Alun Kenwood.]

The Battlefront

BATTLE OF THE JARAMA RIVER

Between the earth and the platinum, smothered
By olive groves and dead Spaniards,
Jarama, pure dagger, you have resisted
The wave of the cruel.

There, from Madrid, came men
With hearts gilded by gunpowder
Like bread made of ash and resistance;
    There they came.

Jarama, between iron and smoke
You were like a branch of fallen crystal,
Like a long line of medals,
    For the victorious.

Neither hollows of burning substance,
Nor angry explosions in the air,
Nor the murky darkness of artillery fire
    Mastered your waters.

Those thirsting for blood drank your water,
Water which they drank with mouth upward:
Spanish water and the soil of olive groves
    Filled them with oblivion.

For a second of water and time the current
Of blood from Moors and traitors
Shimmered in your light like the fish
    In a fountain of bitterness.

The coarse-grained flour of your people
Bristled everywhere with metal and bones,
Formidable, like a field of wheat, like the noble earth
    That they defended.

Jarama, my words are inadequate to speak
Of the splendor and mastery of your regions,
And my hand is too weak:
    There your dead remain.

And there also remain your sorrowful sky,
Your stony peace and your foaming current;
And the undying eyes of your people
    Watch over your banks.

— Pablo Neruda, *España en el corazón: Himno a las glorias del pueblo
en la guerra 1936–1939*, 1937

[Poem translated by Alun Kenwood.]

Seve's new friends always sang this hymn [Cara al Sol].[17] Their united voices gave it an aggressive harmony, the sound of a military march. It was a poetic and youthful hymn. Only youth could understand all that of dying in a shirt embroidered by a woman. Only youth could sing of death because it felt so far away. Death could come, but the death they were awaiting was a beautiful one, like a damsel, not a worn-out, old death, with household remedies, spittle, and varicose veins. It was an athlete's death. There was something magnificent in the night, and in the sea that ebbed and flowed, and in the deep, profound murmur that sang also in his breast.

— M. Pombo Angulo, *La sombra de la bandera*, 1969
[Excerpt translated by Alun Kenwood.]

Sometimes the men bent double on themselves, sometimes they seemed to explode, sometimes they stopped as though surprised and slowly bent forward, looking for death as if for a young girl lying in the green meadows, a girl who should be treated gently, with whom one must proceed sweetly and discreetly. [. . .] And all of them were honest sinners, old Christians, who believed in the Holy Trinity, in the Communion of Saints, in the forgiveness of sins, in the life everlasting, in the resurrection of the dead, amen.

— Rafael García Serrano, *La ventana daba al río*, 1963
[Excerpt translated by Alun Kenwood.]

The Heroes

THE TOWER OF EL CARPIO

Bird-beloved tower, fled are your doves,
Your swallows swift and your martens;
The crows have crowded them out,
And the vultures awaiting carcasses,
Your desecrated nests of peace

17. *Cara al Sol* was the hymn of the Falangists.

Are turned into nests of murder;
Machine-gun beaks spit lead and flame
Into the windows of workers' homes.

In the tower the curate's soft hands,
And the jowls of the fat caciques,
Give the orders, and sprinkle death
Over the workers in the streets.
No one dares come near this church
Which sings with a choir of machine-guns
Whose incense is gunpowder, the church
Which the clergy have turned to an arsenal,
Its bell tower into gun turrets.

Empty is the square; the shunned streets
Leading into the square are empty.
The tower has made a desert.
But the siege goes on. Our militia
Do not flinch: the town will not be
A prey to the perch of vultures.
See, underneath the olive trees
Men swarming, clenched fists raised –
Fists to the sky that the tower blackens.

Eight men leave the crowd, step forth;
Their hearts are deep in willing death;
Their pockets deep with dynamite,
Eight miners make an offering
Before this church, an offering of their lives
For the humanity this church betrays.

They climb into an open truck.
'Faster,' cry these hurriers to their doom;
'Faster,' echo back the hollow streets.
The housefronts and the paving stones
Have taken on the hue of shrouds.
Pallid are the eight faces; pallid
The walls beside, as if blanched with awe.

139

Has there been seen in the world
Sacrifice so stainless, heroism so pure,
Such a proud pacing into death,
As these miners in the open truck
Riding the mortal streets.
The bullets come, and one by one
The miners topple; one by one
Their names stand up, and stand forever
Risen to height of immortality.

The truck arrives
With three alive.
They stand at the root of the tower
That they will soon uproot;
They gaze down the impossible street
That they have passed, and think
Of the impossible return; but not long.

They dig the ground and pierce the walls
Preparing their own sepulchre.
Then peals the thunder from their hands.
And when, among the olive trees,
Triumphant thunder echoes back,
The tower crashes to the earth.

Dull heap of stones and shapeless hill,
Soon as the wonder settles, like the dust,
Becomes a glorious monument.
Dynamite sticks for funeral tapers –
Never was heroes' burial so sublime –
Never such a funeral salute!

Dull heap of stones and hill of ruin,
Where three brave hearts now lie entombed,
Is far more eloquent
Than any splendid Alcazar.

The tower toppled to the earth
Has strengthened our foundations,

Cemented there with heroes' blood.

Our strength renewed, our ardour fired, –

Millions heed the valorous example.

Thus was El Carpio stormed!

Long live the armed people!

— Manuel Altolaguirre, *International Literature*, July 1937

[Freely translated by I. Schneider and S. Williams.]

SHORT PRAYER FOR A HERO OF THE REPUBLIC

A book remained at the edge of his dead waist,

A book was sprouting from his dead corpse.

They carried off the hero,

And his mouth, corporeal and ominous, entered our breath;

We all sweated under the weight of our navels;

The moons were following us on foot;

The dead man was also sweating from sadness.

And a book, at the battle for Toledo,

A book, a book behind, a book above, was sprouting from the
    corpse.

Poetry of the purple cheekbone, between saying it

And keeping it quiet;

Poetry in the moral message that had accompanied

His heart.

The book remained and nothing else, for there are no

Insects in his tomb,

And at the edge of his sleeve the air remained soaking itself

And becoming gaseous, infinite.

We all sweated, under the weight of our navels,

The dead man was also sweating from sadness

And a book, I saw it feelingly,

A book, a book behind, a book above

Abruptly sprouted from the corpse.

— César Vallejo, *España, aparta de mí este cáliz*, 1940

[Poem translated by Alun Kenwood.]

THE ONE WHO WAS SHOT

. . . .

José did not die. Look at him!

Resurrected, he has not died;

For he did not die, just as

The people will never die.

Guns and bullets may seek

To wound your breast.

Bombs and cannons may try

To break your body.

But the people live on and conquer,

A people flawless and fearless,

Who in a bloody dawn

Look like a rising sun.

— Vicente Aleixandre, *Romancero de la guerra civil*, 1936
[Excerpt translated by Alun Kenwood.]

LIKE AN AMADIS OF GAUL[18]

Where will she be, that betrothed

Who hid in her breast

My squadron pistol

When the Hammers and Sickles

Patrolled the corners

Of the startled street?

. . . .

She fell murdered for love of me

In the Country House,

Fragrant with oaks

And morning breezes.

. . . .

Death – red banners –

Wandered among the oaks

18. Amadis of Gaul was a legendary medieval hero who embodied all the knightly ideals and inspired numerous accounts of romance and chivalry.

142

– In cool silk stockings –
Dressed as a militia woman.

. . . .

And when lead rips wide
The Blue Shirt embroidered
By the irises of her hands
With thread of blood and silver,
I will go, a Knight on the Sun,
Across the Sky to seek her
With five Arrows of light,
Like an Amadis of Gaul.

 — Federico de Urrutia, *Poemas de la Falange eterna*, 1938

[Excerpt translated by Alun Kenwood.]

WOMEN

Red Amazons,
Warriors against the cold,
With heads held high
And proud chest forward,
And your mouth red
As a fiery oven
In which there swells
The clamor of a shout.
You are all
Flowers of heroism,
Giving in the moments
Of greatest danger
Courage to the one who struggles
Face to face with the enemy,
And your own blood
To the one who who falls wounded.

 — Luis de Tapia, *La Libertad*, 24 July 1936

[Poem translated by Alun Kenwood.]

Once again Michelle's hand was a source of energy, a fountain of peace, a vigorous stream, that tiny hand which had the strength of whole provinces, which represented men and ideas, villages and cities, rivers, woods and mountains, regiments, legionnaires, banners, friends, the smoke from encampments, well-stocked cartridge belts, regulation-issue wine, the solid bond of comrades in arms, the honest voice of the bugle, the incense of gunpowder, everything, everything.

— Rafael García Serrrano, *La ventana daba al río*, 1963
[Excerpt translated by Alun Kenwood.]

THE MAN OF THE MOMENT

Strong boots, a thick blanket,
A gun, a pistol; it is the man.
A hairy chin, an uncut beard,
Spit and curses,
A determined step, a fixed gaze,
Sleeping in his clothes; it is the man.
It is the man of the moment.
This is the only man you see,
In the street, on trains, in doorways,
Come rain or sun,
Among overturned chairs
And flickering lamps,
Among filthy papers
Pushed by the winter gusts.
The whole city is his,
And it doesn't matter to him
Where he lays his head to rest
From the fatigues of ten nights.
It seems he has never had
Neither herd nor toils,
Nor family to care for him,
Nor women to enjoy.
He drinks, he sings, he fights and falls

144

(For to fall belongs to men).
He would like to be his own master and be
At one with all other men.
He wants a book, bread, respect,
A bed, toil, entertainment,
And all the things
Which man makes for man
Or which nature gives
For man to take.
Under the winter rains
And surrounded by severe cannons,
I see him throughout the devastated city,
Serious and noble,
Like a shoot in search of its roots.
This is the man.

— José Moreno Villa, *Romancero de la guerra civil*, 1936

[Poem translated by Alun Kenwood.]

MASS

When the battle was over,
And the combatant was dead, a man came up to him
And said "Don't die; I love you so!"
But the corpse, alas! went on dying.

And two came up, and said to him again:
"Don't leave us! Be Brave! Come back to life!"
But the corpse, alas! went on dying.

Twenty came up to him, a hundred, a thousand, five
    hundred thousand,
Crying out: "So much love, and yet powerless against death!"
But the corpse, alas! went on dying.

Millions of men surrounded him,
With a common plea: "Don't leave us, brother!"
But the corpse, alas! went on dying.

145

Then all the men of the earth
Surrounded him; the corpse looked at them sadly, deeply
moved;
He sat up slowly,
Embraced the first man; started to walk. . .
— César Vallejo, *España, aparta de mí este cáliz*, 1940
[Poem translated by Alun Kenwood.]

Death and Destruction

REPULSIVE VISIONS

We are living a dark night of bad times,
Where nightmares and fear of sad dreams are intertwined in
our eyes.
Darkness is the fertile womb of all monsters
And shadows only create shadows soiled by the soot of the
abysses.
All the doves have become crows.
The earth is sterile and rough with dry thistles. The rivers have
sunk,
And down their course comes a multitude of famished rats
That squeal and scamper and leap about the fields and invade
the cities,
And come in through the windows of the buildings and crawl
into the open mouths of the Christian dwellers.
The gravity of the bells disturbs the profound mystery of the
shadows.
It is Death arriving. Look at him. He comes in his old chariot of
rotten timbers from tombs,
Pulled by the skeletons of two old donkeys from which rooks
peel off the last remnants of flesh.
His shining skull is dreadful as it turns from side to side, imperi-
ously
Killing with his eyes of fire. His skeleton stretches out and
shrinks again before the closed windows.

146

Through them and through the walls in the darkness its scythe
enters, dripping blood,
And he yanks out his victims caught by the stomach, the edge of
the blade deep in the greenish tangle of their guts.
And off he goes, off he goes, with his chariot of dead, amidst a
tribute of bells, glinting crosses and litanies of crazed priests,
Toward the fields through which those hurricane horses of
plague and war have passed.

What a long and so dark night, bright spirits, brotherly men of
tomorrow!
What world of nightmares and of cadavers of vagrant repulsive
visions do we live in?. . .

— César M. Arconada, *Vivimos en una noche oscura,* 1936

[Excerpt translated by Alun Kenwood.]

What we need are recent ruins, new ashes, fresh rubble; the broken apse, the burnt beams and the shattered stained-glass windows were necessary to purify all the psalms.

We were anxious to offer mutilated cloisters and columns and fallen plaster. But that was because Spain was dozing.

We have already had sufficient years of panoramic views, too many tourist Kodaks aimed at the military architecture of our fortresses, an excess of peaceful pigeons in the cornices of our palaces.

In the Escorial the corpses of the kings were growing cold from tedium, the illuminated manuscripts and the embroidered chasubles were tiring of the glass of their display cases, and Toledo, whose pointed towers resemble the diagram of a fever, had given us no relics since the sixteenth century.

That's how the rich citizens of the powerful countries loved us. Those happy men [. . .] loved us for our dull, decadent folklore.

Picturesque Spain; a weekend for the photograph album, the dancing of flamenco, the immolating of bulls, the swinging of the hips of the dancers before the blond men from the North, who wear the generous expressions of conquerors.

But Toledo has now been destroyed; that's to say, built.

A virile, vigilant, unexpected Spain displays on the table its

147

plans of ruined cities, exalts the heroic architecture of its under-mined fortresses.

A new task will confront the tour guides of the future; there will no longer be any need to pause before the livid cadaver of Count Orgaz in his electric oils,[19] or before the Bible of San Luis,[20] speck-led with drops of gold and reddened with tiny virgins holding apples, but rather piles of rubble and dust will have to be climbed, the catacombs of the new epic will have to be visited, contempo-rary galleries surveyed, and magnificent heroes of ballads evoked, the same ones as those who catch trams in our cities, have girl-friends in our families, smile at us and stretch out their hands to us.

Comrades, don't let those bourgeois Jeremiahs, those right-wing Marxists or those pot-bellied, egotistical prophets frighten you.

It is not true that Spain is in ruins. Toledo has never been more whole.

The danger for a historic city and a fatherland with a great lin-eage doesn't lie in ruins but in museums.

The ivory images in glass cases with a catalog number and a red silk rope around them to keep us at a distance should grieve us more than those Christs burnt by Red barbarism and shock us more than those virgins and archangels decapitated on the thresh-ing floors of the villages.

Blessed be the ruins because in them are faith and hate and pas-sion and enthusiasm and struggle and the souls of men.

This Alcazar in ruins puts back into hot circulation all its vener-able treasures.

Alfonso VI came in through this archway with his armed guards, but so did General Varela* with his soldiers and militia men. So we are united once and for all to the dead, and they are resurrected by our deaths.

With the joyful spring of the Falange already comes the thawing of the display cases. The chalices and swords, frozen long ago amidst a dark race with eyes half-closed, now flow in a lively stream. [. . .]

That is how we love Spain – just as she is, with her faith intact,

19. "Count Orgaz" is a reference to El Greco's famous painting, *The Burial of Count Orgaz*, which can be seen in the church of San Tomé in Toledo.
20. "The Bible of San Luis" is the thirteenth-century French Bible that San Luis, King of France, gave to Ferdinand III, King of Spain. The three volumes are kept in the Cathedral Vestry.

even though all her Romanesque churches be burnt ruins; with
her blood heroic, though all her fortresses be demolished.
This is our Spain; poorer but glorious. [. . .]
Because we have known pain, we now know the beauty of ruins.

— Agustín de Foxá, "Arquitectura hermosa de las ruinas," *Vértice*,
April 1937

[Excerpt translated by Alun Kenwood.]

Appeals for International Support

WORKERS OF THE WORLD

Workers of the world:
Come to the aid of Spain,
Free Spain,
Worthy, proletarian Spain!
Put into her hands
The powerful weapons
That you produce with yours
In factories of war!
Send aeroplanes
So that they may give wings to the people
In these conflicts
And in these wars!

— Luis de Tapia, *La Libertad*, 9 September 1936

[Poem translated by Alun Kenwood.]

GATHER THIS VOICE

Nations of the earth, homelands of the sea, brothers
Of the world and of nothingness:
Inhabitants, lost and far
From our view, more than from our hearts.

Here I have an impassioned voice,
Here I have an embattled and violent life,
Here I have a murmur, here I have a life.

Open I am, look, like a wound.
Submerged I am, look, I'm submerged
In the midst of my people and their ills.
Wounded I go, wounded and badly wounded,
Bleeding through trenches and hospitals.

Men, worlds, nations,
Pay heed, listen to my bloodied cry,
Gather together the impulses of my grief
In your spacious hearts,
For I clutch my soul when I sing.

Singing I defend myself
And I defend my people when the barbarians
Of this crime imprint their hooves
Of thunder and gunpowder upon my people.

This is their work, this:
They pass by, razing like whirlwinds,
And, before their fatal wrath,
The horizons are weapons and the roads, death.

The weeping that pours through valleys and balconies
Deluges the stones and upon the stones it works,
And there isn't space for so much death
And there isn't wood for so many coffins.

Caravans of dejected bodies.
All is bandages, suffering and handkerchiefs:
All is stretchers where the strength
And wings of the wounded are broken.

Blood, blood on trees and ground,
Blood upon the waters, blood on the walls,
And a dread that Spain will collapse
Beneath the weight of the blood that soaks through its meshes
Right down to the bread that is eaten.

Nations, men, worlds,
Gather together this wind
That leaves these mouths of impassioned breath
And from these hospitals of the dying.

Apply your ears
To my clamor of a violated people,
To the lament of so many mothers, to the outcries
Of so many bright beings whom grief has devoured.

Breasts that would push and wound the mountains,
Look at them now without milk or beauty,
And see the white brides and their black eyelashes,
Fallen and submerged in an obscure nap.

Apply the passion of your entrails
To this people that dies with an invincible gesture
Scattered by lips and brow,
Beneath those implacable aeroplanes
That snatch terribly,
Terribly, ignominiously, daily,
Children from the hands of their mothers.

Cities of work and innocence,
Generations of youth sprouting from the oaks,
Trunks of bronze, bodies of power
Rest there rushed into ruin.

A future of dust approaches,
Some incident is approaching
In which nothing will remain:
Neither stone upon stone nor bone upon bone.

Spain is not Spain; it's an immense grave,
A vast cemetery, red and bombarded:
The barbarians want it that way.

The earth will become a dense and desolate heart,
If you, nations, men, worlds,
With the whole of my people
And with your people on our flanks,
Don't break their ferocious fangs.
Madrid, 15 Jan. 1937.

— Miguel Hernández, *Poetas de la España leal,* 1937
[Poem translated by Alun Kenwood.]

SPAIN, TAKE THIS CUP FROM ME

Children of the world,
If Spain should fall – I'm just supposing –
If her forearm
Should fall from the sky gripped
In the halter of two terrestrial sheets;
Children, what an age, that of the concave temples!
How early in the sun what I was telling you!
How soon the old noise in your chest!
How old your 2 in your notebook!

Children of the world,
Mother Spain is shouldering the burden of her womb;
She's our teacher with her birches,
She's mother and teacher,
Cross and wood, for she gave you height,
Vertigo and division and addition, children;
It rests with her, judicial parents!

If Spain should fall – I'm just supposing –
If she should fall from the earth downwards,
Children, how are you going to stop growing!
How the year is going to punish the month!
How your teeth will remain at ten,
The diphthong in downstroke, the medal in tears!
How the little lamb will remain
Tethered by the leg to the great inkwell!
How you are going to descend the steps of the alphabet
To the letter where grief was born!

Children,
Children of the warriors, in the meantime
Lower your voices, for this moment Spain is distributing
Her energy among the animal kingdom,
The small flowers, the comets and men.
Lower your voices, for she's
In her hardship, which is great, not knowing

What to do, and in her hand is
The skull, talking and talking and talking,
That skull with the tress,
The skull of life!

Lower your voices, I tell you;
Lower your voices, the chant of the syllables, the weeping
Of matter and the lesser murmur of the pyramids, and even
That of the temples which function with two stones!
Lower your breath, and if
The forearm descends,
If the birches sound, if it is night,
If the sky fits into two terrestrial limbos,
If there's noise in the sound of the doors,
If I'm late,
If you don't see anyone, if blunt pencils
Frighten you, if mother
Spain should fall – I'm just supposing –
Go out, children of the world; go out and look for her! . . .

— César Vallejo, in *César Vallejo: A Selection of His Poetry*, 1988
[Translated by James Higgins.]

Disillusionment and Defeat

CONVERSATION BETWEEN A CATALAN COMMUNIST AND ANDALUSIAN ANARCHIST

"What blasted resistance?" says Farnals. "It's all Negrín. They shall not pass. Die standing up. But those in the know, off they go. They flee and leave in the stockade whoever it might be. All those who went to France in January, not to mention those who left earlier, are now in America or on their way there. In Paris and Bordeaux there are committees that look after nothing else, and we're still here playing at resistance and waiting for the boats that they can easily spare there. It's our own fault for being such twits and swallowing any fat lies that came with the endorsement of the party. How long ago did the Russians decide that we were lost? I don't know, that's for sure."

"It's the revenge," points out Cuatero, "of the North against the South, of Aragon and Catalonia against New Castile. Don't look at me like that! The Castilians and the Andalusians stopped the Catalans from going to America for centuries. Now they're getting their revenge. . ."

CONVERSATION BETWEEN A COMMUNIST AND AN ANARCHIST

"What do they [the Francoists] say about you, the Communists. They call you fanatics, that is, that you see everything through your faith, that you're mad, which is the same thing. Because of that, you are capable of great things while we, in good faith, indecisive, doubtful and hypothetical, will do nothing because we don't know what to believe in nor do we have anything to grab hold of. That's why the Fascists have beaten us. Though they have no faith, they at least count on having the means of allowing themselves the luxury of seeming to have one."

"You're a traitor," says Vicente Dalmases, walking away.

"Because I don't share your idea about what makes the world go around? To be a traitor, my lad, I would have had to be unfaithful to my ideas. I've always believed this."

Vicente turns round angrily:

"That's why we lost, with people like you in our ranks."

"What ranks? The army ranks? Spain has always had three heads and six arms, and of course one body, like Geryon.[21] But not in the sense of his unmatched harmony. We've never understood each other simply because we can't. We would all have to be born again in an instant. And then what would be the result?"

"Communism. . ."

"Bah! If there were ever Communism in Spain it would have three heads as well."

A DISILLUSIONED COMMUNIST

"There are no boats, are there?"

Gregorio Murcia parsimoniously takes out his Communist party card and tears it in two, throws the pieces on the floor and stamps on them.

"What's the good of doing that?"

21. In classical mythology Geryon was king of three provinces in Spain, from which circumstance the ancients made him a three-headed monster with three bodies. He was killed by Hercules.

"None, but don't let them tell me now or ever to believe that the
workers of Odessa and Constantinople, along with those of New
York or Buenos Aires, care or worry about the luck or destiny of
their "brothers." No, don't let them come to me with tales at this
stage. Don't let them tell me that all those millions of them
couldn't arm a few boats and come for us. With next to nothing,
with a few paltry pesetas from the workers along the Mediterranean, from just the dockworkers. . . And they leave us here abandoned, lost, ruined, and they couldn't care less. They'd better not
come to me now, talking about solidarity. What crap, what
absolute bullshit."

— Max Aub, *Campo de los almendros*, 1968
[Excerpts translated by Alun Kenwood.]

Celebration and Lament

Every village celebrated the triumph in its own special way. In one
it was all rockets and youths in shirtsleeves saluting with their arms
held high. In another all the girls congregated in the square in
regional dress, and came out to meet us with bunches of flowers
and waving silk handkerchiefs. [. . .] Not only priests but civil
guards emerged from goodness only knows where. They were
wearing their habits or uniforms, but they seemed to be lacking
something or to have something too much. No doubt the fact that
they were unaccustomed to appearing in public in their usual
clothes made them feel somewhat self-conscious. Some men and
women kept their distance, and from their doorways or windows
watched us, half-satisfied and half-disappointed. I particularly
sought out with my eyes those whose silent lips and whose expressions showed that the scene didn't please them. There weren't
only Reds, demoralized inside, irritated against their wills, citizens
who'd fought for a lost cause and found themselves in ridicule,
but also there were staunch Nationalists who, during their months
of imprisonment and persecution, when they had pictured victory
to themselves, had imagined it as more wanton, more violent,
more exalted. It was something like when one was a child, and the
bishop or the mayor came to the school. It always turned out less
an event than one had hoped for.

— José Luis Castillo Puche, *El vengador*, 1956
[Excerpt translated by Alun Kenwood.]

TESTIMONY

I want to leave
On record
What is happening.

I go to the balcony,
I lean
Over.

I see crepe,
Spears,
Around the coffin
In which
Lies
Happiness.

A man
Raises
The terrible
Banner.
His voice sounds
Like a muffled
Drum.
    Then
Silence.
    Only
A crying
Child.

These are the funeral rites of freedom.

       — José Agustín Goytisolo, *Obras completas*, 1973
[Poem translated by Alun Kenwood.]

RISE UP AGAIN, SPAIN

Rise again, Spain, from amidst the black crepe
Of mourning for your immortal dead,
Light of peace in astral paths,
Dawn in the sky and in our hearts.

When your legions put down their arms,
In fields of triumph will be heard
A fervent ringing of metals,
The iron of anvils and the bronze of prayers.

The vanquished now united to the victor,
Metal blades turned to ploughshares
In your newly green, blooming fields.

The glory of your true heroes,
By keeping vigil and fending off oblivion,
Will fill the heavens with stars.

— Felipe Sassone, *Antología poética del alzamiento, 1936–1939,* 1940
[Poem translated by Alun Kenwood.]

A SPANIARD SPEAKS OF HIS HOMELAND

The beaches, the high plains
Sleeping in the golden sun,
The hillocks, the fertile expanses
In peace, alone, distant;

The castles and hermitages,
The farmhouses and convents,
Life with history
All so sweet to the memory,

They, the eternal
Victorious Cains,
Tore me away from it all.
All they leave me is exile.

A divine hand
Raised your soil in my body
And there a voice arranged
For your silence to speak.

With you I was alone,
Believing only in you;

157

To think your name now
Poisons my dreams.

How can a rose live
If it is torn out of the soil?

Bitter are the days
Of the life lived
Only in a long wait
And fed on memories.

One day, you by then free
Of their lies,
Will seek me out. Then
What will a dead man have to say?

— Luis Cernuda, *Las nubes* (1937–40)
in *La realidad y el deseo*, 1970

[Poem translated by Alun Kenwood.]

The New Spain

Franco was the first real ruler in my life because from the beginning it was clear that he was the one and only, that his power was
indisputable and omnipresent, that he had managed to insinuate
himself into every house, school, cinema, and café, do away with
spontaneity and variety, arouse a religious, uniform fear, stifle con-
versations and laughter so that no one's voice was louder than anyone else's. Remember that I was nine years old when I began to
see his picture everywhere, in the newspapers and on the walls,
smiling beneath that military beret with the tassels, and then later
on in the school classrooms, on the newsreels, and on stamps. And
the years went by and there was always his effigy, and nothing but
his effigy. The others were satellites; his reign was absolute. If he
were ill, no one knew it. It was as if sickness and death would never
overtake him. So when he died I reacted in the same way as other
people – I couldn't believe it. [. . .] All the years of his reign came
tumbling down on top of me. To me they felt like a homogeneous
block, like a dark brown mountain range such as the ones you see
on geophysical maps. The only thing I realized [. . .] was that I am

incapable of discerning the passage of time during that period, or of differentiating the war years from the postwar ones. It struck me that Franco had paralyzed time.

— Carmen Martín Gaite, *El cuarto de atrás*, 1983

[Excerpt translated by Alun Kenwood.]

British Responses to the War

Poets of the 1930s
Introduction

JOHN LEONARD

For many radical young Britons, Spain became the place of necessary, active opposition to the reactionary tide that seemed to be gathering in all of Europe. The war in fact tested all their years of idealistic analysis, as the example of George Orwell preeminently shows. Left-wing poets found their polemics reworked, as the war forced them to focus on the point of tension, and clash, between ideas of individual value and collective necessity.

In reading the work of the poets selected here, it is useful to remember that only one of them spent more than several weeks in Spain. John Cornford (1915–1936) who arrived as a Communist volunteer in August 1936, fought with a POUM contingent at Perdiguera and Huesca on the Aragon front and was killed near Lopera at the end of December. Sylvia Townsend Warner (1893–1978), also a Communist party member, spent three weeks with the English Red Cross unit in Barcelona in August 1936, and returned briefly in July 1937 to Madrid as a delegate to the Congress of the Association of International Writers in Defence of Culture. W. H. Auden (1907–1973) who was leftist in politics at the time but not a member of a party, wrote to a friend upon going: "I shall probably be a bloody bad soldier, but how can I speak to/for them without becoming one?"[1] He arrived in Barcelona in January 1937, went on to Valencia where he spent several weeks unwillingly assigned to propaganda duty, and managed a short visit to the front at Sarinera. He returned to England disillusioned by much of what he had seen, but would not give the enemy advantage by saying so publicly. "Spain" was published as a pamphlet in April. Stephen Spender (1909–1989) made a slightly more mobile visit during the same period, on behalf on the *Daily Worker*, while

1. H. Carpenter, ed., *W. H. Auden, A Biography* (London, 1981), 207.

briefly and uncomfortably enrolled as a Communist party member. He returned to Madrid for a short visit in July to attend the Writers' Congress. Finally, Louis MacNeice (1907-1956), who was sympathetic to the Left but the least political of the poets surveyed here, holidayed in Spain at Easter 1936: this is the visit that he recalls in the extract from *Autumn Journal,* a book-length diary poem written between August and December 1938.

When politics are taken seriously as a fit subject for poetry, the modernist assumption that a poem is autonomous is undermined. Priorities begin to be inverted in the question whether poetry is an effective medium for politics. The poet's own sense of vocation is affected, as questions of audience and of class become more conscious and crucial. Even so, for the poets represented here, poetry seems to have been as much a medium for the testing of ideas as it was for their dissemination. A strongly lyrical mode was retained – with its inherited weight of assumptions of autonomy – concerning the poem, but also concerning the individuality of human perceptions within it. Warner's "Benicasim" and Cornford's "A Letter from Aragon," for example, are notable for their patient and delicate focus on one place, one event. As befits their respective roles as visitor and combatant, Warner observes from a little distance, while Cornford is in the midst, but each centers his work on the primacy of human experience – both individual and communal – during a crisis, while aware of the hard necessity that exists at the periphery of their vision. The poems here by Spender also display the tact of one who will not intrude, but they are intense, from a resolved sense of the war as an individual and communal tragedy. In his long career as a poet, Spender has seemed to be sporadic and not always tuned, but his Spanish Civil War poems must surely stand among the finest lyrical poems of their time. They are formed in the tradition of the lyric, which values the individual's fate above all else, but they also specify community. Cornford, in "Poem," written for his friend Margot Heinemann in England, writes a lyric of love and fear that is traditional. This is the "pity of war" as Wilfred Owen – and any soldier in a trench – knows it. But to Cornford, what he wrote of Kirov, the popular Communist assassinated in Leningrad in 1934, seems to have been just as basic: "Only in constant action was his constant certainty found." The conundrum of private need and public necessity is mercilessly turned over in Auden's "Spain," of which the version given here is the original. Auden revised it drastically in 1939, then rejected it entirely from 1956, because the conclusion, he thought, equated goodness with success. The whole poem is in fact riddled with a powerful ambivalence. A vertigo of contemporary existence – which might or might not carry the possibility of choice – dominates the poem. Its emblems chart the raw material of the politics of the time, ranging from the individual psyche to the cultural landscape of Europe. To Auden, as to all of these poets, it was more than Republican Spain that hung in the balance.

SERGEI MIRONOVITCH KIROV[2]

Nothing is ever certain, nothing is ever safe,
Today is overturning yesterday's settled good.
Everything dying keeps a hungry grip on life.
Nothing is ever born without screaming and blood.

Understand the weapon, understand the wound:
What shapeless past was hammered to action by his deeds,
Only in constant action was his constant certainty found.
He will throw a longer shadow as time recedes.

— John Cornford, *Understand the Weapon, Understand the Wound:
Selected Writings of John Cornford,* 1976

A LETTER FROM ARAGON

This is a quiet sector of a quiet front.

We buried Ruiz in a new pine coffin,
But the shroud was too small and his washed feet stuck out.
The stink of his corpse came through the clean pine boards
And some of the bearers wrapped handkerchiefs round their
   faces.
Death was not dignified.
We hacked a ragged grave in the unfriendly earth
And fired a ragged volley over the grave.

You could tell from our listlessness, no one much missed him.

2. John Cornford wrote "Sergei Mironovitch Kirov" while at Cambridge University.

This is a quiet sector of a quiet front.
There is no poison gas and no H.E.[3]

But when they shelled the other end of the village
And the streets were choked with dust
Women came screaming out of the crumbling houses,
Clutched under one arm the naked rump of an infant.
I thought: how ugly fear is.

This is a quiet sector of a quiet front.
Our nerves are steady; we all sleep soundly.

In the clean hospital bed my eyes were so heavy
Sleep easily blotted out one ugly picture,
A wounded militiaman moaning on a stretcher,
Now out of danger, but still crying for water,
Strong against death, but unprepared for such pain.

This on a quiet front.

But when I shook hands to leave, an Anarchist worker
Said: 'Tell the workers of England
This was a war not of our own making,
We did not seek it.
But if ever the Fascists again rule Barcelona
It will be as a heap of ruins with us workers beneath it.'

— John Cornford, *John Cornford: A Memoir*, 1938

POEM

[Retitled "To Margot Heinemann"]

Heart of the heartless world,
Dear heart, the thought of you
Is the pain at my side,
The shadow that chills my view.

The wind rises in the evening,
Reminds that autumn is near.

3. "H. E." is the abbreviation for high explosive shells.

I am afraid to lose you,
I am afraid of my fear.

On the last mile to Huesca,
The last fence for our pride,
Think so kindly, dear, that I
Sense you at my side.

And if bad luck should lay my strength
Into the shallow grave,
Remember all the good you can;
Don't forget my love.

— John Cornford, *John Cornford: A Memoir*, 1938

BENICASIM[4]

Here for a little we pause.
The air is heavy with sun and salt and colour.
On palm and lemon-tree, on cactus and oleander
A dust of dust and salt and pollen lies.
And the bright villas
Sit in a row like perched macaws,
And rigid and immediate yonder
The mountains rise.

And it seems to me we have come
Into a bright-painted landscape of Acheron.
For along the strand
In bleached cotton pyjamas, on rope-soled tread,
Wander the risen-from-the-dead,
The wounded, the maimed, the halt.
Or they lay bare their hazarded flesh to the salt
Air, the recaptured sun,
Or bathe in the tideless sea, or sit fingering the sand.

---

4. At Benicasim on the east coast of Spain is the Rest Home for the convalescent wounded of the Spanish People's Army, and the Villa dedicated to Ralph Fox, supported by the Spanish Medical Aid. [Original footnote.]

But narrow is this place, narrow is this space
Of garlanded sun and leisure and colour, of return
To life and release from living. Turn
(Turn not!) sight inland:
There, rigid as death and unforgiving, stand
The mountains – and close at hand.

— Sylvia Townsend Warner, *Collected Poems*, 1980

SPAIN

Yesterday all the past. The language of size
Spreading to China along the trade-routes; the diffusion
        Of the counting-frame and the cromlech;
Yesterday the shadow-reckoning in the sunny climates.

Yesterday the assessment of insurance by cards,
The divination of water; yesterday the invention
        Of cartwheels and clocks, the taming of
Horses. Yesterday the bustling world of the navigators.

Yesterday the abolition of fairies and giants,
The fortress like a motionless eagle eyeing the valley,
        The chapel built in the forest;
Yesterday the carving of angels and alarming gargoyles.

The trial of heretics among the columns of stone;
Yesterday the theological feuds in the taverns
        And the miraculous cure at the fountain;
Yesterday the Sabbath of witches; but to-day the struggle.

Yesterday the installation of dynamos and turbines,
The construction of railways in the colonial desert;
        Yesterday the classic lecture
On the origin of Mankind. But to-day the struggle.

Yesterday the belief in the absolute value of Greek,
The fall of the curtain upon the death of a hero;
        Yesterday the prayer to the sunset
And the adoration of madmen. But to-day the struggle.

As the poet whispers, startled among the pines,
Or where the loose waterfall sings compact, or upright
      On the crag by the leaning tower:
'O my vision. O send me the luck of the sailor.'

And the investigator peers through his instruments
At the inhuman provinces, the virile bacillus
      Or enormous Jupiter finished:
'But the lives of my friends. I inquire. I inquire.'

And the poor in their fireless lodgings, dropping the sheets
Of the evening paper: 'Our day is our loss, O show us
      History the operator, the
Organiser, Time the refreshing river.'

And the nations combine each cry, invoking the life
That shapes the individual belly and orders
      The private nocturnal terror:
'Did you not found the city state of the sponge,

'Raise the vast military empires of the shark
And the tiger, establish the robin's plucky canton?
      Intervene. O descend as a dove or
A furious papa or a mild engineer, but descend.'

And the life, if it answers at all, replies from the heart
And the eyes and the lungs, from the shops and squares of the
      city:
      'O no, I am not the mover;
Not to-day; not to you. To you, I'm the

'Yes-man, the bar-companion, the easily-duped;
I am whatever you do. I am your vow to be
      Good, your humorous story.
I am your business voice. I am your marriage.

'What's your proposal? To build the just city? I will.
I agree. Or is it the suicide pact, the romantic
      Death? Very well, I accept, for
I am your choice, your decision. Yes, I am Spain.'

Many have heard it on remote peninsulas,
On sleepy plains, in the aberrant fisherman's islands
      Or the corrupt heart of the city,
Have heard and migrated like gulls or the seeds of a flower.

They clung like burrs to the long expresses that lurch
Through the unjust lands, through the night,
Through the alpine tunnel;
      They floated over the oceans;
They walked the passes. All presented their lives.

On that arid square, that fragment nipped off from hot
Africa, soldered so crudely to inventive Europe;
      On that tableland scored by rivers,
Our thoughts have bodies; the menacing shapes of our fever

Are precise and alive. For the fears which made us respond
To the medicine ad. and the brochure of winter cruises
      Have become invading battalions;
And our faces, the institute-face, the chain-store, the ruin

Are projecting their greed as the firing squad and the bomb.
Madrid is the heart. Our moments of tenderness blossom
      As the ambulance and the sandbag;
Our hours of friendship into a people's army.

To-morrow, perhaps the future. The research on fatigue
And the movements of packers; the gradual exploring of all the
      Octaves of radiation;
To-morrow the enlarging of consciousness by diet and breathing.

To-morrow the rediscovery of romantic love,
The photographing of ravens; all the fun under
      Liberty's masterful shadow;
To-morrow the hour of the pageant-master and the musician,

The beautiful roar of the chorus under the dome;
To-morrow the exchanging of tips on the breeding of terriers,
      The eager election of chairmen
By the sudden forest of hands. But to-day the struggle.

To-morrow for the young the poets exploding like bombs,
The walks by the lake, the weeks of perfect communion;
     To-morrow the bicycle races
Through the suburbs on summer evenings. But to-day the
  struggle.

To-day the deliberate increase in the chances of death,
The conscious acceptance of guilt in the necessary murder;
     To-day the expending of powers
on the flat ephemeral pamphlet and the boring meeting.

To-day the makeshift consolations: the shared cigarette,
The cards in the candlelit barn, and the scraping concert,
     The masculine jokes; to-day the
Fumbled and unsatisfactory embrace before hurting.

The stars are dead. The animals will not look.
We are left alone with our day, and the time is short, and
     History to the defeated
May say Alas but cannot help nor pardon.

             — W. H. Auden, *Selected Poems*, 1979

TWO ARMIES

Deep in the winter plain, two armies
Dig their machinery, to destroy each other.
Men freeze and hunger. No one is given leave
On either side, except the dead, and wounded.
These have their leave; while new battalions wait
On time at last to bring them violent peace.

All have become so nervous and so cold
That each man hates the cause and distant words
Which brought him here, more terribly than bullets.
Once a boy hummed a popular marching song,
Once a novice hand flapped the salute;
The voice was choked, the lifted hand fell,
Shot through the wrist by those of his own side.

171

From their numb harvest all would flee, except
For discipline drilled once in an iron school
Which holds them at the point of a revolver.
Yet when they sleep, the images of home
Ride wishing horses of escape
Which herd the plain in a mass unspoken poem.

Finally, they cease to hate, for although hate
Bursts from the air and whips the earth like hail
Or pours it up in fountains to marvel at,
And although hundreds fall, who can connect
The inexhaustible anger of the guns
With the dumb patience of these tormented animals?

Clean silence drops at night when a little walk
Divides the sleeping armies, each
Huddled in linen woven by remote hands.
When the machines are stilled, a common suffering
Whitens the air with breath and makes both one
As though these enemies slept in each other's arms.

Only the lucid friend to aerial raiders,
The brilliant pilot moon, stares down
Upon the plain she makes a shining bone
Cut by the shadow of many thousand bones.
Where amber clouds scatter on no-man's-land
She regards death and time throw up
The furious words and minerals which kill life.

— Stephen Spender, *The Still Centre*, 1939

ULTIMA RATIO REGUM[5]

The guns spell money's ultimate reason
In letters of lead on the Spring hillside.
But the boy lying dead under the olive trees
Was too young and too silly

5. The first version was "Regum Ultima Ratio," published in *New Statesman and Nation*, 15 May 1937.

To have been notable to their important eye.
He was a better target for a kiss.
When he lived, tall factory hooters never summoned him
Nor did restaurant plate-glass doors revolve to wave him in.
His name never appeared in the papers.
The world maintained its traditional wall
Round the dead with their gold sunk deep as a well,
Whilst his life, intangible as a Stock Exchange rumour, drifted
  outside.

O too lightly he threw down his cap
One day when the breeze threw petals from the trees.
The unflowering wall sprouted with guns,
Machine-gun anger quickly scythed the grasses;
Flags and leaves fell from hands and branches;
The tweed cap rotted in the nettles.

Consider his life which was valueless
In terms of employment, hotel ledgers, news files.
Consider. One bullet in ten thousand kills a man.
Ask. Was so much expenditure justified
On the death of one so young, and so silly
Lying under the olive trees, O world, O death?

                    — Stephen Spender, *The Still Centre*, 1939

A STOPWATCH AND AN ORDNANCE MAP

A stopwatch and an ordnance map.
At five a man fell to the ground
And the watch flew off his wrist
Like a moon struck from the earth
Marking a blank time that stares
On the tides of change beneath.
All under the olive trees.

A stopwatch and an ordnance map.
He stayed faithfully in that place
From his living comrade split

173

By dividers of the bullet
That opened wide the distances
Of his final loneliness.
All under the olive trees.

A stopwatch and an ordnance map.
And the bones are fixed at five
Under the moon's timelessness;
But another who lives on
Wears within his heart for ever
The space split open by the bullet.
All under the olive trees.

— Stephen Spender, *The Still Centre*, 1939

FALL OF A CITY

All the posters on the walls,
All the leaflets in the streets
Are mutilated, destroyed, or run in rain,
Their words blotted out with tears,
Skins peeling from their bodies
In the victorious hurricane.

All the names of heroes in the hall
Where the feet thundered and the bronze throats roared
FOX and LORCA claimed a history on the walls,[6]
Are now angrily deleted
Or to dust surrender their gold
From golden praise excluded.

All the badges and salutes
Torn from lapels and from hands,
Are thrown away with human sacks they wore,
Or in the deepest bed of mind
They are washed over with a smile
Which launches the victors when they win.

6. Both Ralph Fox and Federico García Lorca were victims of the war.

All the lessons learned, unlearnt;
The young, who learned to read, now blind
Their eyes with an archaic film;
The pleasant relapses to a stumbling tune
Following the donkey's bray;
These only remember to forget.

But somewhere some word presses
In the high door of a skull, and in some corner
Of an irrefrangible eye
Some old man's memory jumps to a child
– Spark from the days of liberty.
And the child hoards it like a bitter toy.

— Stephen Spender, *The Still Centre*, 1939

THE BOMBED HAPPINESS

Children, who extend their smile of crystal,
And their leaping gold embrace,
And wear their happiness as a frank jewel,
Are forced in the mould of the groaning bull
And engraved with lines on the face.

Their harlequin-striped flesh,
Their blood twisted in rivers of song,
Their flashing, trustful emptiness,
Are trampled by an outer heart that pressed
From the sky right through the coral breast
And kissed the heart and burst.

This timed, exploding heart that breaks
The loved and little hearts, is also one
Splintered through the lungs and wombs
And fragments of squares in the sun,
And crushing the floating, sleeping babe
Into a deeper sleep.

Its victoried drumming enters
Above the limbs of bombed laughter

175

The body of an expanding State
And throbs there and makes it great,
But nothing nothing can recall
Gaiety buried under these dead years,
Sweet jester and young playing fool
Whose toy was human happiness.

— Stephen Spender, *New Statesman and Nation*, 4 February 1939

PORT BOU[7]

As a child holds a pet
Arms clutching but with hands that do not join
And the coiled animal looks watches the gap
To outer freedom in animal air.
So the earth-and-rock flesh arms of this harbour
Embrace but do not endorse the sea
Which, through a gap, vibrates in the open sea
Where ships and dolphins swim and above is the sun.
In the bright winter sunlight I sit on the stone parapet
Of a bridge; my circling arms rest on a newspaper
Empty in my mind as the glittering stone
Because I search for an image
And seeing an image I count out the coined words
To remember the childish headlands of the harbour.
A lorry halts beside me with creaking brakes
And I look up at warm waving flag-like faces
Of militiamen staring down at my French newspaper.
'How do they write of our struggle, over the frontier?'
I hold out the paper, but they refuse,
They did not ask for anything so precious
But only for friendly words and to offer me cigarettes.
In their smiling faces the war finds peace, the famished mouths
Of the rusty carbines brush against their trousers,

7. The first version was "Port Bou – Firing Practice," published in *New Writing*, Autumn 1938.

Almost as fragilely as reeds;

And wrapped in a cloth – old mother in a shawl –

The terrible machine-gun rests.

They shout, salute back as the truck jerks forward

Over the vigorous hill, beyond the headland.

An old man passes, his running mouth,

With three teeth like bullets, spits out: 'pom-pom-pom'.

The children run after; and, more slowly, the women;

Clutching their clothes, follow over the hill;

Till the village is empty, for the firing practice,

And I am left alone on the bridge at the exact centre

Where the cleaving river trickles like saliva.

At the exact centre, solitary as a target,

Where nothing moves against a background of card-board
   houses

Except the disgraceful skirring dogs; and the firing begins,

Across the harbour mouth from headland to headland,

White flecks of foam gashed by lead in the sea,

And the echo trails over its iron lash

Whipping the flanks of the surrounding hills.

My circling arms rest on the newspaper,

My mind seems paper where dust and ink fall,

I tell myself the shooting is only for practice,

And my body seems a cloth which the machine-gun stitches

Like a sewing machine, neatly, with cotton from a reel;

And the solitary, irregular, thin 'paffs' from the carbines

Draw on long needles white threads through my navel.

— Stephen Spender, *The Still Centre*, 1939

AND I REMEMBER SPAIN

And I remember Spain

   At Easter ripe as an egg for revolt and ruin

Though for a tripper the rain

   Was worse than the surly or the worried or the haunted faces

With writing on the walls –
  Hammer and sickle, Boicot, Viva, Muerra [sic]; .

With café-au-lait brimming the waterfalls,
  With sherry, shellfish, omelettes.
With fretted stone the Moor
  Had chiselled for effects of sun and shadow;
With shadows of the poor,
  The begging cripples and the children begging.
The churches full of saints
  Tortured on racks of marble –
The old complaints
  Covered with gilt and dimly lit with candles
With powerful or banal
  Monuments of riches or repression
And the Escorial
  Cold for ever within like the heart of Philip.
With ranks of dominoes
  Deployed on café tables the whole of Sunday
With cabarets that call the tourist, shows
  Of thighs and eyes and nipples.
With slovenly soldiers, nuns,
  And peeling posters from the last elections
Promising bread of guns
  Or an amnesty or another
Order or else the old
  Glory veneered and varnished
As if veneer could hold
  The rotten guts and crumbled bones together.
And a vulture hung in air
  Below the cliffs of Ronda and below him
His book-winged shadow wavered like despair
  Across the chequered vineyards.
And the boot-blacks in Madrid
  Kept us half an hour with polish and pincers
And all we did

In that city was drink and think and loiter.
And in the Prado half-
    wit princes looked from the canvas they had paid for
(Goya had the laugh –
    But can what is corrupt be cured by laughter?)
And the day at Aranjuez
    When the sun came out for once on the yellow river
With Valdepeñas burdening the breath
    We slept a royal sleep in the royal gardens;
And at Toledo walked
    Around the ramparts where they throw the garbage
And glibly talked
    Of how the Spaniards lack all sense of business.
And Avila was cold
    And Segovia was picturesque and smelly
And a goat on the road seemed old
    As the rocks or the Roman arches.
And Easter was wet and full
    In Seville and in the ring on Easter Sunday
A clumsy bull and then a clumsy bull
    Nodding his banderillas died of boredom.
And the standard of living was low
    But that, we thought to ourselves, was not our business;
All that the tripper wants is the *status quo*
    Cut and dried for trippers.
And we thought the papers a lark
    With their party politics and blank invective;
And we thought the dark
    Women who dyed their hair should have it dyed more often.
And we sat in trains all night
    With the windows shut among civil guards and peasants
And tried to play piquet by a tiny light
    And tried to sleep bolt upright;
And cursed the Spanish rain
    And cursed their cigarettes which came to pieces
And caught heavy colds in Cordova and in vain

179

Waited for the right light for taking photos.
And we met a Cambridge don who said with an air
　'There's going to be trouble shortly in this country',
And ordered anis, pudgy and debonair,
　Glad to show off his mastery of the language.
But only an inch behind

　This map of olive and ilex, this painted hoarding,
Careless of visitors the people's mind
　Was tunnelling like a mole to day and danger.
And the day before we left
　We saw the mob in flower at Algeciras
Outside a toothless door, a church bereft
　Of its images and its aura.
And at La Linea while
　The night put miles between us and Gibraltar
We heard the blood-lust of a drunkard pile
　His heaven high with curses;
And next day took the boat
　For home, forgetting Spain, not realising
That Spain would soon denote
　Our grief, our aspirations;
Not knowing that our blunt
　Ideals would find their whetstone, that our spirit
Would find its frontier on the Spanish front,
　Its body in a rag-tag army.

— Louis MacNeice, *Autumn Journal* (1939) in *Collected Poems*, 1949

George Orwell and *Homage to Catalonia*

KEVIN FOSTER

Homage to Catalonia is Orwell's "honest" account of his six months of service with the POUM in the Spanish Civil War. According to Orwell's biographer, Bernard Crick, it is "closer to a literal record than anything he wrote." Franz Borkenau, Herbert Read, and Naomi Mitchison each commended Orwell's "truthfulness," and "honesty and objectivity." Yet *Homage to Catalonia* is more than a purely literal record of Orwell's experiences in Spain. It is also a richly symbolic account of one man's search for "comradeship and respect" with the workers, the euphoria of its realization, the despair of its eventual loss, and a commemoration of its incorruptible truths.

The narrative opens with Orwell's realization of the genuine fraternity made possible by the political climate unique to Catalonia, manifested in the handshake of the Italian militiaman: "It was as though his spirit and mine had momentarily succeeded in bridging the gulf of language and tradition and meeting in utter intimacy." Freed by the Catalan dialect from the class-consciousness that had tainted his relationships with the working classes in Britain, war inducts Orwell into a democracy of suffering. But for Orwell, Spain is a continual struggle with languages, both vernacular and political, and the "gulf of language" continually threatens to open up and to swallow him and his new-found sense of identification with his comrades. *Homage to Catalonia* is an alphabet soup of conflicting factions – POUM, PSUC,* FAI, CNT, UGT, JCI,* JSU – who battle with guns and bombs on Barcelona's streets and in words, pictures, and posters in their conflicting newspapers and manifestos. Orwell's memoir attempts to establish for himself and his readers the stable system of signification that the warring parties eschewed and his well-thumbed dictionary could not provide. Indeed, it is an inability to control language, or more specifically, meaning, that ultimately undoes the POUM and hastens Orwell's

181

final expulsion from Spain. The access to the international media enjoyed by POUM's enemies ensured the faction's translation from a Marxist sect into a fascist fifth-column. The language that had liberated Orwell from the shackles of his class-consciousness thus eludes his control, and he is sent scuttling back into bourgeoisie costume and its protective inflections for safety.

If the Italian militiaman's handshake inducted Orwell into a universal comradeship, then the handclasp of the "little officer" that closes the narrative and demonstrates the survival of such fraternity at a purely personal level just as surely marks the end of broader political unity. The "little officer" accompanies Orwell from army to police headquarters in pursuit of a letter that, it is hoped, will help release Orwell's friend and former commander, George Kopp, who was arrested and imprisoned after the suppression of the POUM. This act of loyalty puts Orwell himself at risk of arrest and possible execution. The "little officer" recognizes Orwell's selfless courage and, in full view of a gallery of police narks and *agents provocateurs*, shakes his hand both as a demonstration of his respect for Orwell and as a public declaration of his *bona fides*. The Italian militiaman had impressed Orwell as a man willing to "throw his life away for a friend." This second, echoing handshake implies that both Orwell and the "little officer" are no less capable of such a gesture. It indicates that the political allegiances in which men traditionally seek fraternity merely frustrate its foundation. True fraternity, Orwell implies, resides in the speechless handclasp of "comradeship and respect," not in the slogans and uniforms of political division: it resides in unity experienced, not uniqueness proclaimed.

Homage to Catalonia therefore offers not only a vivid, literal account of Orwell's time in Spain, it also celebrates a spirit and experience of comradeship that political factionalism cannot crush, nor its corrupted idiom taint.

Homage to Catalonia

In the Lenin Barracks in Barcelona, the day before I joined the militia, I saw an Italian militiaman standing in front of the officers' table. He was a tough-looking youth of twenty-five or six, with reddish-yellow hair and powerful shoulders. His peaked leather cap was pulled fiercely over one eye. He was standing in profile to me, his chin on his breast, gazing with a puzzled frown at a map which one of the officers had open on the table. Something in his face deeply moved me. It was the face of a man who would commit murder and throw away his life for a friend – the kind of face you would expect in an Anarchist, though as likely as not he was a Communist. There were both candour and ferocity in it; also the pathetic reverence that illiterate people have for their supposed superiors. Obviously he could not make head or tail of the map; obviously he regarded map-reading as a stupendous intellectual feat. I hardly know why, but I have seldom seen anyone – any man, I mean – to whom I have taken such an immediate liking. While they were talking round the table some remark brought it out that I was a foreigner. The Italian raised his head and said quickly:

'*Italiano?*'

I answered in my bad Spanish: '*No, Inglés. Y tú?*'

'*Italiano.*'

As we went out he stepped across the room and gripped my hand very hard. Queer, the affection you can feel for a stranger! It was as though his spirit and mine had momentarily succeeded in bridging the gulf of language and tradition and meeting in utter intimacy. I hoped he liked me as well as I liked him. But I also knew that to retain my first impression of him I must not see him again; and needless to say I never did see him again. One was always making contacts of that kind in Spain.

I mention this Italian militiaman because he has stuck in my memory. With his shabby uniform and fierce pathetic face he typifies for me the special atmosphere of that time. He is bound up with all my memories of that period of the war – the red flags in Barcelona, the gaunt trains full of shabby soldiers creeping to the front, the grey war- stricken towns farther up the line, the muddy, ice-cold trenches in the mountains.

This was in late December 1936, less than seven months ago as I write, and yet it is a period that has already receded into enormous distance. Later events have obliterated it much more completely than they have obliterated 1935, or 1905 for that matter. I had come to Spain with some vague notion of writing newspaper articles, but I had joined the militia almost immediately, because at that time and in that atmosphere it seemed the only conceivable thing to do. The Anarchists were still in virtual control of Catalonia and the revolution was still in full swing. To anyone who had been there since the beginning it probably seemed even in December or January that the revolutionary period was ending; but when one came straight from England the aspect of Barcelona was something startling and overwhelming. It was the first time that I had ever been in a town where the working class was in the saddle. Practically every building of any size had been seized by the workers and was draped with red flags or with the red and black flag of the Anarchists; every wall was scrawled with the hammer and sickle and with the initials of the revolutionary parties; almost every church had been gutted and its images burnt. Churches here and there were being systematically demolished by gangs of workmen. Every shop and cafe had an inscription saying that it had been collectivised; even the bootblacks had been collectivised and their boxes painted red and black. Waiters and shop-walkers looked you in the face and treated you as an equal. Servile and even ceremonial forms of speech had temporarily disappeared. Nobody said '*Señor*' or '*Don*' or even '*Usted*'; everyone called everyone else 'Comrade' and 'Thou', and said '*Salud*' and '*Buenos días*'. Tipping was forbidden by law; almost my first experience was receiving a lecture from a hotel manager for trying to tip a lift-boy. There were no private motor-cars, they had all been commandeered, and all the trams and taxis and much of the other transport were painted red and black. The revolutionary posters were everywhere, flaming from the walls in clean reds and blues that made the few remaining advertisements look like daubs of mud. Down the Ramblas, the wide central artery of the town where crowds of people streamed constantly to and fro, the loudspeakers were bellowing revolutionary songs all day and far into the night. And it was the aspect of the crowds that was the queerest thing of all. In outward appearance it was a town in which the wealthy classes had practically ceased to exist. Except for a small number of women and foreigners there were no 'well-dressed' people at all. Practically everyone wore rough working-class clothes, or blue overalls, or some variant of the militia uniform. All this was queer and moving. There was much in it that I did not understand, in some ways I did not even like it, but I recognised it immediately as a state of affairs worth fighting for. Also I believed that things were as they appeared, that this was really a workers' State and that the entire bourgeoisie had either fled, been killed, or voluntarily come over to the workers' side; I did not realise that great number of well-to-do bourgeoisie were disguising themselves as proletarians for the time being.

* * *

The road wound between yellow infertile fields, untouched since last year's harvest. Ahead of us was the low sierra that lies between Alcubierre and Saragossa. We were getting near the front line now, near the bombs, the machine-guns, and the mud. In secret I was frightened. I knew the line was quiet at present, but unlike most of the men about me I was old enough to remember the Great War, though not old enough to have fought in it. War, to me, meant roaring projectiles and skipping shards of steel; above all it meant mud, lice, hunger, and cold. It is curious, but I dreaded the cold much more than I dreaded the enemy. The thought of it had been haunting me all the time I was in Barcelona; I had even lain awake at nights thinking of the cold in the trenches, the stand-to's in the grisly dawns, the long hours on sentry-go with a frosted rifle, the icy mud that would slop over my boot-tops. I admit, too, that, I felt a kind of horror as I looked at the people I was marching among. You cannot possibly conceive what a rabble we looked. We straggled along with far less cohesion than a flock of sheep; before we had gone two miles the rear of the column was out of sight. And quite half of the so-called men were children – but I mean literally children, of sixteen years old at the very most. Yet they were all happy and excited at the prospect of getting to the front at last. As we neared the line the boys round the red flag in the front began to utter shouts of '*Visca POUM!*' '*Fascistas mari-cones!*' and so forth – shouts which were meant to be war-like and menacing, but which, from those childish throats sounded as pathetic as the cries of kittens. It seemed dreadful that the defenders of the Republic should be this mob of ragged children carrying worn-out rifles which they did not know how to use. I remember wondering what would happen if a Fascist aeroplane passed our way – whether the airman would even bother to dive down and give us a burst from his machine-guns. Surely even from the air he could see that we were not real soldiers?

As the road struck into the sierra we branched off to the right and climbed a narrow mule-track that wound round the mountain-side. The hills in that part of Spain are of a queer formation, horseshoe-shaped with flattish tops and steep sides running down into immense ravines. On the higher slopes nothing grows except stunted shrubs and heath, with the white bones of the limestone sticking out everywhere. The front line here was not a continuous line of trenches, which would have been impossible in such mountainous country; it was simply a chain of fortified posts, always known as 'positions', perched on each hill-top. In the distance you could see our 'position' at the crown of the horseshoe; a ragged barricade of sand-bags, a red flag fluttering; the smoke of dug-out fires. A little nearer, and you could smell a sickening sweetish stink that lived in my nostrils for weeks afterwards. Into the cleft immediately behind the position all the refuse of months had been tipped – a deep festering bed of breadcrusts, excrement, and rusty tins.

The company we were relieving were getting their kits together. They had been three months in the line; their uniforms were caked with mud, their boots falling to pieces, their faces mostly bearded. The captain commanding the position, Levinski by name, but known to everyone as Benjamin, and by birth a Polish Jew, but speaking French as his native language, crawled out of his dug-out and greeted us. He was a short youth of about twenty-five, with stiff black hair and a pale eager face which at this period of the war was always very dirty. A few stray bullets were cracking high overhead. The position was a semi-circular enclosure about fifty yards across, with a parapet that was partly sand-bags and partly lumps of limestone. There were thirty or forty dug-outs running into the ground like rat-holes. Williams, myself, and Williams's Spanish brother-in-law made a swift dive for the nearest unoccupied dug-out that looked habitable. Somewhere in front an occasional rifle banged, making queer rolling echoes among the stony hills. We had just dumped our kits and were crawling out of the dug-out when there was another bang and one of the children of our company rushed back from the parapet with his face pouring blood. He had fired his rifle and had somehow managed to blow out the bolt; his scalp was torn to ribbons by the splinters of the burst cartridge-case. It was our first casualty, and, characteristically, self-inflicted. In the afternoon we did our first guard and Benjamin showed us round the position. In front of the parapet there ran a system of narrow trenches hewn out of the rock, with extremely primitive loopholes made of piles of limestone. There were twelve sentries, placed at various points in the trench and behind the inner parapet. In front of the trench was the barbed wire, and then the hillside slid down into a seemingly bottomless ravine; opposite were naked hills, in places mere-cliffs of rock, all grey and wintry, with no life anywhere, not even a bird. I peered cautiously through a loophole, trying to find the Fascist trench.

'Where are the enemy?' Benjamin waved his hand expansively.

'Over zere'.

(Benjamin spoke English – terrible English.)

'But *where?*'

According to my ideas of trench warfare the Fascists would be fifty or a hundred yards away. I could see nothing – seemingly their trenches were very well concealed. Then with a shock of dismay I saw where Benjamin was pointing; on the opposite hill-top, beyond the ravine, seven hundred metres away at the very least, the tiny outline of a parapet and a red and yellow flag – the Fascist position. I was indescribably disappointed. We were nowhere near them! At that range our rifles were completely useless. But at this moment there was a shout of excitement. Two Fascists, greyish figurines in the distance, were scrambling up the naked hill-side opposite. Benjamin grabbed the nearest man's rifle, took aim, and pulled the trigger. Click! A dud cartridge; I thought it a bad omen.

* * *

At the beginning I had ignored the political side of the war, and it was only about this time that it began to force itself upon my attention. If you are not interested in the horrors of party politics, please skip; I am trying to keep the political parts of this narrative in separate chapters for precisely that purpose. But at the same time it would be quite impossible to write about the Spanish war from a purely military angle. It was above all things a political war. No event in it, at any rate during the first year, is intelligible unless one has some grasp of the inter-party struggle that was going on behind the Government lines.

When I came to Spain, and for some time afterwards, I was not only uninterested in the political situation but unaware of it. I knew there was a war on, but I had no notion what kind of a war. If you had asked me why I had joined the militia I should have answered: 'To fight against Fascism,' and if you had asked me what I was fighting *for*, I should have answered: 'Common decency.' I had accepted the *News Chronicle-New Statesman* version of the war as a defence of civilisation against a maniacal outbreak by an army of Colonel Blimps in the pay of Hitler. The revolutionary atmosphere of Barcelona had attracted me deeply, but I had made no attempt to understand it. As for the kaleidoscope of political parties and trade unions, with their tiresome names – PSUC, POUM, FAI, CNT, UGT, JCI, JSU, – they merely exasperated me. It looked at first sight as though Spain were suffering from a plague of initials. I knew that I was serving in something called the POUM (I had only joined the POUM militia rather than any other because I happened to arrive in Barcelona with ILP papers), but I did not realise that there were serious differences between the political parties. At Monte Pocero, when they pointed to the position on our left and said: 'Those are the Socialists' (meaning the PSUC), I was puzzled and said: 'Aren't we all Socialists?' I thought it idiotic that people fighting for their lives should *have* separate parties; my attitude always was, 'Why can't we drop all this political nonsense and get on with the war?' This of course was the correct 'anti-Fascist' attitude which had been carefully disseminated by the English newspapers, largely in order to prevent people from grasping the real nature of the struggle. But in Spain, especially in Catalonia, it was an attitude that no one could or did keep up indefinitely. Everyone, however unwillingly, took sides sooner or later. For even if one cared nothing for the political parties and their conflicting 'lines', it was too obvious that one's own destiny was involved. As a militiaman one was a soldier against Franco, but one was also a pawn in an enormous struggle that was being fought out between two political theories. When I scrounged for firewood on the mountainside and wondered whether this was really a war or whether the *News Chronicle* had made it up, when I dodged the Communist machine-guns in the Barcelona riots, when I finally fled from Spain with the police one jump behind me - all these things happened to me in that particular way because I was serving in the POUM militia and not in the PSUC. So great is the difference between two sets of initials!

* * *

All of us were lousy by this time; though still cold it was warm enough for that. I have had a big experience of body vermin of various kinds, and for sheer beastliness the louse beats everything I have encountered. Other insects, mosquitoes for instance, make you suffer more, but at least they aren't resident vermin. The human louse somewhat resembles a tiny lobster, and he lives chiefly in your trousers. Short of burning all your clothes there is no known way of getting rid of him. Down the seams of your trousers he lays his glittering white eggs, like tiny grains of rice, which hatch out and breed families of their own at horrible speed. I think the pacifists might find it helpful to illustrate their pamphlets with enlarged photographs of lice. Glory of war, indeed! In war *all* soldiers are lousy, at least when it is warm enough. The men who fought at Verdun, at Waterloo, at Flodden, at Senlac, at Thermopylae – every one of them had lice crawling over his testicles. We kept the brutes down to some extent by burning out the eggs and by bathing as often as we could face it. Nothing short of lice could have driven me into that ice-cold river.

* * *

When we went on leave I had been a hundred and fifteen days in the line, and at the time this period seemed to me to have been one of the most futile of my whole life. I had joined the militia in order to fight against Fascism, and as yet I had scarcely fought at all, had merely existed as a sort of passive object, doing nothing in return for my rations except to suffer from cold and lack of sleep. Perhaps that is the fate of most soldiers in most wars. But now that I can see this period in perspective I do not altogether regret it. I wish, indeed, that I could have served the Spanish Government a little more effectively; but from a personal point of view – from the point of view of my own development – those first three or four months that I spent in the line were less futile than I then thought. They formed a kind of interregnum in my life, quite different from anything that had gone before and perhaps from anything that is to come, and they taught me things that I could not have learned in any other way.

The essential point is that all this time I had been isolated – for at the front one was almost completely isolated from the outside world: even of what was happening in Barcelona one had only a dim conception – among people who could roughly but not too inaccurately be described as revolutionaries. This was the result of the militia-system, which on the Aragon front was not radically altered till about June 1937. The workers' militias, based on the trade unions and each composed of people of approximately the same political opinions, had the effect of canalising into one place all the most revolutionary sentiment in the country. I had dropped more or less by chance into the only community of any size in Western Europe where political consciousness and disbelief in capitalism were more normal than their opposites. Up here in Aragon one was among tens of thousands of people, mainly though not entirely of working-class origin, all living at the same level and mingling on terms of equality. In theory it was perfect equality, and even in practice it was not far from it. There is a sense in which it would be true to say that one was experiencing a foretaste of Socialism, by which I mean that the prevailing atmosphere was that of Socialism. Many of the normal motives of civilised life – snobbishness, moneygrubbing, fear of the boss, etc. – had simply ceased to exist. The ordinary class-division of society had disappeared to an extent that is almost unthinkable in the money-tainted air of England; there was no one there except the peasants and ourselves, and no one owned anyone else as his master. Of course such a state of affairs could not last. It was simply a temporary and local phase in an enormous game that is being played over the whole surface of the earth. But it lasted long enough to have its effect upon anyone who experienced it. However much one cursed at the time, one realised afterwards that one had been in contact with something strange and valuable. One had been in a community where hope was more normal than apathy or cynicism, where the word 'comrade' stood for comradeship and not, as in most countries, for humbug. One had breathed the air of equality. I am aware that it is now the fashion to deny that Socialism has anything to do with equality. In every country in the world a huge tribe of party-hacks and sleek little professors are busy 'proving' that Socialism means no more than a planned state-capitalism with the grab-motive left intact. But fortunately there also exists a vision of Socialism quite different from this. The thing that attracts ordinary men to Socialism and makes them willing to risk their skins for it, the 'mystique' of Socialism, is the idea of equality; to the vast majority of people Socialism means a classless society, or it means nothing at all. And it was here that those few months in the militia were valuable. For the Spanish militias, while they lasted, were a sort of microcosm of a classless society. In that community where no one was on the make, where there was a shortage of everything but no privilege and no boot-licking, one got, perhaps, a crude forecast of what the opening stages of Socialism might be like. And, after all, instead of disillusioning me it deeply attracted me. The effect was to make my desire to see Socialism established much more actual than it had been before. Partly, perhaps, this was due to the good luck of being among Spaniards, who, with their innate decency and their ever-present Anarchist tinge, would make even the opening stages of Socialism tolerable if they had the chance.

* * *

Everyone who has made two visits, at intervals of months, to Barcelona during the war has remarked upon the extraordinary changes that took place in it. And curiously enough, whether they went there first in August and again in January, or, like myself, first in December and again in April, the thing they said was always the same: that the revolutionary atmosphere had vanished. No doubt to anyone who had been there in August, when the blood was scarcely dry in the streets and militia were quartered in the smart hotels, Barcelona in December would have seemed bourgeois; to me, fresh from England, it was liker to a workers' city than anything I had conceived possible. Now the tide had rolled back. Once again it was an ordinary city, a little pinched and chipped by war, but with no outward sign of working-class predominance.

* * *

About midday on 3 May a friend crossing the lounge of the hotel said casually: 'There's been some kind of trouble at the Telephone Exchange, I hear.' For some reason I paid no attention to it at the time.

That afternoon, between three and four, I was half-way down the Ramblas when I heard several rifle-shots behind me. I turned round and saw some youths, with rifles in their hands and the red and black handkerchiefs of the Anarchists round their throats, edging up a side-street that ran off the Ramblas northward. They were evidently exchanging shots with someone in a tall octagonal tower – a church, I think – that commanded the side-street. I thought instantly: 'It's started!' But I thought it without any very great feeling of surprise – for days past everyone had been expecting 'it' to start at any moment. I realised that I must get back to the hotel at once and see if my wife was all right. But the knot of Anarchists round the opening of the side-street were motioning the people back and shouting to them not to cross the line of fire. More shots rang out. The bullets from the tower were flying across the street and a crowd of panic-stricken people was rushing down the Ramblas, away from the firing; up and down the street you could hear snap-snap-snap as the shopkeepers slammed the steel shutters over their windows. I saw two Popular Army officers retreating cautiously from tree to tree with their hands on their revolvers. In front of me the crowd was surging into the Metro station in the middle of the Ramblas to take cover. I immediately decided not to follow them. It might mean being trapped underground for hours.

At this moment an American doctor who had been with us at the front ran up to me and grabbed me by the arm. He was greatly excited.

'Come on, we must get down to the Hotel Falcon.' (The Hotel Falcon was a sort of boarding-house maintained by the POUM and used chiefly by militiamen on leave.) 'The POUM chaps will be meeting there. The trouble's starting. We must hang together.'

'But what the devil is it all about?' I said.

The doctor was hauling me along by the arm. He was too excited to give a very clear statement. It appeared that he had been in the Plaza de Cataluña when several lorry-loads of armed Civil Guards had driven up to the Telephone Exchange, which was operated mainly by CNT workers, and made a sudden assault upon it. Then some Anarchists had arrived and there had been a general affray. I gathered that the trouble earlier in the day had been a demand by the Government to hand over the Telephone Exchange, which, of course, was refused.

As we moved down the street a lorry raced past us from the opposite direction. It was full of Anarchists with rifles in their hands. In front a ragged youth was lying on a pile of mattresses behind a light machine-gun. When we got to the Hotel Falcon, which was at the bottom of the Ramblas, a crowd of people was seething in the entrance hall; there was a great confusion, nobody seemed to know what we were expected to do, and nobody was armed except the handful of Shock Troopers who usually acted as guards for the building. I went across to the Comité Local of the POUM, which was almost opposite. Upstairs, in the room where militiamen normally went to draw their pay, another crowd was seething. A tall, pale, rather handsome man of about thirty, in civilian clothes, was trying to restore order and handing out belts and cartridge-boxes from a pile in the corner. There seemed to be no rifles as yet. The doctor had disappeared – I believe there had already been casualties and a call for doctors – but another Englishman had arrived. Presently, from an inner office, the tall man and some others began bringing out armfuls of rifles and handing them round. The other Englishman and myself, as foreigners, were slightly under suspicion and at first nobody would give us a rifle. Then a militiaman whom I had known at the front arrived and recognised me, after which we were given rifles and a few clips of cartridges, somewhat grudgingly.

There was a sound of firing in the distance and the streets were completely empty of people. Everyone said that it was impossible to go up the Ramblas. The Civil Guards had seized buildings in commanding positions and were letting fly at everyone who passed. I would have risked it and gone back to the hotel, but there was a vague idea floating round that the Comité Local was likely to be attacked at any moment and we had better stand by. All over the building, on the stairs, and on the pavements outside, small knots of people were standing and talking excitedly. No one seemed to have a very clear idea of what was happening. All I could gather was that the Civil Guards had attacked the Telephone Exchange and seized various strategic spots that commanded other buildings belonging to the workers. There was a general impression that the Civil Guards were 'after' the CNT and the working class generally. It was noticeable that, at this stage, no one seemed to put the blame on the Government. The poorer classes in Barcelona looked upon the Civil Guards as something rather resembling the Black and Tans, and it seemed to be taken for granted that they had started this attack on their own initiative. Once I heard how things stood I felt easier in my mind. The issue was clear enough. On one side the CNT, on the other side the police. I have no particular love for the idealised 'worker' as he appears in the bourgeois Communist's mind, but when I see an actual flesh-and-blood worker in conflict with his natural enemy, the policeman, I do not have to ask myself which side I am on.

* * *

I have tried to write objectively about the Barcelona fighting, though, obviously, no one can be completely objective on a question of this kind. One is practically obliged to take sides, and it must be clear enough which side I am on. Again, I must inevitably have made mistakes of fact, not only here but in other parts of this narrative. It is very difficult to write accurately about the Spanish war, because of the lack of non-propagandist documents. I warn everyone against my bias, and I warn everyone against my mistakes. Still, I have done my best to be honest.

* * *

It must have been three days after the Barcelona fighting ended that we returned to the front. After the fighting – more particularly after the slanging-match in the newspapers – it was difficult to think about this war in quite the same naively idealistic manner as before. I suppose there is no one who spent more than a few weeks in Spain without being in some degree disillusioned. My mind went back to the newspaper correspondent whom I had met my first day in Barcelona, and who said to me: 'This war is a racket the same as any other'. This remark had shocked me deeply, and at that time (December) I do not believe it was true; it was not true even now, in May; but it was becoming truer. The fact is that every war suffers a kind of progressive degradation with every month that it continues, because such things as individual liberty and a truthful press are simply not compatible with military efficiency.

* * *

One morning it was announced that the men in my ward were to be sent down to Barcelona today. I managed to send a wire to my wife, telling her that I was coming, and presently they packed us into buses and took us down to the station. It was only when the train was actually starting that the hospital orderly who travelled with us casually let fall that we were not going to Barcelona after all, but to Tarragona. I suppose the engine-driver had changed his mind. 'Just like Spain!' I thought. But it was very Spanish too that they agreed to hold up the train while I sent another wire, and more Spanish still that the wire never got there.

They had put us into ordinary third-class carriages with wooden seats, and many of the men were badly wounded and had only got out of bed for the first time that morning. Before long, what with the heat and the jolting, half of them were in a state of collapse and several vomited on the floor. The hospital orderly threaded his way among the corpse-like forms that sprawled everywhere, carrying a large goatskin bottle full of water which he squirted into this mouth or that. It was beastly water; I remember the taste of it still. We got into Tarragona as the sun was getting low. The line runs along the shore a stone's throw from the sea. As our train drew into the station a troop-train full of men from the International Column was drawing out, and a knot of people on the bridge were waving to them. It was a very long train, packed to bursting-point with men, with fieldguns lashed on the open trucks and more men clustering round the guns. I remember with peculiar vividness the spectacle of that train passing in the yellow evening light; window after window full of dark, smiling faces, the long tilted barrels of the guns, the scarlet scarves fluttering – all this gliding slowly past us against a turquoise-coloured sea.

'*Extranjeros* – foreigners', said someone. 'They're Italians.'

Obviously they were Italians. No other people could have grouped themselves so picturesquely or returned the salutes of the crowd with so much grace – a grace that was nonetheless because about half the men on the train were drinking out of up-ended wine bottles. We heard afterwards that these were some of the troops who won the great victory at Guadalajara in March; they had been on leave and were being transferred to the Aragon front. Most of them, I am afraid, were killed at Huesca only a few weeks later. The men who were well enough to stand had moved across the carriage to cheer the Italians as they went past. A crutch waved out of the window; bandaged forearms made the Red Salute. It was like an allegorical picture of war; the trainload of fresh men gliding proudly up the line, the maimed men sliding slowly down, and all the while the guns on the open trucks making one's heart leap as guns always do, and reviving that pernicious feeling, so difficult to get rid of, that war *is* glorious after all.

* * *

Kopp was not *incommunicado* and we got a permit to see him without difficulty. As they led us through the steel doors into the jail, a Spanish militiaman whom I had known at the front was being led out between two Civil Guards. His eye met mine; again the ghostly wink. And the first person we saw inside was an American militiaman who had left for home a few days earlier; his papers were in good order, but they had arrested him at the frontier all the same, probably because he was still wearing corduroy breeches and was therefore identifiable as a militiaman. We walked past one another as though we had been total strangers. That was dreadful. I had known him for months, had shared a dug-out with him, he had helped to carry me down the line when I was wounded; but it was the only thing one could do. The blue-clad guards were snooping everywhere. It would be fatal to recognise too many people.

* * *

Then Kopp began telling us about the papers that had been taken from him when he was arrested. Among them was a letter from the Ministry of War, addressed to the colonel commanding engineering operations in the Army of the East. The police had seized it and refused to give it back; it was said to be lying in the Chief of Police's office. It might make a very great difference if it were recovered.

I saw instantly how important this might be. An official letter of that kind, bearing the recommendation of General Pozas,* would establish Kopp's bona fides. But the trouble was to prove that the that letter existed; if it were opened in the Chief of Police's office one could be sure that some nark or other would destroy it. There was only one person who might possibly be able to get it back, and that was the officer to whom it was addressed. Kopp had already thought of this, and he had written a letter which he wanted me to smuggle out of the jail and post. But it was obviously quicker and surer to go in person. I left my wife with Kopp, rushed out, and, after a long search, found a taxi. I knew that time was everything. It was now about half past five, the colonel would probably leave his office at six, and by tomorrow the letter might be God knew where – destroyed, perhaps, or lost somewhere in the chaos of documents that was presumably piling up as suspect after suspect was arrested. The colonel's office was at the War Department down by the quay. As I hurried up the steps the Assault Guard on duty at the door barred the way with his long bayonet and demanded 'papers'. I waved my discharge ticket at him; evidently he could not read, and let me pass, impressed by the vague mystery of 'papers'. Inside, the place was a huge complicated warren running round a central courtyard, with hundreds of offices on each floor; and, as this was Spain, nobody had the vaguest idea where the office I was looking for was. I kept repeating: *'El coronel –, jefe de ingenieros, Ejército de Este!'* People smiled and shrugged their shoulders gracefully. Everyone who had an opinion sent me in a different direction; up these stairs, down those, along interminable passages which turned out to be blind alleys. I had the strangest sensation of being in a nightmare: the rushing up and down flights of stairs, the mysterious people coming and going, the glimpses through open doors of chaotic offices with papers strewn everywhere and typewriters clicking; and time slipping away and a life perhaps in the balance.

However, I got there in time, and slightly to my surprise I was granted a hearing. I did not see Colonel ——, but his aide-de-camp or secretary, a little slip of an officer in smart uniform, with large and squinting eyes, came out to interview me in the ante-room. I began to pour forth my story. I had come on behalf of my superior officer, Major Jorge Kopp, who was on an urgent mission to the front and had been arrested by mistake. The letter to Colonel —— was of a confidential nature and should be recovered without delay. I had served with Kopp for months, he was an officer of the highest character, obviously his arrest was a mistake, the police had confused him with someone else, etc., etc., etc,. I kept piling it on about the urgency of Kopp's mission to the front, knowing that this was the strongest point. But it must have sounded a strange tale, in my villainous Spanish which relapsed into French at every crisis. The worst was that my voice gave out almost at once and it was only by violent straining that I could produce a sort of croak. I was in dread that it would disappear altogether, and the little officer would grow tired of trying to listen to me. I have often wondered what he thought was wrong with my voice – whether he thought I was drunk or merely suffering from a guilty conscience.

However, he heard me patiently, nodded his head a great number of times, and gave a guarded assent to what I said. Yes, it sounded as though there might have been a mistake. Clearly the matter should be looked into. *Mañana –*. I protested. Not *mañana!* The matter was urgent; Kopp was due at the front already. Again the officer seemed to agree. The came the question I was dreading:

'This Major Kopp – what force was he serving in?'

The terrible word had to come out: 'In the POUM militia'.

'POUM!'

I wish I could convey to you the shocked alarm in his voice. You have got to remember how the POUM was regarded at that moment. The spy-scare was at its height; probably all good Republicans did believe for a day or two that the POUM was a huge spying organisation in German pay. To have to say such a thing to an officer in the Popular Army was like going into the Cavalry Club immediately after the Red Letter scare and announcing yourself a Communist. His dark eyes moved obliquely across my face. Another long pause, then he said slowly:

'And you say you were with him at the front. Then you were serving in the POUM militia yourself?'

'Yes'.

He turned and dived into the colonel's room. I could hear an agitated conversation. 'It's all up', I thought. We should never get Kopp's letter back. Moreover I had to confess that I was in the POUM myself, and no doubt they would ring up the police and get me arrested, just to add another Trotskyist to the bag. Presently, however, the officer reappeared, fitting on his cap, and sternly signed to me to follow. We were going to the Chief of Police's office. It was a long way, twenty minutes' walk. The little officer marched stiffly in front with a military step. We did not exchange a single word the whole way. When we got to the Chief of Police's office a crowd of the most dreadful-looking scoundrels, obviously police narks, informers, and spies of every kind were hanging about outside the door. The little officer went in; there was a long, heated conversation. You could hear voices furiously raised; you pictured violent gestures, shrugging of the shoulders, banging on the table. Evidently the police were refusing to give the letter up. At last, however, the officer emerged, flushed, but carrying a large official envelope. It was Kopp's letter. We had won a tiny victory – which as it turned out, made not the slightest difference. The letter was duly delivered, but Kopp's military superiors were quite unable to get him out of jail.

The officer promised me that the letter should be delivered. But what about Kopp? I said. Could we not get him released? He shrugged his shoulders. That was another matter. They did not know what Kopp had been arrested for. He would only tell me that the proper enquiries would be made. There was no more to be said; it was time to part. And then there happened a strange and moving thing. The little officer hesitated a moment, then stepped across, and shook hands with me.

I do not know if I can bring home to you how deeply that touched me. It sounds a small thing, but it was not. You have got to realise what was the feeling of the time – the horrible atmosphere of suspicion and hatred, the lies and rumours circulating everywhere, the posters screaming from the hoardings that I and everyone like me was a Fascist spy. And you have got to remember that we were standing outside the Chief of Police's office, in front of that filthy gang of tale-bearers and *agents provocateurs,* any one of whom might know that I was 'wanted' by the police. It was like publicly shaking hands with a German during the Great War. I suppose he had decided in some way that I was not really a Fascist spy; still, it was good of him to shake hands.

— George Orwell, *Homage to Catalonia,* 1938

French Responses to the War

Introduction

COLIN NETTELBECK

Hitler's rise to power in Germany in 1933 exacerbated France's already severe domestic conflicts. Social, economic, political, and religious problems were all inextricably linked to the possibility of confrontation with a traditional enemy whose aggressive stance could not but be threatening. Studies of France's foreign policies at this time reveal confusion and contradiction, and if there was any general trend, it was that of a nation willing to try anything, and with some desperation, to avoid a war that at the same time it believed inevitable.

France's inner turmoil surfaced with bitter passion at the time of the Stavisky Affair in early 1934. Serge Alexander Stavisky was an urbane and clever swindler who had built up a vast financial empire, implicating police and politicians in a series of elaborate confidence tricks. When the scandal broke, the government handled it so badly that not only was the administration of the day toppled, but the very bases of the parliamentary institutions of the Republic were called into question. For the nationalists of the political Right, Stavisky, a Russian Jew, became the focus of anti-Semitic and anti-Bolshevik sentiment. Stirred by the extremists of the Action Française, conservative groups laid siege to the Assemblée Nationale, sparking the 6 February riots in the Place de la Concorde, where many were killed. Two days later, a counterrally by the Left – the Radical, Socialist, and Communist parties – resulted in more deaths. More than symbolically, the riots of February 1934 mark the emergence of a public conflict of ideologies. For some, France was in a state of latent civil war. Certainly the level of conflict in political and intellectual circles was high, and would remain so for the rest of the prewar period, sustained by a vitriolic press that was largely unconstrained by laws of libel or defamation.

From the early 1930s, many anti-Fascist groups had sprung up in France, and after the 1934 riots they stimulated the creation, in

July 1935, of the Rassemblement Populaire. This Front Populaire, as it soon came to be called, enjoyed the enthusiastic participation of the major political parties of the Left and Center-Left, the major union organizations, as well as numerous intellectual, cultural, and professional associations. By the time of the 1936 national elections, the movement had been formed into a political machine, with a program that, despite the hysterical ravings of the Right, won the favor of the electorate. In May 1936, the Front Populaire became a government.

Its leader was Léon Blum (1872–1950), the head of the Socialist party. He was a distinguished and cultivated writer and member of parliament, a committed idealist and pacifist, and a member of the powerful Conseil d'État. Admired by his followers, Blum, with his internationalist philosophy and Jewish origins, was the very incarnation of everything that the Right feared and hated. Never at ease in the rough-and-tumble of the political arena, he was doomed to preside over the most debilitating polarization of public opinion in the history of the Third Republic.

The lasting achievements of the Front Populaire were in the field of social justice for workers: the introduction of the forty-hour week and of paid holidays. Legislation emphasizing cultural development and the needs of the young also had long-term significance. Generally, however, the election divided rather than unified the national spirit. In a Europe where the expression of a strong French position was becoming more and more imperative, Blum's government, while buoyed by the enthusiasm for many of its social reforms, was lacking clear direction or commitment in its foreign policy. This was painfully evident at the outbreak of the Civil War in Spain.

The sets of extracts that follow represent three different aspects of the French disarray. The first is a speech by Blum himself, and it typifies both the subtlety of his thought and the overwhelming sense of powerlessness that he felt. The second is taken from an essay by Georges Bernanos (1888–1948), who had made his name as a novelist and polemicist in the decade after World War I. A committed Catholic and a royalist, he had as a young man been a militant in the extreme right-wing Action Française, and later had written a eulogy of one of France's leading anti-Semites, Edouard Drumont. Bernanos had gone to Spain in 1934 in the hope of finding a cheaper place to live for his large and impoverished family. When the Spanish Civil War broke out, it was not surprising, given his background, that he at first sympathized with the

Falangists. His change of mind, and his vigorous attacks on the whole Francoist "crusade," were perceived as all the more powerful because he was known as a pillar of conservative values. The third set of texts are from newspaper articles by Antoine de Saint-Exupéry (1900-1944), who successfully combined the life of a man of action – as a pilot – and the more contemplative life of a writer. As a pilot, he had many extraordinary adventures, both as a pioneer of civil aviation networks in Europe, North Africa, and South America, and as a military test pilot. These experiences were often the starting point for his novels and essays, but his writings also raise a range of philosophical and moral questions about the human condition. Steeped in the traditions of individual freedom and comradeship, he had great difficulty in coping with the ideological conflicts of the 1930s. The dismay he felt during his visits as a journalist to Spain during the war is indicative of a wider French awakening to the inadequacy of traditional values in the Europe of Hitler and Mussolini.

Speech to the House of Representatives (La Chambre des Députés) 6 December 1936[1]

THE WAR IN SPAIN AND THE POLITICS OF NON-INTERVENTION

Our foreign policy has been inspired by two simple principles: the determination to place France's interests above all others, and the conviction that France has no greater interest than that of peace, the certainty that peace for France is inseparable from peace for Europe. All the groups in the majority, and I am sure the whole House, are in agreement on these principles.

I shall not accuse anyone of trying to push us directly or indirectly toward war. Everyone in France wants peace. Everyone is equally ardent in expressing this wish, and I have no doubt, equally sincere. Everyone understands that neither war, nor consequently peace, can today be contained within national borders, and that a people can only preserve itself from the scourge by contributing to preserve all others from it. [Applause on the far left, the left and in the center.]

However, gentlemen, despite this fundamental agreement, I am obliged to remark that our questioners have been rather discreet in praising us. Most of the opposition speakers, and first and foremost my friend Paul Reynaud,[2] have come forward in turn to claim that because of the composition of the majority[3] and the demands of our domestic program we are condemned, in the international sphere, either to self-contradiction or to impotence. And furthermore, on what may be the gravest of current issues – it is certainly the most emotional – the Spanish question, our common desire for peace nonetheless leaves us in disagreement, in practice, with one of the groups of the majority, the group made up by the Communist party.

I have dealt with this question elsewhere. I have never spoken of it before the House. Although, in reality, I have nothing to add to

1. This was the closing speech of a long debate on the government's foreign policy. In it, Blum raised the question of a vote of confidence, which the government won, 350 to 171. The Communist party abstained.

2. Paul Reynaud (1878–1966) was an influential right-wing independent. He would be Prime Minister at the time of France's collapse in 1940, at which time he handed power over to Marshall Pétain – who had been ambassador to Franco's Spain!

3. The Popular Front's governmental majority was a coalition of left-wing parties, including the French Communist party.

204

the declarations of my friend Mr. Yvon Delbos,[4] with whom I have always shared the most loyal and affectionate sense of solidarity, the House will no doubt permit me to furnish some personal explanations. I repeat, as was said by the Minister of Foreign Affairs, that as far as we are concerned, there is only one legal government in Spain, or, to put it better, only one government. The principles of what might be called democratic law coincide in this respect with the undisputed rules of international law.

I recognize that France's direct interest includes and calls for the presence of a friendly government on Spanish soil, and one that is free of certain other European influences. I have no hesitation in agreeing that the establishment in Spain of a military dictatorship too closely bound by links of indebtedness to Germany and Italy would represent not only an attack on the cause of international democracy, but a source of anxiety – I do not wish to put it more strongly – for French security, and hence a threat to peace. [Applause on the far left, the left, and on various benches in the center and on the right.] In that respect, I agree with the argument that Mr. Gabriel Péri[5] presented to the House. In fact, I deplore that such an obvious truth was not perceived from the start by all of French and international public opinion, and that it has been obscured by Party passion and resentment. Let me add – and I do not think that anyone in this House will pay me the insult of being surprised – that I do not intend for a single moment to deny the personal friendship tying me to the Spanish socialists, and to many republicans: it still attaches me to them, despite the bitter disappointment they feel and express about me today.

I know all that. I feel it all. And to take this sort of public confession through to its conclusion, I shall add that since 8 August,[6] a certain number of our hopes and expectations have in fact been disappointed; that all of us were hoping that the noninterference pact, which we had put into effect in advance, would be signed more promptly; that we were counting on the other governments' keeping more closely to their commitments. The policy of noninterference, in many respects, has not produced all we expected of

4. Yvon Delbos (1885–1956), representative from Dordogne, was a member of the Radical-Socialist party and minister for foreign affairs under Blum, and later minister for education (1939–1940).
5. Gabriel Péri (1902–1941), Communist party spokesman on foreign affairs and member of the Central Committee, was also a journalist for *L'Humanité*. He was executed by the Germans in 1941.
6. The nonintervention pact was supposed to take effect 8 August 1936.

it. True. But, gentlemen, is that a reason to condemn it? Here we must, all of us, make a very thorough analysis.

If it is true that in the name of international freedom, and in the name of French security, we must at all costs prevent the rebellion on Spanish soil from succeeding, then I declare that the conclusions reached by Mr. Gabriel Péri and Mr. Thorez[7] do not go far enough. It is not enough to denounce the noninterference agreement. It is not enough to reestablish free arms trade between France and Spain. Free arms trade between France and Spain would not be adequate aid, far from it. No! To assure the success of Republican legality in Spain, we would have to go further, much further. We would have to take a much greater step.

In conditions such as we have them at present, the truth of the matter is – and events have proved it – that the arming of a government can really only be done by another government. To be really effective, aid must be governmental. This is true from the point of view of materials, and from the point of view of recruitment. It would have to include, by way of equipment, levying arms from our own stocks, and by way of a sign-up of volunteers, levying troops from our units. That, in effect, is what the Minister for Foreign Affairs was saying yesterday, in a statement that I do not believe Mr. Maurice Thorez interpreted correctly, because it pinpointed this particular case. Let me quote it: 'But there has become such a great flood of them. . .' – he is speaking of the flood of foreign volunteers – '. . . and above all, it could become so significant, that one wonders if there is not a risk of the responsibility of the various States becoming involved, and that would mean a peril perhaps even graver than that deriving from massive and direct arms shipments.' What does this come down to? It comes down to saying that freedom of trade, whatever we did, and whether we liked it or not, and whatever our initial intentions and resolutions, would inevitably become de facto intervention, and a less and less disguised form of intervention. Those are the logical consequences, and the practical ones.

And yet, they are not being proposed. A moment ago, on this floor, Mr. Maurice Thorez vehemently denied that he was proposing them. Why? Precisely because we feel so clearly, gentlemen, the dangers and risks they conceal; because they would add yet another risk and danger to those that already weigh so heavily on

7. Maurice Thorez (1900–1964), representative from Ivry, was secretary general of the Communist party.

peace. And conversely, the policy of noninterference , despite the strains, despite the surprises, disappointments and anguish it may have caused, has at least diminished those risks and dangers. [Lively applause on the far left, the left and in the center.] We have been told that we had exaggerated them, that we had, after all, yielded to threat rather than to real peril. We have been assured that if, during August, we had held firmly to the ground of international law – and to hold strictly to the ground of international law would have meant claiming our right to help the legal government while forbidding Germany, Italy and Portugal to help the rebels – we have been assured that we would then have forced the authoritarian States to retreat. We have been confronted with the objection that, in any case, the arms race and buildup would not have led to the terrible and dramatic consequences we feared, given that since the end of October, the U.S.S.R., after Germany and Italy, to reestablish the balance, has proceeded to deliver arms to the Spanish Republic, and yet war has not occurred.

Gentlemen, I believe on the contrary that last August, Europe was on the brink of war, and I believe that it was saved from war by the French initiative. [Lively applause on the far left, the left, and in the center.] I cannot prove it, of course. I cannot prove that without the Pact, war would have broken out, because, precisely, the Pact was signed. But I hold this conviction deeply, and although I cannot go into all the details of the indications and evidence here, I can nevertheless assure the House that I am not alone in this feeling, and I do not mean just in France, but outside France as well; and among the evidence I have in mind, there are certain things that might surprise the House.

On the other hand, I am inclined to dispute the argument based on Soviet deliveries. Why? Well, gentlemen, because there is a hypothesis that, for my own part, I consider highly plausible. I believe that if the delivery of Russian arms has been able to balance the German and Italian ones without provoking armed conflict, it is precisely because of the psychological lull, the kind of lowering of the European temperature that the noninterference pact had allowed to occur; it is because of the beginnings of European organization that formed around the London Committee. However, if the temperature were to rise, if the London organization fell apart, if each nation reclaimed its freedom to act independently, would the danger not reappear? And do you not see many indications that it is in fact reappearing? Therefore, should the solution not be, today as before, in Geneva as in London, to obtain a consolidation of the organization, so that the commitments cease at last to be fraudulent, and their validity at last be guaranteed? What we sought earlier in the Pact, should we not seek it now, above all, in strict and efficient enforcement? [Applause on the far left, the left, and some center benches.]

That is my conviction, gentlemen, and it is one I share with the Minister for Foreign Affairs and the rest of the government. And let me moreover take my idea further. Even assuming that the criticisms levelled at us were well founded, what would that imply? Nobody can doubt, and nobody has disputed our intentions. Our intention has been to preserve peace, and nobody questions that. Our goal is known: it is peace.

What might we be criticized for? For overshooting the goal? For having been too afraid of war? For doing too much for peace? If we have committed any error, gentlemen, that would have to be it. Well, we can live with such reproaches. [Lively and extended applause on the far left, the left, and in the center.] And if we have to choose, we prefer to have overstated the risk of war than to have underestimated it. If we have had to err, we prefer to have done too much for peace than too little. We prefer to have sinned, if we have sinned at all, through excess rather than through insufficiency. You must by now be realizing that we are reaching the heart of the issue.

Some of our friends in the majority, and also, I know, some of my friends in the opposition, are afraid that we are going too far in our desire for peace; or rather, they are afraid that our desire for peace may mislead us. They believe that war is averted through firmness, and that conversely, a pusillanimous zeal for peace runs the risk of bringing war closer and making it more certain. They think that all our positions are being surrendered, given up one by one without being defended. The spirit of daring and enterprise is encouraged by our weaknesses, concessions, and capitulations. The authoritarian States, which are better adapted to secret preparations and surprise initiatives, are getting into the habit of placing Europe before a set of faits accomplis; and thus, we are told, we end up eroding from the base the conditions essential to peace, by trying to set aside or ward off every possibility of war.

That is the argument. I think I understand what truth it contains. I myself remember having spoken, in July in Geneva, of this epidemic of examples, and of what, I said, was worse still – the epidemic of successes. But I quoted the thought of a statesman of a century ago. 'I have never given an ultimatum,' he said, 'without being prepared to enforce it with a gun.' It will perhaps happen one day, that we will be faced with some circumstance too threatening for the essential conditions of peace, and be driven to say: 'No, not that. It is impossible to go any further.' It will perhaps happen one day that we will say that, as one must say it, but only as one has the right to say it [Applause on the far left, the left, in the center, and on various benches on the right.], that is, with the calm and firm resolution to face the extreme consequences of our word. [Applause on the same benches.]

Every government worthy of France may be reduced to envisaging that, if it involves the integrity of our soil, or the integrity of the territories protected by our signature; if it involves respecting the obligations we have contracted, either through the general pact of the League of Nations, or through the particular pacts and agreements that underpin it. Such possibilities cannot, alas, be excluded, or driven from our minds. Let me make quite clear that the government would of course fight desperately to avoid them or ward them off. [Applause on the far left, the left, and various center benches.] It would be prepared for the most extreme effort possible. Never, in any circumstances, will it resign itself to that most deadly of ideas – the idea that war is inevitable. [Applause on the far left, the left and in the center.] But if, despite everything, this danger were ever to get too close, there is at least one supreme duty that would weigh upon us. Responsible as we are for the safety of our country, as long as we hold the direction of its affairs in our hands, our duty would be to make certain that this terrible moment did not occur in such conditions, Thorez, that France would in fact risk isolation – where we would find Europe hesitant, or more than hesitant, and France divided. And I believe that by invoking, as I have just done, that supreme duty, I have furnished the supreme justification of our position. [Lively applause on the far left, the left, in the center and on various benches on the right.]

Gentlemen, I have said what is most important, but as you will understand, I do not wish to end on such a gloomy note. I spoke a moment ago of a desperate struggle. That was a manner of speaking, but I do not in any way give up – and indeed I shall never give up – the hope of turning away from Europe the unspeakable catastrophe that at times seems to hang over it. This hope is not composed of illusions, and it is not inflated with vanity; I can feel it strengthening within me whenever I make the effort to see Europe as a whole, and to review, to enumerate in Homeric fashion, all the forces of peace.

My friend Mr. Paul Reynaud has spoken of our inertia. I was surprised, but flattered, to find on his tongue the already popular formula: 'Blum in action.' [Applause on various benches on the far left and the left. Smiles.] I do not think he has given a fair assessment of the work accomplished by the government, and especially by the Minister of Foreign Affairs, in its six months of quite hardworking existence. We are not isolated in Europe. We have, to a large extent, put into effect the closing statement of our ministerial declaration: 'to recreate confidence in a peaceful Europe.'

It is not appropriate here to draw up the balance-sheet of a situation created by events that already go back a number of years, and moreover, it is not possible to draw up a diplomatic balance-sheet in the way that my friend Vincent Auriol[8] once drew up, in this House, an economic and financial summary of the state of affairs we inherited. Mr. Yvon Delbos showed you yesterday what the current situation was. He gave pride of place to the close and cordial nature of our relations with England, and quite rightly, for our other friends are unanimous in recognizing and declaring that the Franco-British agreement affects everything, and all other international relations. And yet where were the relations between France and Great Britain after the Ethiopian affair, and after its direct consequence, the crisis of 6 February?[9] [Bravo! Bravo! on the far left and the left.] There is a fact to which Mr. Paul Reynaud, almost exactly a year ago in this same House, seemed to me to attach more value.

The House was well aware of it, because yesterday it greeted with unanimous applause the climax of Mr. Yvon Delbos's speech, when he declared that all of France's armed forces, spontaneously and immediately, would come to the aid of Great Britain in the event of an unprovoked attack, as to the aid of Belgium. We have moreover upheld the reality and truth of the Franco-Soviet Pact,[10] which we discuss openly and without embarrassment: and I imagine that nobody here, even its opponents, would tolerate any foreign pressure for us to abandon it. [Applause on the far left, the

8. Vincent Auriol (1884–1966), representative from Haute-Garonne, was minister of finance, and, after World War II, became president of France.

9. The antiparliamentarian riots provoked by the right-wing *ligues* on 6 February 1934 in the Place de la Concorde not only led to fifteen deaths and over one thousand other casualties, they brought down the government of the day, and put the Third Republic under the greatest strain it had known since World War I. For both Left and Right, the date became a symbol of France's internal tensions, and of the apparent imminence of civil war.

10. The Franco-Soviet Pact was signed in May 1935. It was followed by a violent protest from Hitler.

left and on various benches in the center.] We have strengthened the links that unite us to the Little Entente,[11] and I hope we can strengthen them further. We have restored the full value of the agreements uniting us with Poland.[12] Our relations with Turkey, despite an occasional difficulty, have never shown deeper marks of friendship. I do not intend to give a full enumeration, but let me add that public opinion in the New World, whether in the Hispanic-American republics, the dominion of Canada, or the United States, manifests most active friendship for us, and we take some pride in finding in President Roosevelt's recent speech a magnificent expression of our own thinking and ideals. [Applause on the same benches.]

In respect to Germany and Italy, have we been inactive? No. We were the ones who in London, in July, made the convocation of the Locarno Conference possible. And we remain ready in every way, on every ground, for any political, economic and technical discussions that might permit a general solution of European problems – that is, the return of Europe to its normal state, which means to say – if you will allow me the expression – putting Europe back on a peace footing. [Bravo! Bravo!] I am referring here to disarmament, as Mr. Pierre-Etienne Flandin[13] expected. I do so neither obsessively nor maliciously. I do so because I have not lost my conviction that disarmament remains a substantial condition for the security of our peoples, and because experience has taught me, as it has taught him, that the idea of disarmament has always emerged when excessive military costs become intolerable, and from the danger that the arms race creates for our peoples. [Applause on the far left and the left.]

There, gentlemen, you have our policy. I believe that it has strengthened France towards the outside. I believe that it has strengthened the republican majority in the country as a whole. We ask the House to approve it.

I have never, in six months, raised before the House the question of a vote of confidence. I did not think I would ever have to do so. And yet I am raising it today. Not that it is my intention for

---

11. The "Little Entente" was a system of alliances with the states that had emerged after the dismantling of the Austro-Hungarian empire: Czechoslovakia, Yugoslavia, and Rumania.

12. France's agreement with Poland dated from 1920, when a French military mission under Weygand helped avert a Bolshevik invasion.

13. Pierre-Etienne Flandin (1889–1958), head of the Democratic Alliance, was prime minister and then minister for foreign affairs in the period immediately preceding the Popular Front government.

a single moment to put a section of the majority[14] under a form of pressure that is neither to my taste nor my custom, nor what I feel. I am doing it because the moment is too serious to allow any confusion or doubt to remain in the public mind.

Just before the Biarritz Congress,[15] speaking at a Radical party function, I declared with some solemnity that I would never for my part accept seeing the Communist party rejected from the majority because of any external pressure. I said that, from my viewpoint, the Popular Front would thereby lose its raison d'être. If today the Communist party had to remove itself voluntarily from the majority – if, by its vote, it had to disavow the government's action in such an important matter, the situation would be the same, and the consequences would be the same. Of course, it has always been, and still is, the Party's own business to weigh up whether a divergence of views, which I have not tried to conceal, any more than it has, [Bravo! Bravo!], should hamper the political and social task that we undertook together six months ago.

For my own part, I am, and remain, a man of my word. I make the fervent wish, not only that we might overcome the difficulty of the moment, but that we should do it in conditions such that tomorrow's common task can be pursued together in full confidence and loyalty. The House knows the circumstances that have led me to address the government's normal majority – what I shall call its organic majority. But I do not wish to leave the floor without making an appeal to the whole House. I ask it to gauge, in a fully conscious way, the effect that the vote we are about to take will have on the world outside. I ask it to do what we, after all, have ourselves done: to overcome cliquishness and fear, and to think only of the two great causes, at once national and universal, which to our mind are inextricably linked: the causes of republican France and of peace. [Lively applause on the left and on various far left and center benches. At these benches the representatives give a standing ovation.]

— Léon Blum, *L'oeuvre*, 1964

[Excerpt translated by Colin Nettelbeck.]

14. This is an allusion to the Communists, who, in fact, abstained.
15. The Biarritz Congress had taken place in late October 1936.

Majorca

Here was a small island, so peaceful, nestling amid almond trees, orange groves, vineyards. Its capital is of no more consequence than any ancient town of our French provinces. The next largest town, Soller, is more like a village. Isolated hamlets stuck along mountainsides or scattered in the plains have no communication save a few bad roads and occasional panting, broken-down lorries. Each of those villages is a closed-in world with its two parties 'Priests' and 'Intellectuals.' (The workmen half-heartedly belong to the 'Intellectuals.') There remains the 'Lord of the Manor,' who is only on view on grand occasions, but there isn't a face he doesn't know, and he has long since made up his mind about the blackguards, who are generally to be seen in company of the priest, his fellow ruler. But none of it matters. Owing to the easy-going charm of Spanish customs, they all live in harmony and dance with each other on feast days.

Overnight, or very nearly, each of those villages had its own search committee, a secret honorary tribunal, generally thus composed: the landowning bourgeois (or his bailiff), the sacristan, the priests's housekeeper, a few law-abiding peasants and their wives, and finally the young men hastily recruited by the new Phalange, too often converted but the day before, eager to pledge themselves, drunk with the horror that a blue shirt and a red tasseled cap can suddenly inspire in ignorant minds.

* * *

I have stated it once, I shall state it again: 500 Phalangistas on 17 July; 15,000 a few weeks later; then 22,000. Far from controlling this lightning recruitment, military authority assists it in every way, for they have a plan. When the time comes, when the job is done, nothing will be easier than to disarm a multitude that by sheer weight of numbers has smashed down the ancient framework, to whom another, cut to its measure, has been supplied: government by police. After which it can be broken up and dispersed in the general mass. The purge will be over.

For purge is the last word of this war; everybody knows it, or is beginning to know it, or will know it soon. The 'Get-it-over' slogan that abject impostors interpret more or less as 'Deliver the tomb of Our Lord,' never meant anything but systematic wiping out of dangerous elements, or those suspected of becoming so. Nothing surprising in that. Such was in 1871 precisely the unanimous desire of the people of Versailles. Two centuries before the French Revolution, the same formulae were used to justify the massacres in the prisons after Saint Bartholomew. In a letter to the Pope, Catherine de Medici compared it to the victory of Lepanto,[16] and the same night, Rome celebrated with rockets and illuminations.

All reigns of Terror are alike, all are of the same origin; you will not get me to distinguish between them. I have seen too much, I know men too well, and I am too old now. Fear disgusts me in everybody, and behind all the fine talk of those butchers, lies fear, and only fear. Massacres are due to fear, hate is but an alibi.

* * *

The purge at Majorca had three rather different phases, plus a preparatory stage. In the course of the latter there were certainly a few summary executions, in private houses, but they retained – or appeared to retain – an aspect of personal vengeance more or less deplored by all, of which details were whispered in secret. Then appeared the General Count Rossi.

Of course, the newcomer was neither a general nor a count, but an Italian official belonging to the Black Shirts. One morning we saw him disembark his scarlet racing car. First he called on the military governor appointed by General Godet.* The governor and his officials received him politely. Emphasizing his remarks with thumps upon the table, he announced himself as the herald of true Fascism. A few days later the general and his staff took up their abode in the prison of San Carlos, and Count Rossi was in control of the Phalange.

In black robes, with a huge white cross on his chest, he tore round the villages, driving his racing car himself; other cars, crammed with men armed to the teeth, strove to keep up with him in a cloud of dust. Every morning the papers told of these oratorical excursions. Accompanied by the alcalde and the priest, in a strange mixed jargon of Spanish, Italian, and Majorcan dialect, he announced the 'Crusade.'

In all fairness let it be said that the Italian government possessed in Palma some less glaring agents than this gigantic brute, who asserted one day at the table of a distinguished lady of Palma –

16. Lepanto. Naval battle fought between the Christian League (under Don Juan of Austria) and the Turks on 17 October 1571. The Turks were heavily defeated. [Original footnote.]

whilst wiping his fingers on the tablecloth – that he required at least 'one woman per day.'

But the particular mission entrusted him was marvellously suited to his gifts: the organizing of Terrorism.

From that time, every night, gangs of his own recruiting commenced operations in the villages and in the very suburbs of Palma. Where these gentlemen were most effective, there was barely any outward change. Always the same gentle knock at the door of a comfortable flat or a workman's cottage, the same crunching of steps in the darkness of the garden, or the same whispering of death on the landing, to which the victim listens from the other side of the wall, his ear to the keyhole, and anguish pinching his heart. 'Follow us.' The same words to the distracted woman; trembling hands struggling into well-worn clothes that a few minutes earlier had been discarded for the night, and the purr of the engine out there in the road. 'Don't wake the kids – what's the use? You're taking me to prison aren't you, señor?'

'Perfectamente,' answers the killer, who sometimes is under twenty.

You climb into the lorry where you find two or three other fellows you know, somber and resigned as yourself, with uncertain eyes. . . Hombre! A screech of brakes and the lorry sets off. A few moments of hope whilst it still keeps to the main road. But now it is slowing down, turning, goes jolting along a hollow earthen pathway.

'Get down!'

You get down, you line up, you press your lips to a medal – or merely to your own thumb nail.

Bang! Bang! Bang!

The bodies are piled against a bank, where the gravedigger will find them next day, their heads burst open, and their necks resting on a hideous cushion of black coagulated blood. I say the gravedigger, because all this has been carefully arranged to take place not far from a cemetery. The alcalde will record in his register: 'So-and-So, So-and-So, So-and-So, died of congestion of the brain.'

* * *

The first phase of the purge lasted four months, in the course of which this foreigner, who was mainly responsible for the slaughter, made a point of being well to the fore in all religious manifestations. He was usually supported by a chaplain picked up on the spot, in army breeches and top boots, a white cross on his chest and pistols stuck in his belt. (That particular priest has since been shot by his own side.)

None would have dared question the discretionary powers of the Italian general. I remember one unhappy priest who humbly begged of him to spare the lives of three young women of Mexican origin, who he deemed to be without malice, after hearing their confession.

'Right,' said the count. 'I'll sleep on it.' The following morning he had his men shoot them down.

* * *

The second phase was the purging of these prisons.

A large number of suspects, both men and women, escaped martial law for lack of any shred of evidence against them on which a court-martial could convict. So they began setting them free in groups, according to their birthplace.

But half-way, the carload would be emptied into a ditch.

I know. . . you don't wish me to go on. How many dead? Fifty? A hundred? Five hundred? The figure I shall tell you was given to me by one of the heads of the Palma Crusade. (The evaluation of the people is a very different one: never mind that.) Early in March 1937, after seven months' civil war, there were three thousand assassinations of this kind. Seven months are two hundred and ten days, which means an average of fifteen executions a day. Let me remind you that this tiny island can easily be crossed in two hours, from one end to the other. So that any inquisitive person with a car, if he took the trouble, could successfully wager that he would witness the blowing-out of fifteen wrong-thinking brains per day. These figures are not unknown to his Lordship the Archbishop of Majorca. . .

I could give many examples of this state of apathy – in the exact sense of the word. But I will confine myself to recording one press interview with some nuns of Porto Christo, which appeared in extenso in all the Palma newspapers: *El Ora, El Almudaina* (subtitle: *Diario Catolico*), *Ultima Hora.* The diminutive town of Porto Christo was the landing-place of the Catalonian troops in August 1936. Actually they were never able to get any further, and re-embarked six weeks later. These nuns ran a boarding school, which, at that time of the year was deserted. The Mother Superior spoke with great animation of the arrival of the 'Reds,' of the first contact of her petrified novices with the Barcelona militia, who brutally ordered them to prepare beds for the wounded. In the midst of the confusion appeared a South American, a kind of giant, pointing a gun and introducing himself thus: 'My sisters, I am a Catholic and a Communist. I'll blow out the brains of the first man who doesn't treat you with respect.'

For two days he exerted himself to the utmost, helped them to bandage the wounded, of which there were ever-increasing numbers, and in rare moments of leisure would indulge in a teasing controversy with the Mother Superior, which she described to the reporter in a manner both humorous and appealing.

At last came the dawn of the third day, and the nun tells the climax of her adventure thus:

'Suddenly we heard guns outside. The wounded became uneasy, the militia rushed out; we threw ourselves on our knees and prayed to Heaven to assist our liberators. Then we heard cries of *Viva España, Arriba España,* and the doors burst open. What more can I say? *Our brave soldiers entered from all sides and settled accounts with the wounded! The South-American was killed last!. . .*'

* * *

The military authorities now became uneasy at the growing disgust surrounding them, which the animosity of the Phalange – all arms and leaders had suddenly been confiscated from them – was likely to render dangerous, so they adopted a third method of purging, the most discreet of all. Here it is, in all its simplicity:

Prisoners deemed undesirable received one morning notice of their discharge, together with a certificate of wrongful arrest. They signed the gaol book, gave a receipt for objects confiscated, tied up their bundle of belongings, in short went through every formality, one by one, required to free the prison administration from any further liability. At two o'clock in the morning they were set free, in couples. That is to say that they found themselves outside the doors in a deserted road, facing a lorry and surrounded by men covering them with revolvers.

'Silence. We're taking you home.'

They were taken straight to the cemetery.

* * *

The person whom good manners suggest that I should refer to as His Lordship the Archbishop of Majorca, signed the collective letter of the Spanish Episcopate. I only hope the pen shook in his senile hand. He cannot have been unaware of these murders. I will tell him so to his face, when and where he pleases. And I will bring him this further testimony: One of the canons of his cathedral whom he knows well, a famous preacher, a doctor of divinity, had always seemed to approve the military authorities without any restriction. This prejudice troubled one of his lady parishioners, though she never dared mention the matter. But when she heard of the facts referred to above, she felt the time had come to speak out.

The creature listened without showing the slightest surprise.

'But surely you can't agree with —'

'I neither agree nor disagree,' came the sinister answer. 'Your Grace has unfortunately no idea of the difficulties of our ministry, in this island. At the last general meeting of parish priests, over which his Lordship presided, we had proof that last year only fourteen percent of Majorcans made their Easter. So grave a situation justifies exceptional measures.'

The 'measures' were indeed 'exceptional'! A few weeks before Easter the religious authorities agreed with the military authorities to take a census of the faithful. Printed forms were distributed for every man woman or child above the age of confirmation to fill in. They were inscribed as follows:

Mr., Mrs., or Miss..

Living at ......Street........No....Floor ....

made his (or her) Easter communion at the Church of

....

On the back of the form were the following words:

You are requested to make your communion in your own parish. Whoever does so at another church must bring a legitimate excuse to the priest of his parish.

An easily detachable perforated counterfoil contained the following instructions:

This form is to be filled in and sent to the priest of your parish. Alternatively it may be placed in the box reserved for the purpose.

Needless to add there were soon queues at all the confessionals. Indeed such was the influx of inexperienced penitents, that the priest of Tereno found it necessary to distribute a further pamphlet, which contained this rather surprising but most opportune advice: *The chief difficulty in the act of confession is not so much the confessing of one's sins as knowing what to say (en no saber que confesar o como expresarse)!* There followed a much condensed 'examination of conscience' formula, and finally this post-scriptum:

N.B. No olvides colocar tu billete del cumplimiento en el cajón del cancel para poder formar el censo.

(Do not forget to place the certificate in the box, so that the census list can be completed.)

Not one priest in Majorca would dare deny that such a proceeding in the very midst of terrorism was bound to induce large numbers of sacrilegious confessions.

What more need be said? God knows the names of the steadfast – a very few – who doubtless believed themselves to be His enemies, yet unknowingly retained sufficient Christian blood in their veins to resent this injury to conscience, and cry NO! in the face of such insolent summonses.

May they find their way to Jesus Christ! May they judge where they were judged, when the time comes!

— Georges Bernanos, *A Diary of My Times*, 1938

[Translated by Pamela Morris.]

In Barcelona

THE INVISIBLE FRONTIER OF THE CIVIL WAR

After Lyon, I banked left towards the Pyrenees and Spain. I am now flying over very clean clouds, summer clouds, clouds for cloud lovers, in which great holes open up, like skylights. That is how I catch a glimpse of Perpignan at the bottom of a well.

I am alone on board, and I am daydreaming, as I bend over Perpignan. I lived here for a few months. At that time, I was testing seaplanes at Saint-Laurent de la Salangue. When my work was done, I would come back to the center of this little town, where it always felt like Sunday. A big square, a café with music, and the evening glass of port. And from my wicker armchair, I would observe provincial life. To me, it seemed like a game, as harmless as a parade of toy soldiers. The prettily painted girls, the indolent strollers, the pure sky. . .

Here are the Pyrenees. I have left the last happy town behind me.

Here is Spain and Figueras. Here there is killing. Ah, the biggest surprise is not that you discover fire and ruins and signs of human distress, but that you discover nothing like that. This town looks like any other. I lean over attentively: nothing has marked this pile of white stones; the church, which I know to be burned out, is shining in the sun. I cannot make out the unhealable wounds. Already dissipated, that pale smoke that carried off the gold-leaf, and melted the woodwork, prayerbooks and sacerdotal treasures into the blue of the sky. Not a single line has changed. Yes, this town looks like any other, sitting at the center of its fan of roads, like the insect in the middle of its silken snare. Like other towns, this one feeds on the fruits of the plain, which are brought up to it along the white roads. And I discover nothing other than the image of that slow digestion, which down through the centuries, has marked the soil, driven away the forests, divided the fields, spread out the nutrient canals. That face of things will never change much. It is already old. I tell myself that a colony of bees, once its hive has been built, in the midst of a hectare of flowers, would know peace. But peace is not granted to colonies of human beings.

Yet for the drama to be seen, it has to be sought out. For it is often played out not in the visible world, but in the human mind. Even in Perpignan, the happy town, a cancer victim behind his hospital window tosses and turns in vain to escape from his pain, as from a pitiless bird of prey. And the peace of the town is affected by it. It is one of the miracles of the human species that there is no suffering or passion that does not radiate out and take on universal importance.

A man in his garret, if he nourishes a strong enough desire, can from his garret set the world ablaze.

Here at last is Gerona, then Barcelona, and I let myself glide down from the heights of my observatory. I perceive nothing here either, except deserted avenues. There are more churches that seem intact, but that are badly damaged. I sense somewhere a barely visible wisp of smoke. Is it one of the signs I have been looking for? Some evidence of that rage that has done such little damage, and made so little noise, but that has ravaged everything? For a civilization is contained entirely in that thin veneer of gold-leaf that one breath can blow away.

And they speak in good faith, the ones who say: 'Where is the terrorism in Barcelona? Apart from a score of buildings that have been burned, where is the city in ashes? Apart from a few hundred dead among twelve hundred thousand inhabitants, where is the slaughter?. . . Where is this bloody frontier and all the shooting over it?. . . '

It is true that I saw peaceful crowds strolling on the Rambla, and if I occasionally bumped into cordons of armed militiamen, to get past them most often required no more than a smile. I did not find the frontier immediately. The frontier in this civil war is invisible, and passes through the human heart. . .

And yet, the very first evening, I touched it. . .

I had taken my place outside a café among some good-natured drinkers, when four armed men came to an abrupt halt in front of us, and giving my neighbor a hard look, silently raised their rifle barrels to his stomach. The man, whose face suddenly began to drip with perspiration, got to his feet and slowly raised his arms, arms like lead. One of the militiamen, having searched him, ran his eyes over a few papers, and then gestured to him to start walking. And the man left his half-finished drink, the last drink of his life, and began to walk. And his two hands held above his head looked like those of a man drowning. 'Fascist,' a woman behind me muttered through her teeth, and she was the only witness to show that she had noticed anything. The man's glass remained there, giving witness to a crazy faith in luck, in indulgence, in life. . .

And I watched him move away, surrounded on all sides by rifles, the man through whom, two steps from me, five minutes before, the invisible frontier passed.

12 August 1936

A Civil War

IS NOT A WAR BUT A DISEASE

So I went with my Anarchist guides. Here is the embarkation station for the troops. We have to meet them over yonder, far from the platforms built for tender farewells, in a wasteland of switches and signals. And we stumble, under the rain, through the labyrinth of shunting tracks. We walk the length of forgotten trains of black wagons, where stiff forms lie under soot-covered tarpaulins. I am struck by this setting, which has lost all human qualities. Settings made of iron are uninhabitable. A ship appears living only as long as man, with his brushes and oils, keeps smearing it with false light. But if you abandon them for a fortnight, a ship, a factory, a railway-line grow dull, and take on the face of death. The stones of a temple, after six thousand years, still burn with the trace of man's passage, but with a little rust, a night of rain, this railway station landscape looks utterly worn out.

221

Here are our men. They are loading their artillery and machine guns onto the trucks. They use their backs, with stifled 'oofs' to struggle against these monstrous insects, these fleshless insects, these packets of shells and skeletons.

And I am surprised by the silence. Not a song, or a cry. The most one hears is the occasional hollow ring of a steel partition when a gun-carriage falls. I hear no human voices.

No uniforms. These men will go to their deaths wearing their work clothes. Black clothes, weighed down with mud. The column, busy with its scrap metal, resembles the denizens of a night-shelter.

I feel a sense of uneasiness, like what I remember once before, in Dakar ten years ago, when we were being attacked by yellow fever. . .

The leader of the group has been whispering to me, and he ends with:

'And we are heading up to Saragossa. . . '

Why is he whispering? The atmosphere reigning here is like a hospital. Yes, that is what I felt. . . A civil war is not a war, it is a disease. . .

These men are not mounting their attack in the heady joy of conquest; they are struggling silently against an epidemic. And no doubt it is the same thing in the opposite camp. This struggle is not about driving an enemy out of one's territory: it is an attempt to cure an illness. A new faith is like the plague. It attacks from within. It spreads through the body unseen. And those on one side, in the street, feel themselves surrounded by the plague-stricken, without being able to recognize them.

That is why they go off in silence, with their instruments of asphyxiation. They have nothing in common with the regiments of national wars, set out on a chessboard of meadows and manipulated by the strategists. In a city in chaos, they have got together as best they could. Barcelona, Saragossa, to all intents and purposes, are composed of the same mix: Communists, Anarchists, Fascists. . . . And the very ones that cling together differ perhaps more from each other than from their adversaries. In a civil war, the enemy is within, one is almost fighting against oneself.

And that is doubtless why this war is taking such a terrible form: there are more firing squads than actual combat. Death, here, is an isolation leper colony. They conduct a purge of the germ-carriers. The Anarchists make home visits and load the diseased onto their carts. And on the other side of the barrier, Franco could

222

make this atrocious comment: 'There are no Communists here any more.' The selection has been done as if by a recruiting review board; it has been done as if by a Medical Officer. . . .

A man, who thought he had a social function, presented himself with his faith, with his eyes burning. . . .

'Exempt from service, for life!'

Under quick-lime or petroleum, the dead are burned in fields of manure. No respect for man. In both the parties, the movements of his mind have been traced like a sickness. Why respect their envelope of flesh? And so this body, which was inhabited by youthful audacity, this body which knew about love, and smiling and self-sacrifice, elicits not even the thought of a decent burial.

And I ponder on our respect for death, and on the white sanatorium where a young woman is gently passing away among her kin, who gather in her last smiles and words like priceless treasure. And it is true that this moment of individual fulfilment will never be repeated. Never again will one hear that same burst of laughter, the same inflection of the voice, or the same quality of exchange. Each individual is a miracle. And for twenty years afterwards, we speak of our dead. . . .

Here, a man is simply stuck against a wall and he spills his guts on the stones. We caught you. We shot you. You didn't think like us. . . .

Ah, this nocturnal departure under the rain is the only one that can render the truth of this war. These men surround me and stare at me, and I read a sort of sad graveness in their eyes. They know what fate awaits them if they are caught. And I am cold. And I suddenly notice that no women have been permitted at this departure. It is an absence that seems reasonable. What is there for them to see, the mothers who when they give birth, do not know what image of truth will later inflame the hearts of their sons, nor what partisans will execute him, according to their justice, when he reaches the age of twenty.

14 August 1936

In Search of the War

I landed yesterday in Lerida, where I spent the night, twenty kilometers from the front, before setting off again for the front itself. This town, close to the line of fire, appeared calmer to me than Barcelona. Cars were moving about properly, without rifles sticking out from the doors. In Barcelona, twenty thousand fingers, day and night, are poised on twenty thousand triggers. And as these meteors bristling with weapons pass endlessly through the crowd, it can be said that a whole town is kept relentlessly in the sights. But the crowd here, whose heart is the direct target, no longer notices it, and goes about its business.

No passer-by goes about here with a revolver swinging in his hand. None of those rather pretentious accessories that cause surprise by the casual way they are carried, like a glove, or a flower. In Lerida, a front-line town, the people are serious: there is no longer any need to play at death.

And yet. . . .

'Make sure your shutters are closed tight. A militiaman across from the hotel has been given the task of putting out any visible lights by firing through the windows.'

We are now driving in the war zone. The barricades are more frequent, and henceforth we will parley each time with the revolutionary committees. Passes are now only valid from one village to the next.

'You want to go on?'

'Yes.'

The Committee president consults a large-scale map on the wall.

'You won't get through. The rebels are occupying the road six kilometers from here . . . You could go around this way . . . that should be clear . . . Unless . . . Somebody was talking about cavalry this morning. . . .'

Reading the front is very difficult. Friendly villages, rebel villages, unsure villages vary in the space of a day. This overlap of conquered and unconquered zones makes me think the thrust must lack backbone. This is no trench-line that separates bitter adversaries with knife-like precision. I have the feeling of sinking into a marsh. In one place the earth is firm under your feet. In another it gives way. . . And we head off again into uncertainty. How much space there is, how much air, between movements! . . . These military actions are strangely lacking in density. . . .

On the outskirts of this village, a winnower is sputtering. In a golden halo, they are working here for the men's bread, and the workers give us a big smile.

This lovely image of peace was so unexpected! . . . But life here seems hardly disturbed by death. A geographic expression comes back to me: one killer per square kilometer . . . and between two killers, it is hard to know who holds the land, this land of harvest and vines. And for a long time I hear the song of the winnower, tireless as a beating heart.

Here we are once again at the furthest point of our advance. A wall of paving-stones overlooks the road and we have six rifles aimed at us. Four men and two women are lying behind this wall. I notice moreover that the two women do not know how to hold a rifle.

'You can't drive any further.'

'Why not?'

'The rebels . . . '

From the village they point out another one, eight hundred meters away, a faithful replica of this one. Over there, no doubt, is a barricade, a faithful replica of ours. And perhaps a winnower, too, preparing rebel blood.

We have sat down on the grass near the militiamen. They put down their rifles and cut themselves some slices of fresh bread.

'Are you from round here?'

'No. Catalans, from Barcelona, Communist party.'

One of the girls stretches, and sits down on the barricade, her hair in the wind. She is a little heavy, but fresh and beautiful. She gives us a radiant smile:

'After the war, I'll stay in this village . . . You're much happier in the country than in town . . . I didn't realize!'

And she looks around her, lovingly, as if touched by a revelation. She had known only the grey suburbs, leaving for the factory in the early morning, the consolation of dreary cafés. Around here, every gesture made seems to belong to some kind of festivity. There she goes, leaping to her feet and running to the fountain. No doubt she has the feeling she is drinking from the very breast of the earth.

'Have you had any fighting here yet?'

'No. Sometimes there's movement in the rebel camp . . . We see a truck, or men . . . We hope they'll advance down the road. But in two weeks, nothing has ever happened.'

They are waiting for their first enemy. In the other village, there are no doubt six similar militiamen waiting for theirs. There are twelve warriors alone in the world. . . .

In two whole days spent at the front, feeling my way along the paths, I did not hear a shot. I observed nothing, except for those familiar roads that led nowhere. They seemed to follow their way through other harvests and vines, but that was another universe. They became forbidden to us like the roads in flooded countries that slope away gently down into the water. On the milestones, you could read: 'Saragossa, 15km . . . '

But Saragossa, like the town of Ys, was sleeping, unreachable, beneath the sea.

Of course, with a bit more luck, we might have ended up at one of those key points where the artillery rumbles and leaders give orders. But there are so few troops, so few leaders, so little artillery. Of course, we might have happened upon marching masses; there are twists of road along the front where people are fighting and dying. But that space remains between them. Everywhere I had occasion to observe it, the front was like an open door.

And, despite the fact that there are strategists and guns and convoys of men, it seems to me that the real war is not happening here at all. Everyone is waiting for something to be born out of the invisible. The rebels are hoping that among the indifferent inhabitants of Madrid, there will be partisans declaring themselves. . . . Barcelona is hoping that Saragossa will have an inspired dream, wake up socialist, and fall. What is on the march is thought; it is thought, rather than soldiers, that is laying sieges. Thought is the great hope and the great enemy. The few bombs from planes, the few shells, and the few armed militiamen do not in themselves, I believe, have the power to conquer. Every dug-in defender is stronger than a hundred assailants. But thought, perhaps, is on the move. . . .

From time to time there is an attack. From time to time, the tree gets a shake . . . Not to uproot it, but to see whether the fruit is ripe . . . Then, a town falls. . . .

16 August 1936

Here They Shoot People as if They were Clearing Trees

AND MEN NO LONGER RESPECT ONE ANOTHER

And here I have touched on a contradiction that I am not able to resolve. For the greatness of man is not made of the destiny of the species alone: every individual is an empire.

When a mine has caved in and collapsed on a single miner, the life of the town is suspended. Comrades, children and wives remain waiting, deeply anxious, while below their feet the rescuers probe with their picks the belly of the earth.

Is it a question of rescuing one unit in the collectivity? Is it a question of saving a human being, as one might save a horse, after weighing up the service it might still render? Ten comrades might perish in the rescue mission – what a poor cost-benefit ratio . . . But it is not a question of saving one termite among all the termites in the anthill, but a mind, an empire whose importance is immeasurable. Beneath the narrow skull of the miner trapped under the beams lies a whole world. Relatives, friends, a home, hot soup in the evening, songs for the feast-days, and perhaps even a social drive, some great universal love. How can one measure man? This one's ancestor once drew a deer on the wall of a cave, and two thousand years later his gesture still shines forth. It moves us. It is continued through us. A human gesture is a source of eternity.

At the risk of our lives, we shall raise up from his mineshaft the miner, who, however solitary, is universal.

But this evening, back in Barcelona, I look out from a friend's window onto a little destroyed cloister. The ceilings have collapsed, the walls have been pierced with gaping holes, one's glance probes the most humble secrets.

And despite myself, I think of those termite hills in Paraguay that I used to gut with a pickaxe to see their mysterious inside. And no doubt, for the conquerors who have gutted this little temple, it was no more than a termite hill. The young nuns, thrust back into the light of day by the mere kick of a soldier's boot, started to run back and forth along the walls, and the crowd was unaware of any drama.

But we are not termites. We are men. For us, it is no longer only the laws of number and of space that count. The physicist in his attic, at the high point of his calculations, is the measure of the importance of the whole city. The cancer patient, awake in the night, is the home of human pain. The solitary miner is perhaps worth the death of a thousand men. I can no longer play at this horrendous arithmetic. If someone says to me: 'What do these dozens of victims matter, compared to a whole population? What are a few burned temples, compared to a city whose life is going on?. . . Where is the terror in Barcelona?' I reject such measurements. The empire of man cannot be surveyed.

* * *

Partridge hunt in the woods. A young woman struck down among her brothers. No, it is not death that horrifies me. It almost seems gentle when it is linked to life; I like to imagine that in this cloister, a day of death was a day of celebration, even. . . . But this sudden and monstrous forgetting of man's essential quality, these algebraic justifications – that is what I reject.

Men no longer respect one another. Soulless bailiffs, they scatter the furniture to the winds without realizing that they are annihilating a kingdom. . . . Here are committees that give themselves the right to purge, in the name of criteria that, even if they change two or three times, leave only corpses behind them. Here is a general, at the head of his Moroccan troops, who condemns whole populations with a peaceful conscience, like a prophet crushing a schism. Here they shoot people as if they were clearing trees. . . .

In Spain, there are populations in movement, but the individual, that universe, from the bottom of his mineshaft, calls in vain for help.

— Antoine de Saint-Exupéry, articles for *L'Intransigeant*,
August 1936

[Reprinted in Antoine de Saint-Exupéry, *Un sens à la vie*, 1956. Excerpt translated here by Colin Nettelbeck.]

German Responses to the War

Introduction

PAVEL PETR

A t the time of the Spanish Civil War, German literature operated under special conditions that set it apart from other literatures and from its own past. Its continuity had been broken, its structure disjointed and fragmented by the mass exodus of many of its best representatives. When, in May 1933, works of banned authors were ceremoniously burnt in German university towns, the list was so comprehensive that the moderately known writer Jan Petersen, upon learning in Paris that his name was not on the list, protested against this undeserved denigration and demanded to be banned and burnt as well. (He was.) The dearth of good writers who would be prepared to serve the new regime was such that Ludwig Renn, incarcerated before he could leave Germany, was approached by an official of the highest order and offered pardon and privileges for a statement of support. (He declined and survived.) By the second half of the 1930s, the relatively small number of right-wing writers of note who initially were willing to join the National Socialist rulers and were accepted by them, had either withdrawn or become unacceptable, or both (Ernst Jünger, Gottfried Benn). In consequence, one of the striking characteristics of the German literary reflection of the Spanish Civil War is the almost complete absence of anti-Republican works of distinction. This phenomenon extends beyond the Spanish War topic: Right-wing works dealing with the German war experience in general, and with the First World War in particular, had by this time also declined in quality and influence. Although such works were encouraged after 1933 and produced in great numbers, only pre-1933 novels of this type had any significant impact in National Socialist Germany.[1]

The Air Force ministry approached Werner Beumelburg, an author of nationalistic war novels, and commissioned a novel that

---

1. Compare Peter Monteath, "Die Legion Condor im Spiegel der Literatur," *Zeitschrift für Literaturwissenschaft und Linguistik* 15:60 (1985), 107.

appeared in 1940 as *Kampf um Spanien*. It is a far from successful attempt to prove that the German soldiers who fought in the Condor Legion represented a further continuation of the glorious traditions of German military history. There are no notable German anti-Republican works written by participants, not only because there was no pool of good writers from which they could emerge, but also because Hitler's Germany did not admit participation in the intervention until after its end. Contemporary German works about the Spanish war simply omitted any mention of it.[2]

On the other hand, the list of German writers who sided with the Republican forces is impressive. It includes Erich Arendt, Johannes R. Becher, Bertolt Brecht, Willi Bredel, Louis Fürnberg, Hermann Kesten, Egon Erwin Kisch, Gustav Regler, Ludwig Renn, Bodo Uhse, and Erich Weinert. Twenty-seven German writers fought in the trenches as members of the International Brigades. The international character of the Brigades was complex: apart from varied forms of a more or less Marxist international ideology, it also mirrored the cultural interaction of European – especially Central European – cultures, where proficiency in other languages was natural and German the most common medium of communication. The Hungarian-born Arthur Koestler wrote all his books prior to 1940 in German; the Austrian Franz Borkenau wrote his account of the Spanish conflict in English; Gustav Regler's novel, *The Great Crusade* (1940), also appeared in English, with an introduction by Ernest Hemingway.

All these German authors – the term German is used here in the widest sense, to incorporate Germans, Austrians, and those who wrote in German – had left the German-speaking lands. For them, the Spanish conflict was not just a new literary topic; rather, it meant personal and political involvement. To them, their participation represented the opportunity to find new importance as individuals, a personal fight against the humiliations of exile and the hope that a defeat of the Spanish form of fascism would mark the beginning of the defeat of its German form. The fight for Madrid was, for these writers, the fight for a junction on the road back to Germany. The intensity of their involvement magnified its darker side as well: under these circumstances, the retreat of the Republican forces acquired the connotations of a tragedy.[3]

2. Monteath, "Die Legion Condor im Spiegel der Literatur," 95.
3. Compare Helmut Kreuzer, "Zum Spanienkrieg. Prosa deutscher Exilautoren," *Zeitschrift für Literaturwissenschaft und Linguistik* 15:60 (1985), 23.

* * *

Of the following sets of extracts, two are taken from works published in 1937: *The Spanish Cockpit* is an eyewitness account by the
Austrian sociologist Franz Borkenau (1900–1957). Contemporary
critics appreciated the integrity of the author's account. Orwell
wrote: "here, at last, amid the shrieking horde of propagandists,
was a grown up person, a man capable of writing dispassionately
even when he knew the facts. [. . .] It is a most encouraging thing
to hear a human voice when fifty thousand gramophones are playing the same tune."[4]

Arthur Koestler's (1905–1983) *Spanish Testament* was written at a
time when its author was still a member of the Communist party.
The translation used for this anthology was published in 1937; the
original German version was published a few months later, in
Switzerland. His nonheroic, truth-seeking report has remained
one of the best known works of its kind. The tension between the
demands of Party discipline and the author's pronounced individ-
ualism, the mixture of sharply observed images, Comintern propaganda, apocalyptic vision, and liberal reasoning resulted in a complex and very personal tapestry, the very unevenness of which
seems to enhance its brilliance. Gustav Regler (1898–1963), like
Koestler a journalist, Communist party member, and later anti-
Communist and novelist, views the events in Spain more as a
sequence of personal encounters than as a struggle between ideologies. His critics point out his vanity and the tendency to stage
events around himself. The extracts in this volume are taken not
from his 1940 novel but from his autobiography, which was published in German in 1958 and translated into English the following year. His reminiscences, filled with psychological portraits that
frequently mirror his own ego, contain enough fascinating narrative material to warrant his appearance in this selection.

---

4. George Orwell, *The Collected Essays* (Harmondsworth: Penguin, 1975),
385–386, 388.

A Diary in Revolution

All the churches had been burnt, with the exception of the cathedral with its invaluable art treasures, which the Generalitat* had managed to save. The walls of the churches are standing, but the interior has in every case been completely destroyed. Some of the churches are still smoking. At the corner of the Ramblas and the Paseo Colon the building of the Cosulich Line (the Italian steamship company) is in ruins; Italian snipers, we are told, had taken cover there and the building had been stormed and burnt by the workers. But except for the churches and this one secular building there has been no arson.

These were the first impressions. After a hasty dinner I went out again, in spite of warnings that the streets would not be safe after dark. I did not see any confirmation of this. Life, as usual in Barcelona, was even more seething after nine o'clock at night. True, the turmoil now abated earlier than in peace times, and long before midnight streets were empty.

Now when I went out the streets were full of excited groups of young men in arms, and not a few armed women as well; the latter behaving with a self-assurance unusual for Spanish women when they appear in public (and it would have been unthinkable before for a Spanish girl to appear in trousers, as the militia-girls invariably do) but with decency. Particularly numerous groups gathered before the fashionable buildings now requisitioned as party centres. The enormous Hotel Colon, dominating the splendid Plaza de Cataluña, has been taken over by the PSUC. The anarchists, with an eye for striking contrasts, have expropriated the offices of the Fomento del Trabajo Nacional, in the fashionable Calle Layetana. The Trotskyists have settled down in the Hotel Falcon, on the Ramblas. A tremendous group of cars and motor-lorries, with one or two armoured cars, was standing before the door of their newly acquired offices, and a group of young people in arms was standing about, in excited and eager discussion.

I do not understand Catalan. I was glad to hear German spoken. In this atmosphere of general enthusiasm there is no difficulty in talking to anybody. I soon discover that one of the militia-women in the group is the wife of a Swiss newspaper correspondent, and now I can begin to gather 'stories'. The care to find out whether they are true or not will come later. Let's listen to what people want to say.

234

A good deal of their talk is of the cruelty of the insurgents, who shoot all their prisoners. Is it the habit of the insurgents only, or among the Government militia too, I ask myself?

A second point discussed, and this with a surprising frankness and *naiveté*, is the problem of foreign help. Among the group I am in conversation with there are already many foreign volunteers, who have come to Spain eager to find a chance to fight fascism arms in hand, after having lived through its unopposed success in their respective countries, or watched its triumph over a large part of Europe. Among this POUM group, exactly as among the young people gathering at the doors of the Colon (the Socialist-Communist Party centre), there are Germans, Italians, Swiss, Austrians, Dutch, a few Americans, and a considerable number of young women of all these nations; the latter sharply contrasted, by their unconcerned behaviour and by the absence of any sort of male chaperoning, from their Spanish sisters, even those who wear arms. All languages are spoken and there is an indescribable atmosphere of political enthusiasm, of enjoying the adventure of war, of relief that sordid years of emigration are passed, of absolute confidence in speedy success. And everybody is friends with everybody in a minute knowing that in twenty-four or forty-eight hours one will have to separate again, when the next transports to the front send people towards different sectors.

* * *

The village bar is full of peasants. The appearance of three foreigners naturally is a big event. They immediately start telling us proudly about their feats. Most of them are anarchists. One man with a significant gesture of the fingers across the throat tells us that they have killed thirty-eight 'fascists' in their village; they evidently enjoyed it enormously. (The village has only about a thousand inhabitants.) They had not killed any women or children, only the priest, his most active adherents, the lawyer and his son, the squire, and a number of richer peasants! At first I thought the figure of thirty-eight was a boast, but next morning it was verified from the conversation of other peasants, who, some of them, were not at all pleased with the massacre. From them I got details of what had happened. Not the villagers themselves had organized the execution, but the Durruti column when it first came through the village. They had arrested all those suspected of reactionary activities, took them to the jail by motor-lorry, and shot them. They told the lawyer's son to go home, but he had chosen to die with his father.

As a result of this massacre the rich people and the Catholics in the next village rebelled; the alcalde mediated, a militia column entered the village, and again shot twenty-four of its adversaries.

What had been done with the property of those executed? The houses, of course, had been appropriated by the committee, the stores of food and wine had been used for feeding the militia. I omitted to ask about money. But the big problem was the land and the rents which the landlords had previously received from their tenants. To my intense surprise, no decision had been taken about this matter, though it was more than two weeks since the executions. The only certain thing was that the land of the deceased continued to be worked as it had been previously: those parts which had been let were still worked by their former tenants, and those formerly managed as an estate and cultivated by agricultural labourers were still functioning in the same way; only instead of the squire it was now the committee which employed the necessary labour. As to the rest, there was only vague talk: the committee would eventually receive 50 per cent of the old rents, the other half being remitted, and half of the expropriated lands would be distributed among the poorer peasants, while the other half would be managed by the committee as collective property of the village. Evidently in this village the agrarian revolution had not been the result of passionate struggle by the peasants themselves, but an almost automatic consequence of the executions, which were themselves but an incident in the civil war. Now most of the peasants were bewildered by the new situation. One of them, among many others, simply said: 'What do I know? They will give an order about it.' I ask: 'Who will give an order?' 'Oh, how do I know? There will be some government,' he replied. This threw a new light upon the vague replies I had got the day before in other villages when inquiring about land expropriation and rent abolition.

We drove northward, to the aviation camp of the Saragossa front, which I visited twice, at noon and at night. There were no anti-aircraft guns, and when I asked about it some of the pilots agreed that it was surprising that the rebels, for no conceivable reason, had omitted to raid it. At night I saw enemy signals given from places not far off, behind the Government lines. In my presence the men discussed how awkward it was that these signals appeared every night, but nobody thought of sending a patrol to investigate. A small troop of rough militia arrived that night, in the gayest spirits, and was quickly and efficiently quartered on the aviation field, in tents, in a very orderly manner. For most of these boys it was their first romantic experience of camping, and they thought very little of the more serious aspects of campaigning which might follow.

Why had the aviators, in contrast with all the other troops, remained faithful to the Government? Pilots, after some years of service in the ordinary regiments, were individually selected for aviation training, and thus the links of regimental *camaraderie* which have been the basis of so many compact risings of the Spanish military against various governments were severed. Moreover, as one of the pilots emphasised, they are selected for technical ability, and that often seems to go hand in hand with a tendency to the Left. After all, modern industrialism does not go well with the Spanish type of Catholic education, and machine-mindedness in Spain, especially among the routine-ridden Spanish officers, must still be something almost revolutionary. This pilot was a liberal patriot without any socialist leanings, and I asked him what he thought of the social upheaval going on around him. 'That will be as it must be,' was his answer, 'now we are fighting in common against the fascists.' But one of his comrades, asked the same question on another occasion, bluntly replied: 'To disaster.' His fellows, although they seemed to agree, hushed him up. Evidently these liberal officers are caught between their allegiance to the republic and their dislike of the anarchists, and are almost in despair about it.

And now we came to the real front. We nearly missed it, it was so tiny. Driving north on the road to Huesca we were stopped at the last moment by a guard on the road; otherwise we should have driven into rebel country without noticing it. As it was, we climbed a hill to the village of Alcalá de Obispo, and then to our surprise found that we were in the front line itself. Up to a mile behind the lines there was nothing to suggest its existence; then we had seen one shell bursting in the distance, but did not hear any sound. Neither was there a 'front' with trenches or with an outstretched line of troops. The 'front' consisted of a concentration of perhaps three hundred men in the village of Alcalá, with a few advance-guards half a mile ahead. There was no contact with the next militia column, which was stationed in a neighbouring village some miles away. Seeing this, I remembered with some amusement the foreign newspaper reports of sanguinary battles, which we imagined were being fought between tens of thousands of men.

It took me some time to realise that I was actually in an artillery bombardment. But when there was a shout of 'Take cover' I noticed that something was happening. From Monte Aragon, one of the chief forts of Huesca, the rebels were shelling what they believed to be the Catalan lines. Fortunately their idea of the position of these lines was entirely erroneous and they were aiming with great exactitude at a spot half a mile from Alcalá, where, as the officers explained, there was nothing but sparrows. A large group of Government soldiers was standing erect on the exposed side of the village, watching the fun. Every single time we heard the singing of a shell we receded a few steps, but were quickly reassured by its bursting in the wrong place.

The day before, the Catalan troops had to evacuate the village of Sietamo under a well-aimed artillery attack, but scouting does not seem to be the strong point of the insurgents, and they had not yet found out the new positions. On the Catalan side artillery observation is hardly better. About six light field-guns were placed in front of the village, and occasionally fired without any adequate direction; two howitzers were placed behind the village but the observer, most incompetently, stood on the church tower almost in front of the guns, and I do not think that the shelling did much damage to the enemy. In this column there was not one single casualty that day, despite an all-day bombardment.

* * *

The gap between ideals and reality is sometimes grotesque, in Spain, and people are completely satisfied with their own good intentions without bothering to put them into effect. In the village committees the anarchists seemed usually to take the lead, and among other achievements they prided themselves upon the abolition of private commerce in the harvests. All crops were now sold direct to the trade unions, I learnt, and I was inclined to admire this extraordinary feat of organization. My curiosity, in one case, went so far as to ask for an interview with the man who was charged with the commercial handling of the main crop, which in this instance was wheat. And then came disappointment. There was no such man; thus there was visible dismay on the faces of the committee members when I asked to see the man who did not exist. After a few minutes they decided to admit that the crops were handled exactly as before, by private merchants. In fact, the problem of the handling of export crops such as the Valencia oranges is far beyond the capacity of small villages. But if the ideals of *comunismo libertario* could not be put into practice, at least it was nice to talk about them.

238

In the borough of Gandía, for the first time in Spain, I was threatened with being shot. I was discussing agrarian problems with the local secretary of the UGT when a messenger came in and asked me to see some gentlemen waiting for me outside. There were four of them wearing a sort of uniform unknown to me, with stripes on the sleeves. They at once proceeded to cross-examine me in police manner about my intentions, and when I explained that in this particular spot I wanted to study the agrarian revolution, they retorted that there was no agrarian revolution in Spain, that my research was dangerous, that Spain was not interested in being known by foreigners now, and that if I wanted to bring news home it was quite enough for me to tell England that the whole people was united and obeyed orders from the Government; I ought to leave Gandía immediately unless I wanted to be 'eliminated.' I told them I was there with a car of the Press department of the Comité Regional Ejecutivo, and would they care to come with me to supervise my departure? They did not want to do this – very wisely. And I did not leave the town. I soon found out that these people belonged to the Seguridad, in other words the ordinary police of the old régime, and of course they had acted upon their own responsibility. But it was difficult to convince my anarchist companions of this, their firm belief being that only communists could behave in such a nasty manner. Even my observation that communist militia-men would not wear stripes did not convince them; communists, they said, imitated enthusiastically every sort of military decoration. I do not believe that this is so, but it was characteristic of the mutual hatred between communist and anarchist.

In the afternoon I attended, in Valencia, a mass meeting of the Popular Front (to which neither the anarchists nor POUM belong). There were about 50,000 enthusiastic people there. When La Pasionaria appeared on the platform enthusiasm reached its climax. She is the one communist leader who is known and loved by the masses, but in compensation there is no other personality in the Government camp loved and admired so much. And she deserves her fame. It is not that she is politically minded. On the contrary, what is touching about her is precisely her aloofness from the atmosphere of political intrigue: the simple, self-sacrificing faith which emanates from every word she speaks. And more touching even is her lack of conceit, and even her self-effacement. Dressed in simple black, cleanly and carefully but without the slightest attempt to make herself look pleasant, she speaks simply, directly, without rhetoric, without caring for theatrical effects, without bringing political *sous-entendus* into her speech, as did all the other speakers of the day. At the end of her speech came a pathetic moment. Her voice, tired from endless addresses to enormous meetings since the beginning of the civil war, failed her. And she sat down with a sad waving gesture of her hands, wanting to express: 'It's no use, I can't help it, I can't say any more; I am sorry.' There was not the slightest touch of ostentation in it, only regret at being unable to tell the meeting those things she had wanted to tell it. This gesture, in its profound simplicity, sincerity, and its convincing lack of any personal interest in success or failure as an orator, was more touching than her whole speech. This woman, looking fifty with her forty years, reflecting, in every word and every gesture, a profound motherliness (she has five children herself, and one of her daughters accompanied her to the meeting), has something of a medieval ascetic, of a religious personality about her. The masses worship her, not for her intellect, but as a sort of saint who is to lead them in the days of trial and temptation.

* * *

One remarkable aspect of the streets becomes more conspicuous with time: the changed position of women. Young working-class girls in hundreds and perhaps thousands are walking up and down the streets, and are especially to be seen in the elegant cafés of the Alcalá and the Gran Via. They collect for the 'International Red Help,' an organisation 'in favour of the victims of class war', here mostly working for the wounded and for relatives of the victims of the civil war; it was sponsored originally all over the world by the Comintern, but is run in Spain by socialists and communists jointly. There is no collecting either in Barcelona or in Valencia, whereas the couples of girls (they never go alone; walking through the streets completely unchaperoned would still be unthinkable for any decent Spanish girl), well dressed in working-class fashion, who ask everybody for a contribution, are almost a nuisance in Madrid, or at least would be were they not so pleasant to look at. They enjoy it enormously; for most of them it is obviously their first appearance in public, and now they are even allowed to talk to foreigners and sit down at their ease in the cafés for a chat with the militia-men.

The revolutionary tribunal, which is starting its activities today, will limit its trials to such cases as fall under established civil or military law; this means that practically only cases of mutiny will come before it. But there is an enormous number of other cases: priests, nobles, and innumerable people of the Right wing who have taken no part in military activity but have either been caught conspiring against the Government or are suspected of having done so. All those cases are outside the competence of the revolutionary tribunal. In the first days of the rebellion the anarchists suggested that every single member of a Right-wing party should be shot; they have the lists, and there are 42,000 members of Gil Robles's Catholic Acción Popular alone. They have been convinced of the inexpediency of this cruel folly, but no one thinks of limiting executions to such cases as might be convicted of high treason by way of regular trial. What happens is that investigation committees of the three proletarian groups in Madrid, communists, socialists, and anarchists, co-operate. Each of them has a list of suspects, and when they arrest one they ask the two other parties their opinion. If they all agree, then the man is either executed or released. If they disagree, closer investigation ensues. It is certainly a rough and ready manner of dealing with an insoluble problem.

For insoluble indeed it seems to be. This, at least, seems to be borne out by another story. On 19 July the newly formed militia put down the military revolt in Madrid by storming the Montana Barracks. Then, after five hours of heavy artillery action, followed by a successful attack, the militia went back to the centre of the town, and was acclaimed by a large crowd. When they reached the Puerta del Sol, a largely reactionary district, they were suddenly fired at from the windows on all four sides of the square. The *asaltos** immediately ordered the crowd, men and women, to crouch down on the pavement, and actually prevented a panic. These Spaniards find street fighting perfectly natural. Anyway, there they had to lie on the pavement, under fire from all sides, for many minutes, until the *asaltos* had entered the houses and cleared the snipers from the windows. So it went on in many parts of the town for many days.

Such an outbreak would be bad enough, but worse are the numerous well-confirmed stories of espionage, treason, desertion of officers, storing of arms by the sympathizers of the rebels, signalling the enemy, and so on *ad infinitum*. Some at least of these tales must be true, and they recall scenes of the French and Russian revolutions, when also the revolutionaries felt surrounded by enemies from every quarter and had to strike in the dark, because there was no time to make sure.

All the air of Madrid is full of stories of terrorism, much more than in Barcelona; and this, as far as I can judge, not so much because the actual amount of terrorism is greater here than in Catalonia (though the proximity of the Guadarrama introduces a specially irritating element) as because in Catalonia the job of exterminating the enemies of the Government is done swiftly and ruthlessly, whereas in Madrid the insufficiency of the administration and the lack of political unity make for friction, uncontrollable individual extravagance, and cruelty, and, last, not least, for an enormous amount of gossip.

One well-confirmed story throws light upon an unexpected aspect of fascism. In an hotel a Spaniard suspected of co-operating with the rebels was arrested. He himself got off by the unreputable but humanly intelligible device of denouncing some of his friends, and was soon released. Not for long, however: his friends in their turn denounced him, with convincing proofs, and he was again arrested, and executed without much delay. But then came a surprising finale. The group of militia who had performed the investigation and the execution were afraid of distressing his widow, actually so afraid as not to dare to tell her. So they went on for more than two weeks pretending her husband was alive, that he had been confined to his native village, and other similar stories. The actual result must have been augmented torture for the family, but the motive was undoubtedly compassion for the widow, who, they said, had nothing to do with the guilt of her husband. The husband appears to have really been guilty of co-operation with the insurgents; at any rate the executioners were genuinely convinced of that. The conception that men ought to be killed for their political opinions, but not women for the opinions they share with their husbands, brothers, and fathers, seems fairly prevalent.

Settling of personal accounts by denouncing a personal enemy as an adversary of the Government was one aspect of terrorism continually mentioned by foreigners in Barcelona, but hardly ever proved in a concrete case. But today, in Madrid, I learned of a case which really falls under the heading of the settling of personal accounts in the worst meaning of the expression. A patient denounces his doctor, to whom he owes some money. Fortunately the arrested doctor hits upon the right interpretation, asking his interrogator, 'Has not X denounced me?' and when the answer is in the affirmative explains the whole story. The denouncer was arrested in his turn, could not deny the existence of the debt in question, and then in the course of a short investigation revealed how completely unfounded were his accusations; he was shot at once. But the case is probably not unique, and the issue not always in favour of the innocent.

From these stories of horror I fled to more peaceful and attractive things: in the afternoon I went to the Prado. A group of young anarchist militiamen were walking through its large rooms. They had certainly not seen a museum in their lives, and were staring, puzzled, at the paintings; they had set out to conquer the privileges of bourgeois education, but found it more difficult than they expected. Still, they not only displayed that good behaviour in unwonted circumstances which is one of the conspicuous merits of the Spanish national character but felt that they were amidst things to be admired and reverenced; probably knew dimly that it was something very beautiful indeed; they spoke with subdued voices and went with light steps; only it was all so puzzling.

* * *

I had hardly settled down in my hotel room in Valencia [. . .] before two members of the secret police presented themselves and took my passport away with them. No such practice had been followed in August, nor had it been followed in January in Barcelona. But in itself it seemed quite intelligible and defensible on many grounds. I soon learned, however, that the department which had got hold of my passport was not a regular body at all. It was an institution calling itself 'Información de la Seguridad General' (Information Department of the General Police), but had been formally dissolved by this same 'Seguridad General'. It was still active nevertheless. I had to go next day to its offices, 15 Plaza Tetuán, in order to fetch my passport. I did not get it at once, however, but was subjected to an interrogatory about my political past centring round the question whether I had ever in my life been a Trotskyist. The denunciation from Barcelona had not arrived then, so I suppose that many other people were subjected to similar interrogatories. When I had proved to their satisfaction that I had never been one, no further interest was taken in my past and I got my passport back next day. Number 15 Plaza Tetuán was directed by foreign communists. Later I heard bitter complaints about its actions in arresting people and keeping them in prison for a long time without due investigation and occasionally shooting the wrong man (for this unofficial police body performed executions). Enmity between them and the ordinary police was patent in the personal relations of the staffs, as far as I could observe them.

It must be explained, in order to make intelligible the attitude of the communist police, that Trotskyism is an obsession with the communists in Spain. As to real Trotskyism, as embodied in one section of the POUM, it definitely does not deserve the attention it gets, being quite a minor element of Spanish political life. Were it only for the real forces of the Trotskyists, the best thing for the communists to do would certainly be not to talk about them, as nobody else would pay any attention to this small and congenitally sectarian group. But the communists have to take account not only of the Spanish situation but of what is the official view about Trotskyism in Russia. Still, this is only one of the aspects of Trotskyism in Spain which has been artificially worked up by the communists. The peculiar atmosphere which today exists about Trotskyism in Spain is created, not by the importance of the Trotskyists themselves, nor even by the reflex of Russian events upon Spain; it derives from the fact that the communists have got into the habit of denouncing as a Trotskyist everybody who disagrees with them about anything. For in communist mentality, every disagreement in political matters is a major crime, and every political criminal is a Trotskyist. A Trotskyist, in communist vocabulary, is synonymous with a man who deserves to be killed. But as usually happens in such cases, people get caught themselves by their own demagogic propaganda. The communists, in Spain at least, are getting into the habit of believing that people whom they decided to call Trotskyists, for the sake of insulting them, are Trotskyists in the sense of co-operating with the Trotskyist political party. In this respect the Spanish communists do not differ in any way from the German Nazis. The Nazis call everybody who dislikes their political régime a 'communist' and finish by actually believing that all their adversaries *are* communists; the same happens with the communist propaganda against the Trotskyists. It is an atmosphere of suspicion and denunciation, whose unpleasantness it is difficult to convey to those who have not lived through it. Thus, in my case, I have no doubt that all the communists who took care to make things unpleasant for me in Spain were genuinely convinced that I actually *was* a Trotskyist. The inferences from which they drew this conclusion were twofold: first, I had been highly critical of the type of bureaucratic tyranny towards which the communists are driving in Spain, and have achieved in Russia, as others have achieved it in Germany and Italy. Second, among many friends and acquaintances, I had some who were Trotskyist. What else but a Trotskyist could a man be, if he is opposed to the totalitarian state and talks to Trotskyists? I repeatedly tried, indirectly, to convey to various communists that they were mistaken, that after all I had published a good many things which proved that I was anything but a Trotskyist; that I did not even take the Trotskyists seriously. It was in vain. I was critical of bureaucratic totalitarianism, hence I was a Trotskyist. I had talked with Trotskyists, hence I was a Trotskyist.

— Franz Borkenau, *Spanish Cockpit: An Eye-Witness Account of the Political and Social Conflicts of the Spanish Civil War*, 1937

Spanish Testament

My stay in Seville was very instructive and very brief.

My private hobby was tracking down the German airmen; that is to say, the secret imports of 'planes and pilots, which at that time was in full swing, but was not so generally known as it is to-day. It was the time when European diplomacy was just celebrating its honeymoon with the Non-Intervention Pact. Hitler was denying having despatched aircraft to Spain, and Franco was denying having received them, while there before my very eyes fat, blond German pilots, living proof to the contrary, were consuming vast quantities of Spanish fish, and, monocles clamped into their eyes, reading the "Völkischer Beobachter."

There were four of these gentlemen in the Hotel Cristina in Seville at about lunch time on 28 August 1936. The Cristina is the hotel of which the porter had told me that it was full of German officers and that it was not advisable to go there, because every foreigner was liable to be taken for a spy.

I went there, nevertheless. It was, as I have said, about two o'clock in the afternoon. As I entered the lounge, the four pilots were sitting at a table, drinking sherry. The fish came later.

Their uniforms consisted of the white overall worn by Spanish airmen; on their breasts were two embroidered wings with a small swastika in a circle (a swastika in a circle with wings is the so-called "Emblem of Distinction" of the German National-Socialist Party).

In addition to the four men in uniform one other gentleman was sitting at the table. He was sitting with his back to me; I could not see his face.

I took my place some tables further on. A new face in the lounge of a hotel occupied by officers always creates a stir in times of civil war. I could tell that the five men were discussing me. After some time the fifth man, the one with his back to me, got up and strolled past my table with an air of affected indifference. He had obviously been sent out to reconnoitre.

As he passed my table, I looked up quickly from my paper and hid my face even more quickly behind it again. But it was of no use; the man had recognized me, just as I had recognized him. It was Herr Strindberg, the undistinguished son of the great August Strindberg; he was a Nazi journalist, and war correspondent in Spain for the Ullstein group.

This was the most disagreeable surprise imaginable. I had known the man years previously in Germany at a time when Hitler had been still knocking at the door, and he himself had been a passionate democrat. At that time I had been on the editorial staff of the Ullstein group, and his room had been only three doors from mine. Then Hitler came to power and Strindberg became a Nazi.

We had no further truck with one another but he was perfectly aware of my views and political convictions. He knew me to be an incorrigible Left-wing liberal, and this was quite enough to incriminate me. My appearance in this haunt of Nazi airmen must have appeared all the more suspect inasmuch as he could not have known that I was in Seville for a newspaper.

He behaved as though he had not recognized me, and I did the same. He returned to his table.

He began to report to his friends in an excited whisper. The five gentlemen put their heads together.

Then followed a strategic manoeuvre: two of the airmen strolled towards the door – obviously to cut off my retreat; the third went to the porter's lodge and telephoned – obviously to the police; the fourth pilot and Strindberg paced up and down the room.

I felt more and more uncomfortable and every moment expected the Guardia Civil to turn up and arrest me. I thought the most sensible thing would be to put an innocent face on the whole thing, and getting up, I shouted across the two intervening tables with (badly) simulated astonishment:

"Hallo, aren't you Strindberg?"

He turned pale and became very embarrassed, for he had not expected such a piece of impudence.

"I beg your pardon, I am talking to these gentlemen," he said.

Had I still had any doubts, this behaviour on his part would in itself have made it patent to me that the fellow had denounced me. Well, I thought, the only thing that's going to get me out of this is a little more impudence. I asked him in a very loud voice, and as arrogantly as possible, what reason he had for not shaking hands with me.

He was completely bowled over at this, and literally gasped. At this point his friend, airman number four, joined in the fray. With a stiff little bow he told me his name, von Bernhardt, and demanded to see my papers.

The little scene was carried on entirely in German.

I asked by what right Herr von Bernhardt, as a foreigner, demanded to see my papers.

Herr von Bernhardt said that as an officer in the Spanish Army he had a right to ask "every suspicious character" for his papers.

Had I not been so agitated, I should have pounced upon this statement as a toothsome morsel. That a man with a swastika on his breast should acknowledge himself in German to be an officer in Franco's army, would have been a positive tit-bit for the Non-Intervention Committee.

I merely said, however, that I was not a "suspicious character," but an accredited correspondent of the London "News Chronicle," that Captain Bolín* would confirm this, and that I refused to show my papers.

When Strindberg heard me mention the "News Chronicle" he did something that was quite out of place: he began to scratch his head. Herr von Bernhardt too grew uncomfortable at the turn of events and sounded a retreat. We went on arguing for a while, until Captain Bolín entered the hotel. I hastened up to him and demanded that the others should apologise to me, thinking to myself that attack was the best defence and that I must manage at all costs to prevent Strindberg from having his say. Bolín was astonished at the scene and indignantly declared that he refused to have anything to do with the whole stupid business, and that in time of civil war he didn't give a damn whether two people shook hands or not.

* * *

Even Terror has its gradations, its evolutionary history, its theory. Danton was a dilettante in the application of Terror, Robespierre was a systematic exponent of it. But the methods of Terror employed by the nineteenth century bear the same relation to those of the twentieth century as does a post-chaise to a motor-car.

Nowadays the aim is no longer to defeat the political opponent but to destroy and exterminate him. This may seem merely to be a nuance; in reality it is a kind of revolution within the realm of Terror – if one may say such a thing.

The Spanish insurgents have adopted in every detail the ultra-modern theory of Terror. This statement too seems to be a platitude. It is not. How concretely and consciously this theory was put into practice, can best be illustrated by a few quotations taken at random from the German Press.

> The Generals looked for guarantees of victory not primarily in military successes, but in a systematic and thorough cleaning-up of the hinterland. . . .[5]

> Fortunately the old attitude of sentimentality has been dissipated among the Nationalists, and every soldier realises that a horrible end is better than endless horrors. . . .[6]

> The Marxist parties are being destroyed and exterminated down to the very last cell far more drastically even than here in Germany. Every house, every flat, every office is kept under constant observation and supervision. . . Every single citizen, moreover, is continually drawn into the whirl of political excitement, made to participate in triumphal celebrations and mass demonstrations. The principle of modern Nationalism 'No opponent but shall be destroyed' is thoroughly carried out. . . Just as here in Germany. . . .[7]

It is difficult to convey any idea of the scenes that occurred during the first few days after the revolt in the districts occupied by the rebels. The reports available are naturally few and far between; and the accounts of fugitives, passed on at second or third hand, are either incomplete or exaggerated. We know how much harm the preposterous atrocity propaganda engaged in by both sides caused during the Great War, and the author shares the repugnance felt by every newspaper man with a conscience at the thought of allowing himself to be drawn into such slimy depths. Nevertheless there is a form of journalistic vanity which is just as dangerous as the indulgence in unscrupulous and tendentious propaganda; I call it "objectivity neurosis." The journalist who is determined at all costs to give proof of his objectivity often succumbs to the temptation of maintaining silence with regard to

5. Kurt Kränzlein in the *Angriff*, 10 November 1936. [Original footnote.]
6. The *Angriff*, 17 September 1936. [Original footnote.]
7. *Essener National-Zeitung*, 13 October 1936. [Original footnote.]

concrete facts, because these facts are in themselves so crude that he is afraid of appearing biased. English journalists in particular, with their traditional feeling for level-headedness and decency, have often had to complain of this difficulty. But a civil war is in itself a somewhat indecent affair.

* * *

So it is all over. Malaga has surrendered.

And I remember Colonel Villalba's* last statement before he stepped into his car: "The situation is a critical one, but Malaga will put up a good fight."

Malaga did not put up a good fight.

The city was betrayed by its leaders – deserted, delivered up to the slaughter. The rebel cruisers bombarded us and the ships of the Republic did not come. The rebel 'planes sowed panic and destruction, and the 'planes of the Republic did not come. The rebels had artillery, armoured cars and tanks, and the arms and war material of the Republic did not come. The rebels advanced from all directions and the bridge on the only road connecting Malaga with the Republic had been broken for four months. The rebels maintained an iron discipline and machine-gunned their troops into battle, while the defenders of Malaga had no discipline, no leaders, and no certainty that the Republic was backing them up. Italians, Moors and Foreign Legionaries fought with the professional bravery of mercenaries against the people in a cause that was not theirs; and the soldiers of the people, who were fighting for a cause that was their own, turned tail and ran away.

It would be far too glib to explain away the catastrophes of Badajoz, Toledo and Malaga simply by pointing to the enemy's superiority in war material. Nor does the fact of the treachery and desertion of the local leaders of Malaga alone suffice as an explanation. The city was in the charge of men who proved incompetent – yet no less great is the responsibility of the Central Government of Valencia, which sent neither ships nor 'planes nor war material to Malaga, and did not have the sense to replace incompetent leaders by good ones. With Malaga Largo Caballero's Government completed the chapter of their mistakes and errors of judgment; they had to go. But a whole string of those who bear the responsibility for the unfortunate course of the Civil War up till now (I am writing these lines in September, 1937) still remain. This is one of those things that fills the friends of Spanish democracy with the gravest concern.

249

The longer one waits for a thing to happen, the more astonished one is when it finally does happen. We had known for days
that Malaga was lost, but we had pictured the end quite different-
ly. Everything had proceeded so terribly silently, noiselessly,
undramatically. Events had shown every sign of coming to a head,
but we were cheated of the climax. In all secrecy the white flag had
been hoisted on the Malaga tower. When, on the morrow, the
enemy's cruisers and 'planes arrived, we expected them to open
fire, and did not realise that there was no longer an enemy, that
we were already living under the domination of the Bourbon flag.

This smooth, slick transition was much more terrifying than anything we had feared. Without our knowing it, while we slept, we
had been delivered up to the tender mercies of General Franco.

The entry of the rebel troops likewise took place in a breathtak-
ingly natural and undramatic fashion.

My diary runs:

1 p.m. An officer wearing the grey steel helmet of the Italian
army appears on the road leading to Colmenar, just opposite our
house.

He looks round and fires a revolver shot into the air. Immediately after this about two hundred infantry come marching down
the road in perfect formation. They are singing Mussolini's hymn,
"Giovinezza."

As they pass by the house they salute us, and the household
staff, who only yesterday assiduously raised their clenched fists,
now, with equal Spanish effusiveness, raise their arms in the Fascist salute. They seem perfectly at ease, but since they look upon
us foreigners as half imbecile, the gardener advises Sir Peter and
me to change our demeanour, too, "because we have a new Government now." It is both tragi-comic and humiliating.

After some time, as more and more troops go by and salute us –
we are all gathered on the balcony as though reviewing a march
past – Sir Peter and I are constrained to raise our arms, too. We
avoid looking at each other.

I drink a tumbler full of cognac.

2 p.m. A company of Italian infantry occupies the neighbouring
hill.

3 p.m. The Italian lieutenant in command of the company on
the hill comes into the garden and asks whether he may wash. He
introduces himself courteously, and Sir Peter gives orders for a
bath to be got ready for him. A few soldiers follow him down from
the hill to get a wash and a drink of water. They do not speak a

word of Spanish. They look pretty worn-out; their behaviour is per-fectly polite.

4 p.m. A storm of hurrahs and clapping is heard coming from the city. The rebels have reached the centre of Malaga.

4.30 p.m. Cars flying the Bourbon flag come driving along the road. Tanks are lumbering down in an endless column for Colme-nar. Shots can be heard from the town at regular intervals. One of the household staff volunteers the suggestion that, since the fight-ing is over, these shots may mean "that the execution of the Red criminals is beginning."

I burn some compromising papers: letters of introduction from the Spanish Embassy and from well-known politicians in Valencia.

It is all up now. We are at the mercy of Queipo de Llano. Unfor-tunately I know him of old.

Once more it was evening, and once more we sat opposite one another on high-backed Victorian armchairs at the formally laid table and ate grilled sardines. The rebels had occupied the town and we had seen nothing of it all, and nothing had happened to us. They might come for us at any moment now – it was most like-ly that they would come at night – but we did not really believe it. In the morning, when I had given the trembling Militiaman his cigarette, I had still had one last impulse to flee. I had half resolved to fetch my typewriter and papers from the house and join the Militiamen. And it was mainly out of indolence that I had not done so. Down below in the town all was chaos and uncertain-ty, and the garden here basked so peacefully in the sun — it seemed highly improbable that things of a disorderly nature could ever happen in this neat and well-kept garden.

I was reminded of a scene from a play about the French Revolu-tion by a German writer of the last century. Danton learns that Robespierre is going to have him arrested on the following day, and he flees from his house at night. He wanders blindly across the dark heath. It is cold and windy and suddenly he has a feeling that it is highly illogical to be wandering at night over a windy heath instead of sleeping at home in his good bed. Robespierre and the Convention seem to him unreal figments of the imagina-tion, and the only common-sense thing to do seems to be to go home to bed and sleep. This he does. "Even should we know in theory," is the substance of this reflections, "even should we know in theory of all the dangers that threaten us, deep down in us there is a smiling voice which tells us that the morrow will be just as yesterday." The next morning he is arrested.

Deep down in us, too, on this last evening was that smiling voice that told us that the morrow would be just as yesterday.

The next morning at 11 a.m. we were arrested.

— Arthur Koestler, *Spanish Testament*, 1937

We Defend Madrid

There was a spirit of intoxication in the people, an infectious eagerness for sacrifice, a hot-blooded unreason and fanatical belief in freedom, which could never lead to the constitution of an orderly State on any earlier pattern. To judge by their outward aspect, the militiamen might have been pushed out into the streets by the French Revolution, and no doubt many of the acts of violence of the first days of the war had been prompted by unconscious imitation of the *sans-culottes*. Anarchist doctrines were far more widespread than one would ever have supposed. They loved to see flags waving, and they built barricades which obstructed traffic more than they served the revolution. They drove in requisitioned Cadillacs up and down the Gran Via with sashes round their waists and Phrygian caps on their heads. No one knew whether the war was going well or ill. When I grew restless amid the fortifications, and asked for a car to take me to the front, they provided one at once.

We drove westward by way of Talavera. No one stopped us. Children were playing in the village streets, and cats lay contentedly on the doorsteps.

"Where is the front?" I asked.

"Wherever they start shooting at us," the driver answered.

We were brought up presently by a grey-stone barricade set diagonally across the road, and a few armed men surrounded our car.

"What's the position?" asked the man in charge of our party.

"They may have reached the next village. We're waiting to hear."

No one seemed to be worrying. The whole war was like this. The enemy was imminent, a constant threat, like that of disease or any other danger, making all life unsafe but at the same time stimulating the deepest powers of resistance. As I came to realise later, this first expedition should have taught me the whole nature of the war; but at the time I only asked, in reasonable astonishment:

"Why do you simply put up barricades at the entrances to the villages? What's to prevent the enemy going round them? Are your flanks secured?"

They laughed without resentment.

"It's not the custom. We only fight on the roads."

I shuddered at this, but it was quite true. The enemy observed the same principle.

* * *

We got silently back into the lorry and drove back to Madrid. I asked them to drop me off at the Palace Hotel, where the Russians were staying. I was in a hurry to see Koltsov.* The thing had become an obsession with me. I felt sure that he would not look the same as he had done in Russia.

I ran into him in the doorway of the hotel. His face was relaxed and there were wrinkles of happiness round his mouth and eyes. He uttered a cry and flung his arms about me and pressed his unshaven cheek to mine. He held me thus for a long time, and it was as though a cramp in both of us was dispelled. Then he said:

"Everything will come right. You'll see."

Some stretcher-bearers went past us carrying a groaning man into the hotel.

"Everything is very unreal," I said.

"It's a dream," said Koltsov, whom I had never heard speak in this way before.

The wounded man caught the sound of German. He heaved himself up on the stretcher and raised his clenched fist. "*Rot Front!*" he said, and then sank back groaning.

"Aren't they wonderful?" said Koltsov.

I let him lead me into the hotel. He had a big room with windows looking over the street. We did not talk very much, being overwhelmed by memories.

* * *

The young man entered the room again, talked hurriedly to Koltsov and vanished as silently as he had come. Koltsov gazed fixedly at me for a moment, as though he were trying to determine whether I could bear to hear some bad news. Then he said:

"We have been ordered to leave the town. Things are getting serious, very serious. I shall stay here as a newspaper correspondent – last impressions before the débacle, and so on. Do you want to come with me?"

"Who's in charge of this International Brigade in Albacete?" I asked.

"André Marty,"' said Koltsov, and looked at me with satisfaction, seeing what I had in mind. Then he picked up his spectacle-case from the table and put it in his pocket. "Let's go," he said.

When we reached the ground floor he nodded towards the hotel lounge, which was packed with wounded. They were all serious cases – amputations destined to turn gangrenous for lack of antiseptics, head-wounds, maimed men who had managed to escape from the Fascists.

"Perhaps they'll be killed in their beds by the Moors this very night," said Koltsov softly, gazing over the bandaged forms that lay so quietly. "But they won't know anything about it until the last moment. Come on, let's go."

Perhaps it was the helplessness of those wounded men that finally altered my mood. A Russian car bore me through the night to Albacete, where I at once reported at the headquarters of the International Brigade and offered my services. I was searched for weapons and then shown into the room of André Marty.

Marty was known to me for the part he had played in the Russian revolution. His French warship had been ordered to fire at the mutinous sailors of the Tsar. Marty had refused, and by doing so had considerably influenced the course of events. I too thought, at first glance, that he really was the right man to assemble volunteers from all over the world and send them to the defence of threatened Madrid.

But it is not so easy to turn a mutinous N.C.O. into the commander of an army, a fact of which the last war furnished notable examples. Marty covered his forgivable inadequacy with an unforgivable, passionate spy-hunt; he was genuinely convinced that many of the volunteers who came to his headquarters were Fascist spies. He put all his energies at the service of his mistrust, and did not shrink from conducting day-long, soul-destroying interrogations, or even from sacrificing the tranquillity of his nights and his peace of mind by promptly liquidating doubtful cases, rather than harm the Republic by what he called "petty-bourgeois indecision."

Frenchman that he was, he permitted himself a certain use of irony in his proceedings. As he invited me to be seated in his office I felt that he had decided upon a cat-and-mouse game.

"Where have you been?" he asked. "What do you think of General Miaja? Are the Republicans going to win?" And then suddenly: "When did you leave Germany? Whom do you know in Paris?

Malraux? Aha! Where is he now? Did you also meet any anarchists?" Then abruptly, this time like a pistol-shot: "Show me your membership card of the POUM!" (This was the Trotskyite organisation of the Catalonian ex-Communists.)

At that time the POUM was quite unknown to me. I was opposed to Trotsky because I felt that his desire for revenge was overriding his reason.

Marty's game was suddenly too much for me. I wanted to jump up and hit him, although I know now that if I had done anything of the kind I should have paid for it with my life. But I controlled myself, considering the cause we were both serving. I produced the letter Koltsov had given me, stating that I was Spanish correspondent for the Moscow-published *Deutsche Zeitung,* and referred Marty to Koltsov if he wished for further information about me. Then I left.

* * *

A motor bicycle came roaring into the yard. The rider jumped off and handed me a dispatch from Lukacz.* All sections were to march immediately to the north of Madrid. The enemy had broken into the university quarter in the western part of the town.

I read it aloud. The men ran to their rifles. I left a small party to attend to the bodies and we marched off in silence. The rain had started again and a cold wind was blowing. No man had a coat.

Thus it began. For days the horses of the Apocalypse rode the clouds above Madrid. We saw the town from a distance. We encircled it north-about, passing through poor districts filled with cheerful inhabitants, and halted for some hours in the outer suburb of Fuencarral. Lukacz sent out patrols which always returned without having made contact with the enemy. Lukacz began to curse. We had no better map than a plan of the town torn out of a *Baedeker.* Finally a tall, thin German appeared, introduced himself as Alexander Maass and said that he was looking for me and my general. Lukacz laughed at this lofty designation and asked him what he wanted. Maass looked at me, scratching his head, as though wondering whether to speak. I assured him that he might. He then said that so far as he could make out there was no proper Command in the whole blasted place, but that if the general would take the whole situation in hand he was ready to go out and explore the ground thoroughly and get back a report by morning. All he asked for was a pair of field-glasses and a few hand-grenades.

"A patrol is not supposed to shoot," said Lukacz, "but take the Commissar with you, and this young man."

He pointed at a dark, gypsy-like youngster of no more than twenty who as a passport showed his camera. I liked the idea of a reporter taking pictures of the front which we ourselves ignored.

The young man disliked the noise of the shells which soon whistled over us, though they exploded far in the country. Later he asked leave to change his pants saying with humour that it was his first battle and that his bowels had been weaker than his feet. His name was Capa. He later covered all the wars of our time, became the mascot of the Western armies and was killed by a mine in Vietnam.

So together we penetrated into no-man's-land. The scrubby woods on the left bank of the Manzanares were hung with rime. Once a hare crossed our path. When we came to the river we found build-up trenches but no one in them. We moved southward and found the same thing. Madrid lay as open to attack as a doe overtaken by hounds. The town had no walls. Its only defence consisted of a young German emigrant called Maass, presently to be joined by one Hans Beimler, the leader of the German contingent, who was stamping around in the bushes trying to establish a front line.

Lukacz was poring over his *Baedeker* map. The Battalion doctor, a German named Heilbrun, was searching for beds and an operating table, so as to be "ready." Ludwig Renn, the pedantic writer, was hastily studying Spanish grammar by the light of a shaded candle – an Archimedes whose cogitations were liable to be interrupted at any moment by an irruption of murderous Africans. The French were practising throwing the hand-grenades which the Spanish had contrived for them out of jam-tins, dynamite and a primitive fuse. Less than a mile away were the Moroccans, with German telescopic sights on their rifles. My Italians were organising themselves under Pacciardi's quiet orders.

Back in Madrid I expected to find universal despair and the still unthreatened western and southern entrances to the town crowded with fugitives. But instead I found the cafés filled with men smoking, and a notice over the bar saying, *"No hay anis, no hay pastel* – no anisette, no cake." The men were playing chess.

In the militia-kitchen, where I was known, I was received with shouts of joy and some of them wept. They told me that Russian ships had arrived from Odessa with cargoes of grain, fats, rifles and field-guns, and Mexico had sent arms as well. Suddenly María Teresa León, the wife of the poet Alberti, appeared and told me

256

that our printing-press was already in operation and that the film-projector was giving shows in all the suburbs. She was full of high spirits and talked optimistically about the situation: Madrid would now shine forth like a mountain of diamonds. She invited me to her car and drove me to the "House of Culture," a charming palace belonging to an absent grandee. It was filled with militiamen and workers who sat waiting in a small concert-hall. An orchestra occupied the platform, and a slightly built man with a baton entered amid loud applause. Maria Teresa explained that he was the Mexican composer, Sylvestre Revueltas, who was conducting his own works. By an almost comical chance a bomb fell near by just as he raised his baton. No one so much as started and the great little man, obviously stimulated by the danger, treated it as though it were no more than an appropriate opening chord.

The music was like a cascade of crystal balls. Then it grew harder, like cooling lava when the sharp edges rattle together as it sinks. It was like the play of lightning along a high-tension cable, and then the music of Mexican songs crept in, to be suddenly resolved in challenging fortissimi which were like storm-bells and cries issuing from throats that had long kept silent.

I was shaken by its savagery, but the audience pressed forward to shake the composer by the hand and beg him to repeat the last movement of the symphony, as though this were an ordinary day and Madrid a town untroubled by problems or enemies. Then they went off, enlivened by the music that had adorned the steely harshness of the revolution with a mixture of vitality and nostalgia.

I got back to my battalions in time to take part in General Miaja's first brush with Franco's forces. Much was later said about Miaja. Republican propaganda needed a hero to put on a pedestal, and the enemy helped in this process, because if they had not ascribed exceptional qualities to their adversary the stemming of Franco's advance that autumn would have appeared an altogether too mortifying defeat. Miaja therefore "held off the enemy with a strong fist and broke the black tide" – so it was said.

As a matter of policy, as well as from a sense of tact, we endorsed this glowing picture when talking to the foreign correspondents and even to the Spanish people.

Only Capa would say bending over his camera: "Have you seen Miaja?"

And the camera would say: "Not here."

The time may now have come when we should approach nearer to historic reality, and the simple truth is as follows:

When, in that autumn of 1936, Franco's Moors were on the verge of perpetrating unthinkable atrocities in the naive, unarmed and daydreaming city of Madrid, they were stopped by those few battalions which were later named the International Brigade. The saviours had no names and will never have any. Their heroes, very different in character but united in their devotion to the cause of the Spanish Republic, were Paul Lukacz; Hans Beimler and Hans Kahle,* the German Communists; the youngster, Alexander Maass, who was the first to make contact with the enemy; Ralph Fox, who was killed, and Ralph Bates,* who survived, both British members of the brave Anglo-Saxon formation called the Lincoln Brigade.

A strong magnetic power emanated from Madrid and these voluntary units. They have called us adventurers and ascribed to us a considerable number of crimes. Koestler in his obituary of Orwell talks about the "sham-fraternity" of the International Brigade. But how could a troop exist and win the most difficult battles if their main duty were that of field-gendarmes, their ambition plunder and their morale a sham-fraternity?

There were also reporters of the *New York Times*, the *Manchester Guardian*, the *News Chronicle*, *L'Oeuvre*; with us were Herbert Mathews and Josephine Herbst, and, the most devoted of all, Martha Gellhorn, witty and humane, of the best St. Louis stock. Her book *The Trouble I've Seen* had shown her sympathy with the unemployed masses during the depression in the USA. Now she saw our brigade in the making, strolled with Pacciardi in no-man's-land, provided the doctor with his first bandages, saw our amateurish weapons and wondered at the almost incredible modesty of our troops. I call her as a witness with special satisfaction, as her testimony can certainly not be called that of an agent of Moscow. And I give my reason for saying so: When in 1939 Finland was invaded by Russia she covered the Finnish and not the Russian front, leaving no doubt as to where her sympathy was and always would be.

Our forces were under observation of the world. The Vatican viewed us with disfavour, quite unjustly, since the Brigade defended the churches and, as a politically educated body, made it a deliberate part of policy to respect the principle of religious toleration. The Vatican was never able to prove that any crime had been committed by the Brigade against any priests. We were installed in the university quarter, in the western sector of the town. From behind barricades of book-shelves, from cellar-windows and sometimes from the rooftops of that very modern,

uncompleted centre of learning, we poured our bullets into the
night.

After the tall Moroccans had been surprised by our few battalions, and mowed down in battles as tragic as they were grotesque
(for no one on Franco's side realised how few we were), we saw no
more enemies, only here and there, at street-corners, the flame of
trench-mortars. The black bodies lay unburied between what were
called "the lines" – the philosophical and legal faculties. My volunteers displayed an indifference to danger which I find it hard to
explain. No one knew exactly where the enemy was, and a surprise
attack might come at any moment, obliging us to turn and fire in
the opposite direction. Out of the uncertainty of the military situation there grew the certainty of gladiators. Men dedicated to life
again discovered the meaning of life. Most of them were *emigrés*
who for three years had suffered humiliation at the hands of the
Paris, Prague and Swiss police. Some had been obliged to report
daily (I repeat, daily) and apply for another day's asylum. Now
they had arms in their hands and a city to defend. The constant
threat of death, which they laughed at or at the least ignored, had
restored their dignity. Many were Jews, and their bullets in the
darkness were aimed at Hitler. They took pleasure in talking of
mercy; this, too, repaired their wounded pride.

Once by daylight a Moor was pointed out to me, standing in the
street below our roof. He had lost his way in the confusion of
buildings and was running back and forth like a hunted animal,
sometimes turning his back to us, sometimes pausing and sniffing
with his nose in the air, but in the wrong direction. We could see
him plainly from above, and an argument arose as to whether he
should be shot. The majority were against it, because one does not
shoot a man in the back, and because after all he was only a man,
a victim of colonialism. This thought cropped up from the beginning, and had no small influence upon our methods of warfare. It
was destined to lead to a notable victory at Guadalajara, in March
1937.

In this case the desire to destroy the enemy triumphed over
principle. The volunteers did not shoot the less well because they
had hesitated, and they were fortified in the last resort by the
hideous memory of Hitler, or simply by the ruthlessness of the
war.

"I've come out of Dachau," said Hans Beimler, the Bavarian
leader of the Germans. He had got away to Prague and then had
become a member of the Central Committee of the exiled Ger-

man Communist Party. He had reason enough for flight. Held in solitary confinement and certain of death, he had strangled the first SS man who came into his cell, exchanged clothes with him and thus made his escape. "The only way we can get back to Germany is through Madrid," Beimler said as we lay side by side on a mattress in Fuencarral. He had been in the fight for forty-eight hours and it was only with difficulty that we could persuade him to take a little rest. But when at last he was persuaded, his almost superhuman intensity and coolness fell away from him. He took my shoes off. "The Moors won't come as quickly as all that," he said, "and a foot can only rest when it can breathe." He awoke us at five. "We'll relieve the look-outs before daylight."

There was something gluttonous in his ardour, as though he were afraid of not getting his fill. He wore a wool-lined jacket and a grey militia-cap adorned with a red star. There was nothing unusual in his face with its high cheekbones, but within a few days he had become the magical centre of all the fighting in the farms round Palacete. There was a German thoroughness in his exercising of command, relieved by a care for the momentary weaknesses of his men, a kindness which was his Bavarian inheritance. He insisted that there should always be at least one stretcher available for his troops; he thought of everything, and he caused me to feel that after all this war could be won, for the example he set was worth battalions.

On 12 December 1936 I found him behind a machine-gun in the north-west of Madrid, among the farm-buildings of Palacete. The long forms of dead Africans lay a short distance in front of him. I was astonished by the lack of hatred in his face. With the cool detachment of a land-surveyor he turned the gun on an enemy patrol which was trying to get under cover behind some buildings. One of them tried to find a way out by rushing straight towards us, and Beimler shot him down within ten yards of our earthwork. Werner, the doctor, came creeping up beside me.

"You'll have to hold out until nightfall," he said. "I have three wounded to get away."

"All right," said Beimler and pointed to the man he had just shot. "What about him?"

Werner, to my consternation, got up and went forward to the African, knelt beside him, felt his pulse and then let the dark-skinned arm fall. Beimler cleared his throat and said glumly:

"A pity the poor devil had to be fighting for Franco!"

That afternoon he heard that there was a weak spot in our line near the river, and he decided to go and investigate. He came to where I was stationed and said that he wanted to try and re-establish the line. Werner pointed to a stretcher that had just arrived. "Fine!" said Beimler, and climbed out over the earthworks. I warned him of the snipers that were in the red house in front of us, but he only laughed. "I'm bullet-proof," he said. Ten minutes later two Germans whom I did not know appeared, picked up the stretcher and dashed off with it. I heard tanks firing from the direction of the Manzanares, evidently to cover Beimler, who must have got through. Greatly relieved, I ordered the men to open fire across our shell-pitted sector. The wood echoed with explosions; the sun broke through the clouds and lit up the birch-trees; and then the two young Germans reappeared, coming slowly and almost solemnly round the end of the earthworks. Beimler lay on the stretcher. His face was colourless; his wool-lined jacket was open, and there was a small hole in his sweater above his heart.

Werner knelt beside him and quickly rose again. "Is it bad?" I asked, voicing the foolish question although I knew what had happened. No blood was coming from the wound because the heart was no longer beating. I wept, and Werner passed me his handkerchief. Then I went through the dead man's pockets. He still carried the hunting-knife he had taken from the SS man he throttled. I found a newspaper-cutting of Stalin's speech promising help for Spain. He had left nothing else behind. I took his jacket and put it on, and was only parted from it in 1940, in a French concentration-camp.

He was laid in state in Madrid, and I delivered the funeral oration. His comrades then bore his body to Barcelona, taking days to do so, because in every village they were held up by peasants and citizens desirous of honouring the foreigner who had died for Spain.

Over-zealous opponents of Communism have since asserted that Beimler was "liquidated" by the GPU.* The thing was not impossible in principle; but in fact he was killed by a Moorish bullet.

— Gustav Regler, *The Owl of Minerva*, 1959

[Translated by Norman Denny.]

American Responses to the War

Introduction

ELAINE BARRY

In comparison with the widespread involvement of Latin American, English, and continental writers in the Spanish Civil War – both as participants and as commenters – the response of American writers seems marginal. Take away Hemingway, whose interest sprang less from political ideology than from an almost mystical attachment to Spain itself, and the American literary response is comparatively small. Reasons for this detachment lie in America's social, economic, and political climate, as well as in its foreign policy. The 1930s in America were scarred by a bitter depression that, especially after the soaring optimism and upward mobility of the Jazz Age, seemed to sound the death knell of the American dream. International socialism never really took hold on American soil (as Steinbeck's *Grapes of Wrath* demonstrates), so there was no groundswell of popular sympathy to support the ideology of the Left in Spain. The Spanish Civil War did not test the conscience of the American nation, which was far more preoccupied with its own internal problems. The isolationist attitudes that later would delay American involvement in the Second World War operated to keep Spain on the margins of America's moral concern.

Yet many American consciences were stirred by the Spanish War and many American writers voiced their opinions. In 1938, the League of American Writers circulated a letter to a thousand American writers and asked them for a response. Four hundred and eighteen replied – among them Sherwood Anderson, William Faulkner, and John Steinbeck. Their statements were published in a pamphlet called *Writers Take Sides*. It was a companion volume to a similar survey of English writers published in England the previous year. Many American writers went to Spain to report if not to fight, and the body of American literary response to the Spanish war (dispatches, poems, short stories, a play, film scripts, a novel) is a solid if not a major contribution to the war's artistic legacy. John Dos Passos, Theodore Dreiser, Upton Sinclair, and Archibald MacLeish are among the better-known contributors; and established journals such as *The New Masses, Harper's, Esquire* and *The New Yorker* spread sympathy for the Republican cause. The American contribution is also notable because it crossed both race and gender lines. The black writer Langston Hughes (there were black soldiers in the International Brigade) wrote a number of poems in 1938: "Air Raid, Barcelona," "Madrid," "October 16," and "Post-Card from Spain." Among the female writers, Dorothy Parker wrote a short story entitled "Soldiers of the Republic"; Lillian Hellman included her experience in Spain in her autobiography *An Unfinished Woman*; Frances Davis, declared to be the first foreign female journalist covering the war, gave a graphic account of her experience in *A Fearful Innocence*; poets Genevieve Taggard and Muriel Rukeyser recorded the event, while Edna St. Vincent Millay wrote the memorable "Say That We Saw Spain Die."

But it is, of course, Hemingway, who dominates any discussion of the American literary involvement in the Spanish Civil War. Long before the war, he had "adopted" Spain as his heartland. He spoke good Spanish, loved the land and the people, viewed the peasant way of life as a vital primitive life force in conflict with urban, technological deracination, and idealized the bullfight as an existential defiance of death. When the war came he contributed his literary reputation and a great deal of personal money as well his services as a soldier to the Republican cause. Apart from his journalistic despatches, Hemingway scripted two important films (*Spain in Flames* and *The Spanish Earth*), wrote his only play (*The Fifth Column*), five short stories ("Under the Ridge," "The Denunciation," "The Old Man at the Bridge," "The Butterfly and the Tank," and "Night Before Battle"), and the novel, *For Whom the Bell Tolls*. No other event in his life fired his imagination and his sympathy as the Spanish war did. His heroes never seem foreigners in Spain; they reflect their author's identification with the country.

The Villages Are the Heart of Spain

1. VILLAGE BEHIND THE LINES

First it was that the driver was late, then that he had to go to the garage to get a mechanic to tinker with the gasoline pump, then that he had to go somewhere else to wait in line for gasoline; and so, in pacing round the hotel, in running up and down stairs, in scraps of conversation in the lobby, the Madrid morning dribbled numbly away in delay after delay. At last we were off. As we passed the Cibeles fountain two shells exploded far up the sunny Castellana. Stonedust mixed with pale smoke of high explosives suddenly blurred the ranks of budding trees, under which a few men and women were strolling because it was Sunday and because they were in the habit of strolling there on Sunday. The shells hit too far away for us to see if anyone were hit. Our driver speeded up a little.

We passed the arch of Carlos Third and the now closed café under the trees opposite the postoffice where the last time I was in Madrid I used to sit late in the summer evenings chatting with friends some of whom are only very recently dead. As we got past the controlposts and sentries beyond the bullring, the grim exhilaration of the besieged city began to drop away from us, and we bowled pleasantly along the Guadalajara road in the spring sunlight.

In a little stone town in a valley full of poplars we went to visit the doctor in charge of the medical work for the Jarama front. He was a small dark brighteyed young man, a C. P. member I imagine; he had the look of a man who had entirely forgotten that he had a life of his own. Evidently for months there had been nothing he thought of, all day and every day, but his work. He took us to one of his base hospitals, recently installed in a group of old buildings, part of which had once been a parochial school. He apologized for it; they had only been in there two weeks, if we came two weeks later we'd see an improvement. We ate lunch there with him, then he promptly forgot us. In spite of the rain that came on, we could see him walking up and down the stony court inside the hospital gate with one member of his staff after another talking earnestly to them. He never took his eyes off whoever he was talking to, as if he were trying to hypnotize them with his own tireless energy. Meanwhile we tried to stimulate our driver, a singularly spineless young man in a black C.N.T. tunic, the son of a winegrower in Alcazar de

267

San Juan, to fix the gasoline pump on the miserable little Citroen sedan we have been assigned to. At last the doctor remembered us again and as our driver had gotten the pump into such a state that the motor wouldn't even start, he offered to take us to the village to which we were bound, as he had to go out that way to pick a site for a new base-hospital. We set out in his Ford, that felt like a racing-car after the feeble little spluttering Citroen.

Rain was falling chilly over the lichengreen stone towns and the tawny hills misted over with the fiery green of new wheat. Under the rain and the low indigo sky, the road wound up and down among the great bare folds of the upland country. Late in the afternoon we came to a square building of lightbrown stone in a valley beside a clear stream and a milldam set about with poplars. The building had been a monastery long ago and the broad valley lands had belonged to the monks. As we got out of the car larks rose singing out of the stubby fields. The building was a magnificent square of sober seventeenth century work. In the last few years it had been used as a huntingclub, but since July, 1936 none of the members of the club had been seen in those parts. A family of country people from Pozorubio had moved out there to escape the air-raids and to do some planting.

They invited us in with grave Castilian hospitality and in a dark stone room we stood about the embers of a fire with them, drinking their stout darkred wine and eating their deliciously sweet fresh bread. With his glass in his hand and his mouth full of bread the doctor lectured them about the war, and the need to destroy the Fascists and to produce as much food as possible. Wheat and potatoes, he said, were as important as machinegun bullets in war.

We stopped at their village, Pozorubio, to load up on bread. We went into the bakery through a dimly lit stone doorway. The baker was at the front, so the women and young boys of the family were doing the baking. The bread had just come out of the oven. 'Yes you can buy as much as you want,' the women said. 'We'd have bread for Madrid if they'd come and get it. Here at least we have plenty of bread.' We stood around for a while in the dry dim room talking and looking into the fire that glowed under the ovens. As we got back into the car with our arms piled high with the big flat loaves the doctor was saying bitterly, 'And in Madrid they are hungry for bread; it's the fault of the lack of transport and gasoline. . . . We must organize our transport.' Then he snapped at his Belgian chauffeur, 'We must get back to headquarters fast, fast.' You could see that he was blaming himself for the relaxed moment he'd spent in the warm, sweetsmelling bakery. As the car lurched over the ruts of the road across the hills, furry black in the rainy night, there went along with us in the smell of the bread something of the peaceful coziness of the village, and country people eating their suppers in the dim roomy stone houses and the sharpsmelling herbs in the fires and the brown faces looking out from the shelter of doorways at the bright stripes of the rain in the street and the gleam of the cobbles and the sturdy figures of countrywomen under their shawls.

2. VILLAGE ON THE VALENCIA ROAD

Fuentedueña is a village of several hundred houses in the province of Madrid. It stands on a shelf above the Tagus, at the point where the direct road to Valencia from Madrid dips down into the river's broad terraced valley. Above it on the hill still tower the crumbling brick and adobe walls of a castle of Moorish work where some feudal lord once sat and controlled the trail and rivercrossing. Along the wide wellpaved macadam road there are a few wineshops and the barracks of the civil guard. The minute you step off the road you are back in the age of packmules and twowheeled carts. It's a poor village and it has the air of having always been a poor village; only a few of the houses on the oblong main square with their wide doors that open into pleasant green courts have the stone shields of hidalgos on their peeling stucco fronts. The town hall is only a couple of offices, and the telephone on the wall that links the village to Madrid. Since July the real center of the town has been on another street, in the house once occupied by the pharmacist, who seems to have been considered hostile, because he is there no more, in an office where the members of the socialist (U.G.T.) Casa del Pueblo meet. Their president is now mayor and their policies are dominant in the village. The only opposition is the C.N.T. syndicalist local which in Fuentedueña, so the socialists claim and I think in this case justly, is made up of small storekeepers and excommission merchants, and not working farmers at all. According to the mayor they all wear the swastika under their shirts. Their side of the story, needless to say, is somewhat different.

At the time of the military revolt in July the land of Fuentedueña was held by about ten families, some of them the descendants, I suppose, of the hidalgos who put their shields on their houses on the main square. Some of them were shot, others managed to get away. The Casa del Pueblo formed a collective out of their lands. Meanwhile other lands were taken over by the C.N.T. local. Fuentedueña's main cash crop is wine; the stocks in the three or four bodegas constituted the town's capital. The Casa del Pueblo, having the majority of the working farmers, took over the municipal government and it was decided to farm the lands of the village in common. For the present it was decided that every working man should be paid five pesetas for every day he worked and have a right to a daily liter of wine and a certain amount of firewood. The mayor and the secretary and treasurer and the muledrivers and the blacksmith, every man who worked was paid the same. The carpenters and masons and other skilled artisans who had been making seven pesetas a day consented, gladly they said, to taking the same pay as the rest. Later, the mastermason told me, they'd raise everybody's pay to seven pesetas or higher; after all wine was a valuable crop and with no parasites to feed there would be plenty for all. Women and boys were paid three fifty. The committees of the U.G.T. and the C.N.T. decided every day where their members were to work. Housing was roughly distributed according to the sizes of the families. There was not much difficulty about that because since the fascist airraids began people preferred to live in the cavehouses along the edges of the hill than in the big rubble and stucco houses with courts and corrals in the center of town, especially since one of them had been destroyed by a bomb. These cavehouses, where in peacetime only the poorest people lived, are not such bad dwellings as they sound. They are cut out of the hard clay and chalky rock of the terraced hillsides facing the river. They have usually several rooms, each with a large coneshaped chimney for light and to carry off the smoke of the fire, and a porch onto which narrow windows open. They are whitewashed and often remarkably clean and neat. Before the civil war the housedwellers looked down on the cavedwellers; but now the caves seem to have definite social standing.

The village produces much wine but little oil, so one of the first things the collective did was to arrange to barter their wine for oil with a village that produced more oil than it needed. Several people told me proudly that they'd improved the quality of their wine since they had taken the bodegas over from the business men who had the habit of watering the wine before they sold it and were ruining the reputation of their vintages. Other local industries taken over by the collective are the bakery and a lime kiln, where three or four men worked intermittently, getting the stone from a quarry immediately back of the town and burning it in two small adobe ovens, and the making of fiber baskets and harness which people make from a tough grass they collect from the hills round about. This was a spare time occupation for periods of bad weather. After the wine crops are wheat, and a few olives.

The irrigation project seemed to loom larger than the war in the minds of the mayor and his councillors. Down in the comparatively rich bottom land along the Tagus the collective had taken over a piece that they were planning to irrigate for truck gardens. They had spent thirteen thousand pesetas of their capital in Madrid to buy pumping machinery and cement. A large gang of men was working over there every day to get the ditches dug and the pump installed that was going to put the river water on the land before the hot dry summer weather began. Others were planting seed potatoes. An old man and his son had charge of a seedbed where they were raising onions and lettuce and tomatoes and peppers and artichokes for planting out. Later they would sow melons, corn and cabbage. For the first time the village was going to raise its own green vegetables. Up to now everything of that sort had to be imported from the outside. Only a few of the richer landowners had irrigated patches of fruits and vegetables for their own use. This was the first real reform the collective had undertaken and everybody felt very good about it, so good that they almost forgot the hollow popping beyond the hills that they could hear from the Jarama river front fifteen miles away, and the truckloads of soldiers and munitions going through the village up the road to Madrid and the fear they felt whenever they saw an airplane in the sky. Is it ours or is it theirs?

Outside of the irrigated bottom lands and the dryfarming uplands the collective owns a considerable number of mules, a few horses and cows, a flock of sheep and a flock of goats. Most of the burros are owned by individuals, as are a good many sheep and goats that are taken out to pasture every day by the village shepherds under a communal arrangement as old as the oldest stone walls. Occasional fishing in the river is more of an entertainment than part of the town economy. On our walks back and forth to the new pumping station the mayor used to point out various men and boys sitting along the river bank with fishing poles. 'All members of the C.N.T.,' he'd say maliciously. 'You'd never find a socialist going out fishing when there was still spring plowing to be done.' 'We've cleaned out the fascists and the priests,' one of the men who was

walking with us said grimly. 'Now we must clean out the loafers.'
'Yes,' said the mayor. 'One of these days it will come to a fight.'

3. FISHING VILLAGE

In San Pol, so the secretary of the agricultural coöperative told me
with considerable pride, they hadn't killed anybody. He was a
small, schoolteacherylooking man in a worn dark business suit. He
had a gentle playful way of talking and intermingled his harsh
Spanish with English and French words. San Pol is a very small
fishing village on the Catalan coast perhaps thirty miles northeast
of Barcelona. It consists of several short streets of pale blue and
yellow and whitewashed houses climbing up the hills of an irregular steep little valley full of umbrella pines. The fishingboats are
drawn up on the shingly beach in a row along the double track of
the railway to France. Behind the railway is a string of grotesque
villas owned by Barcelona business men of moderate means. Most
of the villas are closed. A couple have been expropriated by the
municipality, one for a coöperative retail store, and another,
which had just been very handsomely done over with a blue and
white tile decoration, to house a municipal pool parlor and gym-
nasium, public baths and showers, a huge airy coöperative barber
shop and, upstairs, a public library and readingroom. On the top
of the hill behind the town a big estate has been turned into a
municipal chicken farm.

The morning I arrived the towncouncil had finally decided to
take over the wholesale marketing of fish, buying the catch from
the fishermen and selling it in Barcelona. The middleman who
had handled the local fish on a commission basis was still in business; we saw him there, a big domineering pearshaped man with a
brown sash holding up his baggy corduroys, superintending the
salting of sardines in a barrel. 'He's a fascist,' the secretary of the
coöperative said, 'but we won't bother him. He won't be able to
compete with us anyway because we'll pay a higher price.'

Then he took me to see a little colony of refugee children from
Madrid living in a beautiful house overlooking the sea with a rich
garden behind it. They were a lively and sunburned bunch of kids
under the charge of a young man and his wife who were attending
to their schooling. As we were walking back down the steep flow-
erlined street (Yes, the flowers had been an idea of the socialist
municipality, the secretary said smiling) it came on to rain. We

272

passed a stout man in black puffing with flushed faced up the hill under a green umbrella. 'He's the priest,' said the secretary. 'He doesn't bother anybody. He takes no part in politics.' I said that in most towns I'd been in a priest wouldn't dare show his face. 'Here we were never believers,' said the secretary, 'so we don't feel that hatred. We have several refugee priests in town. They haven't made any trouble yet.'

He took me to a fine building on the waterfront that had been a beach café and danceplace that had failed. Part of it had been done over into a little theatre. 'We won a prize at the Catalonia drama festival last year, though we're a very small town. There's a great deal of enthusiasm for amateur plays here.' We had lunch with various local officials in the rooms of the choral society in a little dining room overlooking the sea. Far out on the horizon we could see the smoke of the inevitable non-intervention warship.

And a fine lunch it was. Everything except the wine and the coffee had been grown within the town limits. San Pol had some wine, they said apologetically, but it wasn't very good. First we had broad beans in olive oil. Then a magnificent dish of fresh sardines. My friends explained that the sardine fishing had been remarkably successful this year, and that fish were selling at war prices so that everybody in town had money in his pocket. They fished mostly at night with floating nets. The board had motors and great batteries of acetylene lights to attract the fish to the surface. The difficult part of the business was to tow the net around the fish and scoop them up without losing them. After the sardines we had roast chicken from the village chickenfarm, with new potatoes and lettuce. Outside of fish they explained new potatoes were their main cash crop. They sold them in England, marketing them through the coöperative of which my friend was secretary. He had been in England that winter to make new arrangements. The coöperative was a number of years old and a member of the Catalan alliance of coöperatives. Of course now, since the movement, they were more important than ever. 'If only the fascists would let us alone.' 'And the anarchists.' somebody added. . . 'We could be very happy in San Pol.'

We drove out of town in the pouring rain. As the road wound up the hill we got a last look at the neat streets of varicolored stucco houses and the terraced gardens and the blue and white and blue and green fishing boats with their clustered lights sticking out above their sterns like insect eyes, drawn up in a row along the shingle beach.

4. THE MEN AT THE TELEPHONE

Barcelona. April 29. The headquarters of the unified Marxist party (P.O.U.M.). It's late at night in a large bare office furnished with odds and ends of old furniture. At a bit battered fake Gothic desk out of somebody's library Nin* sits at the telephone. I sit in a mangy overstuffed armchair. On the settee opposite me sits a man who used to be editor of a radical publishing house in Madrid.

We talk in a desultory way with many pauses about old times in Madrid, about the course of the war. They are telling me about the change that has come over the population of Barcelona since the great explosion of revolutionary feeling that followed the attempted military coup d'etat and swept the fascists out of Catalonia in July. 'You can even see it in people's dress,' said Nin from the telephone laughing. 'Now we're beginning to wear collars and ties again but even a couple of months ago everybody was wearing the most extraordinary costumes. . .you'd see people on the street wearing feathers.' Nin was wellbuilt and healthylooking and probably looked younger than his age; he had a ready childish laugh that showed a set of solid white teeth.

From time to time as we were talking the telephone would ring and he would listen attentively with a serious face. Then he'd answer with a few words too rapid for me to catch and would hang up the receiver with a shrug of the shoulders and come smiling back into the conversation again. When he saw that I was beginning to frame a question he said, 'It's the villages. . . They want to know what to do.' 'About Valencia taking over the police services?' He nodded. 'What are they going to do?' 'Take a car and drive through the suburbs of Barcelona, you'll see that all the villages are barricaded. . . The committees are all out on the streets with machine guns.' Then he laughed. 'But maybe you had better not.' 'He'd be all right,' said the other man. 'They have great respect for foreign journalists.' 'Is it an organized movement?' 'It's complicated. . . in Bellver our people want to know whether they ought to move against the anarchists. In other places they are with them. . . . You know Spain.'

It was time for me to push on. I shook hands with Nin and with a young Englishman who also is dead now, and went out into the rainy night. Since then Nin has been killed and his party suppressed. The papers have not told us what has happened in the villages.

274

But already that April night the popular movement in Catalonia seemed doomed, hemmed in by ruthless forces of worldpolitics too big for it. Perhaps these men already knew it. They did not have the faces of men who were betraying their country or their cause, but there was no air of victory about them.

The trade union paper had just been installed in a repaired building where there had once been a convent.

The new rotary presses were not quite in order yet and the partitions were unfinished between the offices in the editorial department. They took me into a little room where they were transmitting news and comment to the trade union paper in the fishing town of Gijon in Asturias on the north coast clear on the other side of Franco's territory. A man was reading an editorial. As the rotund phrases (which perhaps fitted in well enough with the American scheme of things for me to accept) went lilting through the silence, I couldn't help being swept by the feeling of the rainy night and the working men on guard with machineguns and rifles at sandbag posts on the roads into villages, and the hopes of new life and liberty and the political phrases pounding confused and contradictory in their ears; and then the front, the towns crowded with troops and the advanced posts and trenches and the solitude between; and beyond, the old life, the titled officers in fancy uniforms, the bishops and priests, the pious ladies in black silk with their rosaries, the arab moors and the dark berbers getting their revenge four hundred and fifty years late for the loss of their cities, and the profiteers and businessmen and squareheaded German traveling salesmen; and beyond again the outposts and the Basque countrypeople praying to God in their hillside trenches and the Asturian miners with their sticks of dynamite in their belts and the longshoremen and fishermen of the coast towns waiting for hopeful news; and another little office like this where the editors crowded around the receiving set that except for blockaderunners is their only contact with the outside world. 'How can the new world full of confusion and crosspurposes and illusions and dazzled by the mirage of idealistic phrases win against the iron combination of men accustomed to run things who have only one idea binding them together, to hold on to what they've got; how can the new world win?' was what I'd liked to have asked the editors of the labor paper in Gijon over the short wave set.

There was a sudden rumble in the distance. The man who was reading stopped. Everybody craned their necks to listen. There it was again. 'No it's not firing, it's thunder,' everybody laughed with relief. They turned on the receiver again. The voice from Gijon came feebly in a stutter of static. They must repeat the editorial. Static. While the operator tinkered with the adjustments the distant voice from Gijon was lost in sharp crashes of static. Black rain was lashing against the window.

—John Dos Passos, *The Villages are the Heart of Spain*, 1937

Under the Ridge

In the heat of the day with the dust blowing, we came back, dry-mouthed, nose-clogged and heavy-loaded, down out of the battle to the long ridge above the river where the Spanish troops lay in reserve.

I sat down with my back against the shallow trench, my shoulders and the back of my head against the earth, clear now from even stray bullets, and looked at what lay below us in the hollow. There was the tank reserve, the tanks covered with branches chopped from olive trees. To their left were the staff cars, mud-daubed and branch-covered, and between the two a long line of men carrying stretchers wound down through the gap to where, on the flat at the foot of the ridge, ambulances were loading. Commissary mules loaded with sacks of bread and kegs of wine, and a train of ammunition mules, led by their drivers, were coming up the gap in the ridge, and men with empty stretchers were walking slowly up the trail with the mules.

To the right, below the curve of the ridge, I could see the entrance to the cave where the brigade staff was working, and their signaling wires ran out of the top of the cave and curved on over the ridge in the shelter of which we lay.

Motorcyclists in leather suits and helmets came up and down the cut on their cycles or, where it was too steep, walking them, and leaving them beside the cut, walked over to the entrance to the cave and ducked inside. As I watched, a big Hungarian cyclist that I knew came out of the cave, tucked some papers in his leather wallet, walked over to his motorcycle and, pushing it up through the stream of mules and stretcher-bearers, threw a leg over the saddle and roared on over the ridge, his machine churning a storm of dust.

Below, across the flat where the ambulances were coming and

going, was the green foliage that marked the line of the river. There was a large house with a red tile roof and there was a gray stone mill, and from the trees around the big house beyond the river came the flashes of our guns. They were firing straight at us and there were the twin flashes, then the throaty, short *bung-bung* of the three-inch pieces and then the rising cry of the shells coming toward us and going on over our heads. As always, we were short of artillery. There were only four batteries down there, when there should have been forty, and they were firing only two guns at a time. The attack had failed before we came down.

'Are you Russians?' a Spanish soldier asked me.

'No, Americans,' I said. 'Have you any water?'

'Yes, comrade.' He handed over a pigskin bag. These troops in reserve were soldiers only in name and from the fact that they were in uniform. They were not intended to be used in the attack, and they sprawled along this line under the crest of the ridge, huddled in groups, eating, drinking and talking, or simply sitting dumbly, waiting. The attack was being made by an International Brigade. We both drank. The water tasted of asphalt and pig bristles.

'Wine is better,' the soldier said. 'I will get wine.'

'Yes. But for the thirst, water.'

'There is no thirst like the thirst of battle. Even here, in reserve, I have much thirst.'

'That is fear,' said another soldier. 'Thirst is fear.'

'No,' said another. 'With fear there is thirst, always. But in battle there is much thirst even when there is no fear.'

'There is always fear in battle,' said the first soldier.

'For you,' said the second soldier.

'It is normal,' the first soldier said.

'For you.'

'Shut your dirty mouth,' said the first soldier. 'I am simply a man who tells the truth.'

It was a bright April day and the wind was blowing wildly so that each mule that came up the gap raised a cloud of dust, and the two men at the ends of a stretcher each raised a cloud of dust that blew together and made one, and below, across the flat, long streams of dust moved out from the ambulances and blew away in the wind.

I felt quite sure I was not going to be killed on that day now, since we had done our work well in the morning, and twice during the early part of the attack we should have been killed and were not; and this had given me confidence. The first time had been when we had gone up with the tanks and picked a place from which to film the attack. Later I had a sudden distrust for the place and we had moved the cameras about two hundred yards to the left. Just before leaving, I had marked the place in quite the oldest way there is of marking a place, and within ten minutes a six-inch shell had lit on the exact place where I had been and there was no trace of any human being ever having been there. Instead, there was a large and clearly blasted hole in the earth.

Then, two hours later, a Polish officer, recently detached from the battalion and attached to the staff, had offered to show us the positions the Poles had just captured and, coming from under the lee of a fold of hill, we had walked into machine-gun fire that we had to crawl out from under with our chins tight to the ground and dust in our noses, and at the same time made the sad discovery that the Poles had captured no positions at all that day but were a little further back than the place they had started from. And now, lying in the shelter of the trench, I was wet with sweat, hungry and thirsty and hollow inside from the now-finished danger of the attack.

'You are sure you are not Russians?' asked a soldier. 'There are Russians here today.'

'Yes. But we are not Russians.'

'You have the face of a Russian.'

'No,' I said. 'You are wrong, comrade. I have quite a funny face but it is not the face of a Russian.'

'He has the face of a Russian,' pointing at the other one of us who was working on a camera.

'Perhaps. But still he is not Russian. Where you from?'

'Extremadura,' he said proudly.

'Are there any Russians in Extremadura?' I asked.

'No,' he told me, even more proudly. 'There are no Russians in Extremadura, and there are no Extremadurans in Russia.'

'What are your politics?'

'I hate all foreigners,' he said.

'That's a broad political program.'

'I hate the Moors, the English, the French, the Italians, the Germans, the North Americans and the Russians.'

'You hate them in that order?'

'Yes. But perhaps I hate the Russians the most.'

'Man, you have very interesting ideas,' I said. 'Are you a Fascist?'

'No. I am an Extremaduran and I hate foreigners.'

'He has very rare ideas,' said another soldier. 'Do not give him too much importance. Me, I like foreigners. I am from Valencia. Take another cup of wine, please.'

I reached up and took the cup, the other wine still brassy in my mouth. I looked at the Extremaduran. He was tall and thin. His face was haggard and unshaven, and his cheeks were sunken. He stood straight up in his rage, his blanket cape around his shoulders.

'Keep your head down,' I told him. 'There are many lost bullets coming over.'

'I have no fear of bullets and I hate all foreigners,' he said fiercely.

'You don't have to fear bullets,' I said, 'but you should avoid them when you are in reserve. It is not intelligent to be wounded when it can be avoided.'

'I am not afraid of anything,' the Extremaduran said.

'You are very lucky, comrade.'

'It's true,' the other, with the wine cup, said. 'He has no fear, not even of the *aviones*.'

'He is crazy,' another soldier said. 'Everyone fears planes. They kill little but make much fear.'

'I have no fear. Neither of planes nor of nothing,' the Extremaduran said. 'And I hate every foreigner alive.'

Down the gap, walking beside two stretcher-bearers and seeming to pay no attention at all to where he was, came a tall man in International Brigade uniform with a blanket rolled over his shoulder and tied at his waist. His head was held high and he looked like a man walking in his sleep. He was middle-aged. He was not carrying a rifle and, from where I lay, he did not look wounded.

I watched him walking alone down out of the war. Before he came to the staff cars he turned to the left and his head still held high in that strange way, he walked over the edge of the ridge and out of sight.

The one who was with me, busy changing film in the hand cameras, had not noticed him.

A single shell came in over the ridge and fountained in dirt and black smoke just short of the tank reserve.

Someone put his head out of the cave where Brigade head-quarters was and then disappeared inside. I thought it looked like a good place to go, but knew they would all be furious in there because the attack was a failure, and I did not want to face them. If an operation was successful they were happy to have motion pictures of it. But if it was a failure everyone was in such a rage there was always a chance of being sent back under arrest.

'They may shell us now,' I said.

'That makes no difference to me,' said the Extremaduran. I was beginning to be a little tired of the Extremaduran.

'Have you any more wine to spare?' I asked. My mouth was still dry.

'Yes, man. There are gallons of it,' the friendly soldier said. He was short, big-fisted and very dirty, with a stubble of beard about the same length as the hair on his cropped head. 'Do you think they will shell us now?'

'They should,' I said. 'But in this war you can never tell.' 'What is the matter with this war?' asked the Extremaduran angrily. 'Don't you like this war?'

'Shut up!' said the friendly soldier. 'I command here, and these comrades are our guests.'

'Then let him not talk against our war,' said the Extremaduran. 'No foreigners shall come here and talk against our war.'

'What town are you from, comrade?' I asked the Extremaduran.

'Badajoz.' he said. 'I am from Badajoz. In Badajoz, we have been sacked and pillaged and our women violated by the English, the French and now the Moors. What the Moors have done now is no worse than what the English did under Wellington. You should read history. My great-grandmother was killed by the English. The house where my family lived was burned by the English.'

'I regret it,' I said. 'Why do you hate the North Americans?'

'My father was killed by the North Americans in Cuba while he was there as a conscript.'

'I am sorry for that, too. Truly sorry. Believe me. And why do you hate the Russians?'

'Because they are the representatives of tyranny and I hate their faces. You have the face of a Russian.'

'Maybe we better get out of here,' I said to the one who was with me and who did not speak Spanish. 'It seems I have the face of a Russian and it's getting me into trouble.'

'I'm going to sleep,' he said. 'This is a good place. Don't talk so much and you won't get into trouble.'

'There's a comrade here that doesn't like me. I think he's an anarchist.'

'Well, watch out he doesn't shoot you, then. I'm going to sleep,'

Just then two men in leather coats, one short and stocky, the other of medium height, both with civilian caps, flat, high-cheek-boned faces, wooden-holstered Mauser pistols strapped to their legs, came out of the gap and headed toward us.

The taller of them spoke to me in French. 'Have you seen a French comrade pass through here?' he asked. 'A comrade with a blanket tied around his shoulders in the form of a bandoleer? A comrade of about forty-five or fifty years old? Have you seen such a comrade going in the direction away from the front?'

'No,' I said. 'I have not seen such a comrade.'

He looked at me a moment and I noticed his eyes were a grayish-yellow and that they did not blink at all.

'Thank you, comrade,' he said, in his odd French, and then spoke rapidly to the other man with him in a language I did not understand. They went off and climbed the highest part of the ridge, from where they could see down all the gullies.

'There is the true face of Russians,' the Extremaduran said.

'Shut up!' I said. I was watching the two men in the leather coats. They were standing there, under considerable fire, looking carefully over all the broken country below the ridge and toward the river.

Suddenly one of them saw what he was looking for, and pointed. Then the two started to run like hunting dogs, one straight down over the ridge, the other at an angle as though to cut someone off. Before the second one went over the crest I could see him drawing his pistol and holding it ahead of him as he ran.

'And how do you like that?' asked the Extremaduran.

'No better than you,' I said.

Over the crest of the parallel ridge I heard the Mausers' jerky barking. They kept it up for more than a dozen shots. They must have opened fire at too long a range. After all the burst of shooting there was a pause and then a single shot.

The Extremaduran looked at me sullenly and said nothing. I thought it would be simpler if the shelling started. But it did not start.

The two in the leather coats and civilian caps came back over the ridge, walking together, and then down to the gap, walking downhill with that odd bent-kneed way of the two-legged animal coming down a steep slope. They turned up the gap as a tank came whirring and clanking down and moved to one side to let it pass.

The tanks had failed again that day, and the drivers coming down from the lines in their leather helmets, the tank turrets open now as they came into the shelter of the ridge, had the straight-ahead stare of football players who have been removed from a game for yellowness.

The two flat-faced men in the leather coats stood by us on the ridge to let the tank pass.

'Did you find the comrade you were looking for?' I asked the taller one of them in French.

'Yes, comrade. Thank you,' he said and looked me over very carefully.

'What does he say?' The Extremaduran asked.

'He says they found the comrade they were looking for.' I told him. The Extremaduran said nothing.

We had been all that morning in the place the middle-aged Frenchman had walked out of. We had been there in the dust, the smoke, the noise, the receiving of wounds, the death, the fear of death, the bravery, the cowardice, the insanity and failure of an unsuccessful attack. We had been there on that plowed field men could not cross and live. You dropped and lay flat; making a mound to shield your head; working your chin into the dirt; waiting for the order to go up that slope no man could go up and live.

We had been with those who lay there waiting for the tanks that did not come; waiting under the inrushing shriek and roaring crash of the shelling; the metal and the earth thrown like clods from a dirt fountain; and overhead the cracking, whispering fire like a curtain. We knew how those felt, waiting. They were as far forward as they could get. And men could not move further and live, when the order came to move ahead.

We had been there all morning in the place the middle-aged Frenchman had come walking away from. I understood how a man might suddenly, seeing clearly the stupidity of dying in an unsuccessful attack; or suddenly seeing it clearly, as you can see clearly and justly before you die; seeing its hopelessness, seeing its idiocy, seeing how it really was, simply get back and walk away from it as the Frenchman had done. He could walk out of it not from cowardice, but simply from seeing too clearly; knowing suddenly that he had to leave it; knowing there was no other thing to do.

The Frenchman had come walking out of the attack with great dignity and I understood him as a man. But, as a soldier, these other men who policed the battle had hunted him down, and the death he had walked away from had found him when he was just over the ridge, clear of the bullets and the shelling, and walking toward the river.

'And that,' the Extremaduran said to me, nodding toward the battle police.

'Is war,' I said. 'In war, it is necessary to have discipline.'

'And to live under that sort of discipline we should die?'

'Without discipline everyone will die anyway.'

'There is one kind of discipline and another kind of discipline,' the Extremaduran said. 'Listen to me. In February we were here where we are now and the Fascists attacked. They drove us from the hills that you Internationals tried to take today and that you could not take. We fell back to here; to this ridge. Internationals came up and took the line ahead of us.'

'I know that,' I said.

'But you do not know this,' he went on angrily. 'There was a boy from my province who became frightened during the bombardment, and he shot himself in the hand so that he could leave the line because he was afraid.'

The other soldiers were all listening now. Several nodded.

'Such people have their wounds dressed and are returned at once to the line,' the Extremaduran went on. 'It is just.'

'Yes,' I said. 'That is as it should be.'

'That is as it should be,' said the Extremaduran. 'But this boy shot himself so badly that the bone was all smashed and there surged up an infection and his hand was amputated.'

Several soldiers nodded.

'Go on, tell him the rest,' said one.

'It might be better not to speak of it,' said the cropped-headed, bristly-faced man who said he was in command.

'It is my duty to speak,' the Extremaduran said.

The one in command shrugged his shoulders. 'I did not like it either,' he said. 'Go on, then. But I do not like to hear it spoken of either.'

'This boy remained in the hospital in the valley since February,' the Extremaduran said. 'Some of us have seen him in the hospital. All say he was well liked in the hospital and made himself as useful as a man with one hand can be useful. Never was he under arrest. Never was there anything to prepare him.'

The man in command handed me the cup of wine again without saying anything. They were all listening; as men who cannot read or write listen to a story.

'Yesterday, at the close of day, before we knew there was to be an attack. Yesterday, before the sun set, when we thought today was to be as any other day, they brought him up the trail in the gap there from the flat. We were cooking the evening meal and they brought him up. There were only four of them. Him, the boy Paco, those two you have just seen in the leather coats and the caps, and an officer from the Brigade. We saw the four of them climbing together up the gap, and we saw Paco's hands were not tied, nor was he bound in any way.

'When we saw him we all crowded around and said, "Hello, Paco. How are you, Paco? How is everything, Paco, old boy, old Paco?"'

'Then he said, "Everything's all right. Everything is good except this" – and showed us the stump.'

'Paco said, "That was a cowardly and foolish thing. I am sorry that I did that thing. But I try to be useful with one hand. I will do what I can with one hand for the Cause."'

'Yes,' interrupted a soldier. 'He said that. I heard him say that.'

'We spoke with him,' the Extremaduran said. 'And he spoke with us. When such people with the leather coats and the pistols come it is always a bad omen in a war, as is the arrival of people with map cases and field glasses. Still we thought they had brought him for a visit, and all of us who had not been to the hospital were happy to see him, and as I say, it was the hour of the evening meal and the evening was clear and warm.'

'This wind only rose during the night,' a soldier said.

'Then,' the Extremaduran went on somberly, 'one of <u>them</u> said to the officer in Spanish, "Where is the place?"'

'Where is the place this Paco was wounded?' asked the officer.'

'I answered him,' said the man in command. 'I showed the place. It is a little further down than where you are.'

'Here is the place,' said a soldier. He pointed, and I could see it was the place. It showed clearly that it was the place.

'Then one of them led Paco by the arm to the place and held him there by the arm while the other spoke in Spanish. He spoke in Spanish, making many mistakes in the language. At first we wanted to laugh, and Paco started to smile. I could not understand all the speech, but it was that Paco must be punished as an example, in order that there would be no more self-inflicted wounds, and that all others would be punished in the same way.

'Then, while the one held Paco by the arm; Paco, looking very ashamed to be spoken of this way when he was already ashamed and sorry; the other took his pistol out and shot Paco in the back of the head without any word to Paco. Nor any word more.'

The soldiers all nodded.

'It was thus,' said one. 'You can see the place. He fell with his mouth there. You can see it.'

I had seen the place clearly enough from where I lay.

'He had no warning and no chance to prepare himself,' the one in command said. 'It was very brutal.'

'It is for this that I now hate Russians as well as all other foreigners,' said the Extremaduran. 'We can give ourselves no illusions about foreigners. If you are a foreigner, I am sorry. But for myself, now, I can make no exceptions. You have eaten bread and drunk wine with us. Now I think you should go.'

'Do not speak in that way,' the man in command said to the Extremaduran. 'It is necessary to be formal.'

'I think we had better go,' I said.

'You are not angry?' the man in command said. 'You can stay in this shelter as long as you wish. Are you thirsty? Do you wish more wine?'

'Thank you very much,' I said. 'I think we had better go.'

'You understand my hatred?' asked the Extremaduran.

'I understand your hatred,' I said.

'Good,' he said and put out his hand. 'I do not refuse to shake hands. And that you, personally, have much luck.'

'Equally to you,' I said. 'Personally, and as a Spaniard.'

I woke the one who took the pictures and we started down the ridge toward Brigade headquarters. The tanks were all coming back now and you could hardly hear yourself talk for the noise.

'Were you talking all that time?'

'Listening.'

'Hear anything interesting?'

'Plenty.'

'What do you want to do now?'

'Get back to Madrid.'

'We should see the General.'

'Yes,' I said. 'We must.'

The General was coldly furious. He had been ordered to make the attack as a surprise with one brigade only, bringing everything up before daylight. It should have been made by at least a division. He had used three battalions and held one in reserve. The French tank commander had got drunk to be brave for the attack and finally was too drunk to function. He was to be shot when he sobered up.

The tanks had not come up in time and finally had refused to advance, and two of the battalions had failed to attain their objectives. The third had taken theirs, but it formed an untenable salient. The only real result had been a few prisoners, and these had been confided to the tank men to bring back and the tank men had killed them. The General had only failure to show, and they had killed his prisoners.

'What can I write on it?' I asked.

'Nothing that is not in the official communiqué. Have you any whisky in that long flask?'

'Yes.'

He took a drink and licked his lips carefully. He had once been a captain of Hungarian Hussars, and he had once captured a gold train in Siberia when he was a leader of irregular cavalry with the Red Army and held it all one winter when the thermometer went down to forty below zero. We were good friends and he loved whisky, and he is now dead.

'Get out of here now,' he said. 'Have you transport?'

'Yes.'

'Did you get any pictures?'

'Some. The tanks.'

'The tanks,' he said bitterly. 'The swine. The cowards. Watch out you don't get killed,' he said. 'You are supposed to be a writer.'

'I can't write now.'

'Write it afterwards. You can write it all afterwards. And don't get killed. Especially, don't get killed. Now, get out of here.'

He could not take his own advice because he was killed two months later. But the oddest thing about that day was how marvelously the pictures we took of the tanks came out. On the screen they advanced over the hill irresistibly, mounting the crests like great ships, to crawl clanking on toward the illusion of victory we screened.

The nearest any man was to victory that day was probably the Frenchman who came, with his head held high, walking out of the battle. But his victory only lasted until he had walked halfway down the ridge. We saw him lying stretched out there on the slope of the ridge, still wearing his blanket, as we came walking down the cut to get into the staff car that would take us to Madrid.

— Ernest Hemingway, "Under the Ridge,"
Hearst Magazines, Inc., 1939

[Reprinted in *The Fifth Column and Four Stories of the Spanish Civil War,* 1969.]

Say That We Saw Spain Die

Say that we saw Spain die. O splendid bull, how well you fought!
Lost from the first.
   . . .the tossed, the replaced, the watchful *torero* with gesture
      elegant and spry,
Before the dark, the tiring but the unglazed eye deploying the
      bright cape,
Which hid for once not air, but the enemy indeed, the authentic
      shape,
A thousand of him, interminably into the ring released . . .
   the turning beast at length between converging colours caught.

Save for the weapons of its skull, a bull
Unarmed, considering, weighing, charging
Almost a world, itself without ally.

Say that we saw the shoulders more than the mind confused, so
      profusely
Bleeding from so many more than the accustomed barbs, the
      game gone vulgar, the rules abused.
Say that we saw Spain die from loss of blood, a rustic reason, in a
      reinforced
And proud punctilious land, no *espada* –
A hundred men unhorsed,
A hundred horses gored, and the afternoon aging, and the crowd
      growing restless (all, all so much later than planned),
And the big head heavy, sliding forward in the sand, and the
      tongue dry with sand, – no *espada*
Toward that hot neck, for the delicate and final thrust, having
      dared thrust forth his hand.

— Edna St. Vincent Millay, Collected Poems, 1956

Glossary of Leading Figures and Political Parties

Alcalá Zamora, Niceto (1877–1949). Lawyer and right-wing Republican. Elected first prime minister of the Republic and later its first president. Deposed in May 1936.

Alfonso XIII (1886–1941). Last king of Spain before the uprising. Dethroned in April 1931, he went into exile.

Alvarez del Vayo, Julio (1891–1974). A member of the Socialist party who became a close ally of the Communists. One of the principal diplomats of the Second Republic during the Spanish Civil War. Argued the Republic's international position before the League of Nations in Geneva.

Aranda Mata, Antonio (1888–1979). One of Spain's most brilliant staff officers. Led the Nationalist uprising in Oviedo and withheld the city against a siege that lasted ninety days. Played a major role in the successful northern campaigns.

Asaltos. See **Assault Guards.**

Assault Guards. Special police units created by the Spanish Republic in 1931 to combat urban violence.

Azaña y Díaz, Manuel (1880–1940). Member of the revolutionary committee that overthrew the monarchy and established the Republic. Headed several cabinets between 1931 and 1933. Elected president of the Spanish Republic in 1936 and held office for two-and-a-half years of the Spanish Civil War. Died in exile in France.

Balmes Alonso, Amadeo (1877–1936). Military governor of Las Palmas who accidentally shot himself dead at target practice.

Bates, Ralph (1899–?). British novelist. Edited *Volunteer for Spain,* the official weekly of the English-speaking battalions of the International Brigades. Later became a fund-raiser and energetic champion of the Republican cause at public méetings in Europe and the U.S.A. Wrote a number of books and articles on Spain, including *Lean Men* and *The Olive Field.*

Beimler, Hans (1895–1936). Communist ex-deputy of the *Reichstag* and commissar of all the Germans in Spain. Led the Thaelmann Battalion. Regler wrote of Beimler's death in *The Owl of Minerva.* The anniversary of Beimler's death inspired "Homage to Hans Beimler" and "Madrid honours Hans Beimler."

Bolín Bidwell, Captain Luis (1894–1969). London correspondent of the Monarchist daily paper, ABC. He chartered the airplane that transported General Franco from the Canary Islands to Morocco at the start of the military uprising. He was sent to Rome by Franco to make a formal request for aircraft and bombs. Later he became the Nationalist press chief, in charge of propaganda and censorship.

Caballero. See **Largo Caballero.**

Calvo Sotelo, José (1893–1936). Political leader of the Monarchist opposition under the Second Republic. His murder by leftist Republican police in July 1936 was the final spark that set off the civil war.

Carlists. Traditional antiliberal Church/king party, with nineteenth-century roots and based mainly in Navarre. Provided the Nationalists with some of their staunchest troops — the *requetés*.

Casares Quiroga, Santiago (1894–1950). Leader of the Galician Autonomy party and a militant anticlerical who inflamed the Right with his public pronouncements and bias. Became prime minister in 1936, but proved ineffectual and was replaced in the early hours of the war. His refusal to distribute arms to the masses at the start of the military rebellion is generally considered a major cause of the early successes of the rebels.

CEDA (*Confederación Española de Derechas Autónomas*). Composite rightwing Catholic party founded in 1933 and led by Gil Robles.

CNT (*Confederación Nacional de Trabajo*). The anarcho-syndicalist trade union founded in 1910 in Barcelona.

Cortes. Spanish parliament, comprising 473 deputies.

Domingo Sanjuán, Marcelino (1884–1939). Catalan deputy and Republican minister; responsible for the failed agrarian law reform.

Durruti, Buenaventura (1896–1936). Perhaps the most famous Spanish anarchist during the civil war. His revolutionary activities in France, South America, and Spain made him a cult figure of revolutionary idealism long after his death. Played a leading role in defeating the military uprising in Barcelona and died in the defense of Madrid at the head of his anarchist battalion.

FAI (*Federación Anarquista Ibérica*). Federation of militant Anarchist groups, founded in 1927. Advocated "libertarian communism" and opposed all forms of state control.

Fox, Ralph (1900–1937). A graduate of Magdalen College, Oxford, and a leading English communist man of letters. Commissar of the British company of the International Brigades. After his death in action, he was claimed by the British Communist party as Byron's successor in dying for a foreign cause.

Franco y Bahamonde, Francisco (1892–1975). Nationalist general, one of the leaders of the 1936 revolt and eventual supreme commander of the Nationalist cause. Dictator of Spain from 1939 until his death in 1975.

FUE (*Federación Universitaria Española*). The main students' union, controlled at the time by the Left.

Generalidad/Generalitat. The autonomous regional government of Catalonia that was created by the Catalan Statute of 1932.

Gil Robles, José María (1898–1980). Fascist leader of the Popular Action Party and CEDA. Was minister of war from 6 May to 9 December 1936.

Goded Llopis, Manuel (1882–1936). General and chief of staff in 1931. Led the failed military uprising in Barcelona. Surrendered to the Republican forces and was executed after trial by court martial.

Ibarruri, Dolores. See **Pasionaria**.

JCI (*Juventud Comunista Ibérica*). A POUM youth movement, very active in Catalonia. Tool of the Soviets. Urged the dissolution of the Cortes and the formation of an assembly based on collective committees of all types.

JONS (*Juntas de Ofensiva Nacional-Sindicalista*). A Fascist group, founded in 1931 and merged with the Falange in 1934.

JSU (*Juventudes Socialistas Unificadas*). Unified Socialist Youth, formed in 1936 from separate Socialist and Communist youth movements.

Kahle, "Hans." An ex-Prussian colonel and communist. Led the German Battalion of the International Brigades and later commanded the XI International Brigade.

Koltsov, Mikhail. *Pravda* correspondent in Spain. Became Karkov in Hemingway's novel *For Whom the Bell Tolls.*

Largo Caballero, Francisco (1869–1946). Labor leader and politician. President of the Socialist party and the UGT. Head of the Spanish government from September 1936 to May 1937.

Lister, Enrique (1907–). Emigrated to Cuba in 1927 and joined the Cuban Communist party. Returned to Spain in 1930 where he was elected head of the Miscellaneous Trades' Syndicate. Studied and worked in Moscow 1931–1934. During the civil war he became one of the most famous militia and army commanders. Between July and November 1938 he fought in the Ebro campaign from where he wrote to Machado. After the defeat of the Republic, he returned to Moscow for six years. Organized guerrilla operations against Franco in 1946–1947. Founded the Spanish Workers' Communist party in 1973 and returned to Spain in November 1977, following the death of Franco.

Lukacz. General in command of the XII International Brigade. He was, in fact, the Hungarian writer Mata Zalka, who had served in the Austrian army in the First World War. Captured by the Russians, he joined the Red Army where he was known under name of "Kémeny." Regler gives an account of his death in *The Owl of Minerva.*

Martínez Barrio, Diego (1883–1965). Founder of the Republican Union party and the most moderate of the Popular Front leaders. Failed in an attempt to form a compromise coalition government on 19 July 1936. Became president of the Republic in 1939.

Marty, André. Megalomaniac Stalinist who commanded the Albacete base of the International Brigades. Regler describes him in *The Owl of Minerva.*

Miaja Menant, José (1878–1954). Professional soldier, promoted to general in 1932. Remained loyal to the Republic and became its most famous soldier. In November 1936 appointed military commander of Madrid and organized its defense. Went into exile in Mexico at the end of the war.

Millán Astray y Terreros, General José (1879–1954). An extreme Nationalist, he had a brilliant military career in Morocco. Famous for his remark: *¡Viva la muerte!* (*Long live death!*). Unsuccessful challenger to Queipo de Llano as chief propagandist of the Nationalists.

Mola Vidal, Emilio (1887–1937). General, leading conspirator, and military commander of Pamplona at the outbreak of the civil war. He took command of the Nationalist forces advancing on Madrid and coined the phrase the "fifth column." Killed in an airplane accident in 1937.

Movement. A mass political movement created to fill the political void on the Nationalist side. In 1937 the Falange and the Carlists were forcibly united to form a single party, which later became known as the Movement. This grouping provided Franco with a political ideology.

Negrín, Juan (1892–1956). Spain's last prime minister during the Second Republic. More responsible than any other Spaniard for the success of Communist policy during the last years of the civil war.

Nelken y Mausberger, Margarita (1898–1968). Writer, art critic, politician. First a Socialist, then a Communist. She later broke with communism.

Nin, Andrés (1892–1937). Once secretary to Trotsky and later leader of the POUM. Executed by the Communists in 1937 in their attempt to destroy their rivals and take control of the Spanish revolution.

Odena, Lina. Anarchist militia leader. Helped to crush the rebel uprising in Almeria at the start of the war. Died a few days later on journey to Granada when she fell into the hands of Falangists and shot herself. Elevated to the category of a national heroine. Lorenzo Varela wrote a moving poem about her death entitled "Lina Odena."

Ossorio y Gallardo, Angel (1873–1946). Republican ambassador to Brussels and Paris.

Pasionaria, La (Dolores Ibarruri) (1895–1981). Labor leader, Communist deputy in the 1936 parliament and general secretary of the Spanish Communist party. At the end of the war, she went into exile in the Soviet Union, where she remained until her return to Spain following the death of Franco. Elected as a Communist deputy to the first democratic parliament in post-Franco Spain.

Patriotic Union Party (Unión Patriótica). A right-wing party that General Primo de Rivera attempted to set up in 1927.

PC (*Partido Conservador*). Conservative party, led by Miguel Maura.

Pemán y Pemartín, José María. Right-wing apologist. The most celebrated of the Nationalist writers.

PNV (*Partido Nacionalista Vasco*). Main Basque Nationalist party, founded in 1895. Proclerical and reactionary, seeking limited autonomy for the Basque provinces.

POUM (*Partido Obrero de Unificación Marxista*). Revolutionary anti-Stalinist Communist party, formed in 1935, with a strong Trotskyist influence. They supported the collectivization of the means of production and Trotsky's concept of permanent revolution.

Pozas Perea, Sebastián (1876–1946). Promoted to general during the dictatorship of Primo de Rivera after a brilliant career in Morocco. Despite his conservative background, a strong supporter of the Republic. Favored arming the people at the start of the uprising, and secured the loyalty of the Civil Guard in several urban centers. Given command of the new Army of the Center when the Republican government abandoned Madrid. Took part in the battles of Jarama and Guadalajara. In May 1937 appointed chief of staff of the Army of the East and restored order after anarcho-syndicalist and POUM elements attempted a revolutionary coup. Emigrated to Moscow at the end of the war.

Prieto y Tuero, Indalecio (1883–1962). Socialist minister who tried to link the Socialist party with middle-class reformists in an attempt to create a progressive force capable of transforming Spanish political life.

Primo de Rivera, Miguel (1870–1930). Captain general of Catalonia and dictator of Spain from 1923 to January 1930. He passed on to his son his contempt for political parties, especially liberalism.

Primo de Rivera, José Antonio (1903–1936). Political leader and son of General Primo de Rivera. Disillusioned with parliamentary liberalism, he moved towards Nationalist, antiliberal, and anti-Marxist, totalitarian ideas. Founded the Spanish Falange in 1933 and became its sole leader. Executed in November 1936 for influencing the rebellion.

PSOE (*Partido Socialista Obrero Español*). Spanish Socialist party, founded in 1897 and led by the triumvirate, Francisco Largo Caballero (Left), Indalecio Prieto (Center) and Julián Besteiro (Right). Sought a collective form of government with the socialization of production.

PSUC (*Partido Socialista Unificado de Cataluña*). United Catalan Socialist party, formed in 1936 from several Socialist and Communist groups. Affiliated to the Comintern, and in effect the Communist party in Catalonia.

Queipo de Llano Sierra, Gonzalo (1875–1951). Career soldier and general in the civil war. Led the successful Nationalist revolt in Andalusia. Took part in the capture of Malaga. Conspicuous for his highly aggressive propaganda broadcasts.

Radicals (*Partido Radical*). Radical party, led by Alejandro Lerroux. Anti-Socialist and an ally of the Fascist parties.

Requetés. Carlist militias.

Sanjurjo Sacanell, José (1872–1936). A highly regarded military officer who rose to the rank of lieutenant general through active service in Morocco. Politically naive, he led the first ill-conceived and abortive coup against the Republic. Supreme commander of the rebels at the start of the war. Killed in an airplane crash in July 1936.

UGT (*Unión General de Trabajadores*). The main Socialist trade union, later under Communist domination.

Varela Iglesias, José (1891–1951). Colonel and later general. Trained the Carlist *requetés*. Dressed as a priest and known as *Tío Pepe* (Uncle Pepe), he travelled about the Pyrenean villages recruiting Carlists to the Nationalist cause. Arrested and imprisoned in Cadiz for plotting, but later released. Fought on the Madrid front.

Villalba Rubio, José (1889–?). Colonel and later general. The most important officer to defect from the Nationalist conspiracy. An ineffective commander of the defense force in Malaga.

Bibliography

General History

Beevor, Anthony *The Spanish Civil War* (London: Orbis, 1982)

Brenan, Gerald *The Spanish Labyrinth* (Cambridge: Cambridge University Press, 1943)

Carr, Raymond *The Civil War in Spain, 1936–1939* (London: Weidenfeld and Nicolson, 1986)

Jackson, Gabriel *A Concise History of the Spanish Civil War* (London/New York: Thames and Hudson, 1974)

Malefakis, Edward *Agrarian Reform and Peasant Revolution in Spain* (New Haven: Yale University Press, 1970)

Payne, Stanley *Falange: A History of Spanish Fascism* (Stanford: Stanford University Press, 1961)

Preston, Paul *The Coming of the Spanish Civil War* (London: Methuen, 1983)

Preston, Paul, ed. *Revolution and War in Spain 1931–39* (London: Methuen, 1984)

Preston, Paul *The Spanish Civil War, 1936–39* (London: Weidenfeld & Nicolson, 1986)

Southworth, Herbert *Guernica! Guernica!* (Berkeley: University of California Press, 1977)

Thomas, Hugh *The Spanish Civil War* (London: Penguin, 1986 [1961])

Tuñón de Lara, Manuel et al., *La guerra civil española 50 años después* (Barcelona: Labor, 1986)

International Aspects

Alexander, Bill *British Volunteers for Liberty* (London: Lawrence and Wishart, 1982)

Castells, Andreu *Las brigadas internacionales de la guerra de España* (Barcelona: Ariel, 1974)

Cattell, David *Soviet Diplomacy and the Spanish Civil War* (Berkeley: University of California Press)

Puzzo, Dante *Spain and the Great Powers, 1936–1941* (New York: Columbia University Press, 1962)

Whealey, Robert *Hitler and Spain. The Nazi Role in the Spanish Civil War, 1936–1939* (Lexington: University Press of Kentucky, 1987)

Biography/Memoirs

Alvarez del Vayo, Julio *The Last Optimist* (New York: Viking, 1950)

Alvarez del Vayo, Julio *Give Me Combat: the Memoirs of Julio W. Alvarez del Vayo* (Boston: Little, Brown and Company, 1973)

Azaña y Díaz, Manuel *Memorias íntimas* (Madrid: Ediciones Españolas, 1939)

Casado, Segismundo *The Last Days of Madrid* (London: Peter Davies, 1939)

Caudwell, Christopher *Scenes and Actions: Unpublished Manuscripts* ed. Jean Dupare and David Margolies (London/New York: Routledge and Kegan Paul, 1986)

Fox, Ralph *Ralph Fox: A Writer in Arms* ed. John Lehmann, T. A. Jackson, and C. Day Lewis (London: Lawrence & Wishart, 1937)

Fraser, Ronald *Blood of Spain: The Experience of Civil War, 1936–1939* (London: Penguin, 1979)

Gil Robles, José María *No fue posible la paz* (Barcelona: Ariel, 1968)

Gregory, Walter *The Shallow Grave. A Memoir of the Spanish Civil War* ed. David Morris and Anthony Peters (London: Gollancz, 1986)

Ibarruri, Dolores *They Shall Not Pass* (London: Lawrence and Wishart, 1967)

Landis, Arthur *The Abraham Lincoln Brigade* (New York: Citadel, 1967)

Langdon-Davies, John *Behind the Spanish Barricades* (New York: Martin Secker Warburg, 1936)

Largo Caballero, Francisco *Mis recuerdos* (Mexico: Alianza, 1954)

MacDougall, Ian, ed. *Voices from the Spanish Civil War: Personal Recollections of Scottish Volunteers in Republican Spain, 1936–39* (Edinburgh: Polygon, 1986)

Maisky, Ivan *Spanish Notebooks* (London: Hutchinson, 1966)

Romilly, Esmond *Boadilla* (London: Macdonald, 1971)

Steer, George *The Tree of Guernica* (London: Hodder and Stoughton, 1938)

Fiction

(Works represented in the anthology have been excluded from the following list.)

Hemingway, Ernest *For Whom the Bell Tolls* (London: Jonathan Cape, 1969)

Koestler, Arthur *Darkness at Noon* (London: Penguin, 1964)

Lewis, Norman *The Day of the Fox* (London: Robinson Publishing, 1957)

Malraux, André *Days of Hope* (London: Routledge and Kegan Paul, 1938; New York: Doubleday, 1967)

Regler, Gustav *The Great Crusade* (New York: Longmans, Green, 1940)

Sartre, Jean-Paul *Le mur* (Paris: Gallimard, 1939)

Serge, Victor *The Case of Comrade Tulayev* (London: Gollancz, 1968); *Birth of Our Power* (London: Gollancz, 1968)

Literary Aspects

Beals Romeiser, John *Red Flags, Black Flags: Critical Essays on the Literature of the Spanish Civil War* (Madrid: Porrua Turanzas, 1982)

Benson, Frederick *Writers in Arms: The Literary Impact of the Spanish Civil War* (New York: New York University Press, 1967)

Ford, Hugh *A Poet's War: British Poets and the Spanish Civil War* (Philadelphia: University of Pennsylvania Press, 1965)

Hanrez, Marc *Les écrivains et la Guerre d'Espagne* (Paris: Pantheon Press, 1975)

Hart, Stephen *"¡No pasarán!" Art, Literature and the Spanish Civil War* (London: Tamesis, 1988)

Hoskins, Katherine *Today the Struggle: Literature and Politics in England during the Spanish Civil War* (Austin: University of Texas Press, 1969)

Lechner, José *El compromiso en la poesía española del siglo XX* (Leiden: Rijksuniversiteit, 1968)

Rodríguez-Puértolas, Julio *Literatura fascista española* (Madrid: Akal, 1986)

Salaün, Serge *La poesía de la guerra de España* (Madrid: Castalia, 1985)

Thomas, Gareth *The Novel of the Spanish Civil War* (Cambridge: Cambridge University Press, 1990)

Weintraub, Stanley, *The Last Great Cause: The Intellectuals and the Spanish Civil War* (London: W. H. Allen, 1968)

Pictorial Images

Carr, Raymond *Images of the Spanish Civil War* (London: Allen and Unwin, 1986)

La guerre civile d'Espagne et le cinéma (*Revue Belge du Cinéma*, no. 17, Autumn 1986)

Gubern, Román *La guerra de España en la pantalla* (Madrid: Filmoteca Española, 1986)

Martin, Rupert *No pasarán: Photographs and Posters of the Spanish Civil War* (Bristol: Arnolfini Gallery, 1986)

Pabellón Español: Exposición Internacional de París, 1937 A catalogue. (Madrid, 1987).

Tisa, John *The Palette and the Flame: Posters of the Spanish Civil War* (New York: International Publishers, 1979)

Vernon, Kathleen, ed. *The Spanish Civil War and the Visual Arts* (Ithaca: Cornell University Press, 1990)

List of Anthologized Texts

The following sources have been used for the Anthology of Texts:

Historical Documents

Díaz-Plaja, F. *La guerra de España en sus documentos* (Barcelona: Marte, 1966)

Enciclopedia ilustrada universal (Madrid: Espasa Calpe, 1940)

League of Nations Official Journal

New Statesman and Nation

Primo de Rivera, J. A. *Obras completas* (Madrid: Editora Nacional, 1942)

American Texts

Dos Passos, J. *The Villages are the Heart of Spain* (Chicago: Esquire-Coronet, 1937)

Hemingway, E. *The Fifth Column and Four Stories of the Spanish Civil War* (New York: Charles Scribner's Sons, 1969)

Millay, E. St. Vincent *Collected Poems* (New York: Harper and Row, 1956)

British Texts

Auden, W. H. *Selected Poems* ed. W. Mendelson (New York: Vintage Books, 1979)

Cornford, J. *John Cornford: A Memoir* ed. Pat Sloan (London: Jonathan Cape, 1938)

MacNeice, L. *Collected Poems* (London: Faber & Faber, 1949)

Orwell, G. *Homage to Catalonia* (Harmondsworth: Penguin, 1986)

Spender, S. *The Still Centre* (London: Faber & Faber, 1939)

New Statesman and Nation

French Texts

Bernanos, G. *A Diary of My Times* trans. Pamela Morris (London: Bodley Head, 1938)

Blum, L. *L'Oeuvre* (Paris: Albin-Michel, 1964)

Saint de Exupéry, A. de *Un sens à la vie* (Paris: Gallimard, 1956)

German Texts

Borkenau, F. *Spanish Cockpit: An Eye-Witness Account of the Political and Social Conflicts of the Spanish Civil War* (London: Pluto, 1986 [1937])

Koestler, A. *Spanish Testament* (London: Gollancz, 1937)

Regler, G. *The Owl of Minerva* trans. Norman Denny (London: Rupert Hart Davis, 1959 [1958])

Hispanic Texts

Books

Alberti, R. *Obra completa* (Madrid: Aguilar, 1988)

Antología poética del alzamiento, 1936–1939 (Cadiz: Establecimientos Cerón y Librería Cervantes, 1939)

Arconada, C. M. *Vivimos en una noche oscura* (Madrid: Publicaciones Izquierda, 1936)

Aub, M. *Campo de las almendras* (Mexico: Joaquín Mortiz, 1968)

Azaña, M. *Obras completas* (Mexico: Oasis, 1967)

Vigil in Benicarló trans. J. and P. Stewart (London: Associated University Presses, 1982 [1939])

Barea, A. *The Forging of a Rebel* trans. Ilsa Barea (London: Faber & Faber, 1946)

Calle Iturrino, E. *Plenitud lírica: obra completa* (Bilbao: Diputación de Vizcaya, 1985)

Castillo Puche, J. L. *El vengador* (Barcelona: Destino, 1956)

Cernuda, L. *La realidad y el deseo* (Mexico: Fondo de Cultura Económica, 1970)

Cunningham, V., ed. *The Penguin Book of Spanish Civil War Verse* (Harmondsworth: Penguin, 1980)

Díaz-Plaja, F. *La guerra de España en sus documentos* (Barcelona: Espasa Calpe, 1966)

Enciclopedia universal ilustrada (Madrid: Espasa Calpe, 1940)

Espina, C. *Retaguardia* (Cordoba: Librería Internacional, 1937)

Fernández, C., ed. *Antología de cuarenta años, 1936-75* (La Corunna: Editora Nacional, 1983)

Foxá, A. de *El almendro y lo espada* (San Sebastian: Editora Nacional, 1940)

Madrid, de corte a checa (San Sebastian: Librería Internacional, 1938)

Fraser, R. *Blood of Spain* (London: Allen Lane, 1979)

García Serrano, R. *La ventana daba al río* (Madrid: Bullón, 1963)

Garfías, P. *Poesía de la guerra española* (Mexico: Minerva, 1941)

Gay, V. *Estampas rojas y caballeros blancos* (Burgos: Editora Nacional, 1937)

Giménez Caballero, E. *Nuestro Madrid* (Madrid: n.p., 1944 [1937])

Gironella, J. M. *Los cipreses creen en Dios* (Barcelona: Planeta, 1953)

Gómez Pardal, C. *España gloriosa y culta, única, patriótica y poética* (La Corunna: Editora Nacional, 1936)

Goytisolo, J. A. *Obras completas* (Madrid: Aguilar, 1973)

Hernández, M. *Viento del pueblo* (Valencia: Socorro Rojo, 1937)

Lehmann, J. *Poems for Spain (1939)* (London: Hogarth Press, 1938)

Machado, M. *Horas de oro: Devocionario poético* (Valladolid: Prensa Castellana, 1938)

Martín Gaite, C. *El cuarto de atrás* (Barcelona: Destino, 1983)

Moreno Villa, J. *Obra poética completa* (Madrid: CSIC, 1987)

Neruda, P. *España en el corazón. Himno a las glorias del pueblo en la guerra 1936–1939* (Santiago de Chile: Ercilla, 1937)

Olmedo, F. G. *El sentido de la guerra española* (Bilbao: El Mensajero del Corazón de Jesús, 1938)

Pemán, J. M. *Poema de la bestia y el ángel* (Saragossa: Jerarquía, 1938)

Poetas de la España leal (Madrid/Valencia: Ediciones Españolas, 1937)

Pombo Angulo, M. *La sombra de la bandera* (Barcelona: Planeta, 1969)

Primo de Rivera, J. A. *Obras completas* (Madrid: Editora Nacional, 1942)

Rodríguez Puértolas, J. *Literatura fascista española* (Madrid: Akal, 1986)

Romancero de la guerra civil — Serie I (Madrid: Ministerio de Instrucción Pública y Bellas Artes, 1936)

Romancero general de la guerra de España (Madrid/Valencia: Ediciones Españolas, 1937)

Selección de poesía: Juegos florales (Vitoria: Ayuntamiento, 1938)

Sender, R. J. *Seven Red Sundays* trans. Sir Peter Chalmers Mitchell (London: Faber and Faber, 1936)

The War in Spain trans. Sir Peter Chalmers Mitchell (London: Faber and Faber, 1937)

Urrutia, F. de *Poemas de la Falange eterna* (Santander: Aldus, 1938)

Vallejo, C. *César Vallejo. A Selection of His Poetry* ed. J. Higgins (Liverpool: Francis Cairns, 1988)

Villén, J., ed. *Antología poética del alzamiento: 1936-1939* (Cadiz: Establecimientos Cerón y Librería Cervantes, 1939)

Ximénez Sandoval, F. *Camisa azul. Retrato de un falangista* (Valladolid: Santarén, 1938)

Press and Periodicals

ABC de Sevilla (Seville edition)
Adelante
Ahora, diario de la juventud (JSU)
La Ametralladora
Arriba
Arriba España
Azul
Daily Worker
Diario vasco
Domingo

Hora de España
International Literature
La libertad
Mono azul
Octubre
El país
Sí
Stajanov
Venceremos
Vértice

Acknowledgments

Every effort has been made to secure permission to reprint copyrighted material. Although regrettably we have failed in a few cases to trace the copyright holder, the editor and publishers gratefully acknowledge permission to reprint the following copyrighted material:

Rafael Alberti: "El quinto regimento" and excerpts from *Radio Sevilla*, by permission of Agente Literario Carmen Balcells. Copyright Rafael Alberti, 1935, by permission of author.

Vicente Aleixandre: "Romance del fusilado" and "Oda a los niños de Madrid matados por ametralladora," by permission of Aguilar S. A. Editores.

Manuel Altolaguirre: "The Tower of El Carpio," trans. I. Schneider and S. Williams, from *The Penguin Book of Spanish Civil War Verse*, ed. Valentine Cunningham, by permission of Penguin Books Ltd. (Penguin Books, 1980), copyright Valentine Cunningham, 1980.

Max Aub: from *Campo de las almendras*, by permission of Max Aub, 1968, and Heirs of Max Aub.

Wystan H. Auden: "Spain" from *W. H. Auden: Collected Poems*, ed. Edward Mendelson. Copyright 1940 and renewed 1968 by W. H. Auden. Reprinted by permission of Random House, Inc.

Manuel Azaña: from *Vigil in Benicarlo* trans. J. and P. Stewart, by permission of Associated University Presses; and from *Obras completas*, by permission of Ediciones Oasis.

Léon Blum: from *L'oeuvre de León Blum 1934–1937*, by permission of Editions Albin Michel.

Franz Borkenau: from *Spanish Cockpit: An Eye-Witness Account of the Political and Social Conflicts of the Spanish Civil War*, by permission of University of Michigan Press.

Gerald Brenan: from *The Spanish Labyrinth*, by permission of Cambridge University Press.

José Luis Castillo Puche: from *El vengador*, by permission of E.diciones Destino.

Cyril Connolly: from "Barcelona," *New Statesman and Nation*, 21 November 1936, by permission of *New Statesman and Nation*.

Luis Cernuda: "Un español habla de su país" from *Poesía completa*, by permission of Sr. Angel María Yanguas Cernuda.

John Dos Passos: *The Villages are the Heart of Spain*, by permission of Mrs. Elizabeth H. Dos Passos, Literary Executor, Estate of John Dos Passos.

León Felipe: from "The Insignia," by permission of Sr. Alejandro Campo Ramírez.

Rafael García Serrano: from *La ventana que daba al río*, by permission of Espasa Calpe, S.A.

Pedro Garfias: "Single front," trans. Tom Wintringham, from *The Penguin Book of Spanish Civil War Verse*, ed. Valentine Cunningham (Penguin

Books, 1980), copyright Valentine Cunningham, 1980.

José María Gironella: from *Los cipreses creen en Dios*, by permission of Editorial Planeta, S. A.

Ernest Hemingway: "Under the Ridge," reprinted in *The Fifth Column and Four Stories of the Spanish Civil War*, Charles Scribner's Sons, an imprint of Macmillan Publishing Company. Copyright 1939 by Hearst Magazines, Inc., renewal copyright 1967 by Mary Hemingway.

Miguel Hernández: "El yunquero", "El fuego" and "Recoged esta voz" from *Poesías completas*, by permission of Dª Lucía Izquierdo García. Copyright Herederos de Miguel Hernández.

Arthur Koestler: from *Spanish Testament*, by permission of Peters, Fraser, and Dunlop.

Manuel Machado: "Una oración para José Antonio," from *Poesía*, by permission of José Rollán Riesco, Literary Executor.

Louis MacNeice: "And I Remember Spain," by permission of Faber and Faber Ltd.

Carmen Martín Gaite: from *El cuarto de atrás*, by permission of Ediciones Destino.

Edna St. Vincent Millay: "Say that We Saw Spain Die," from *Collected Poems*, Harper and Row. Copyright 1939, 1967 by Edna St. Vincent Millay and Norma Millay Ellis. Reprinted by permission of Elizabeth Barnett, Literary Executor.

José Moreno Villa: "Madrid, frente de lucha," "El hombre del momento," by permission of Sr. José Moreno Nieto.

Pablo Neruda: "Explico algunas cosas" and "Batalla del Río Jarama," from *España en el corazón: Himno a las glorias del pueblo en la guerra 1936-1939* (Santiago de Chile: Ercilla, 1937), by permission of Fundación Pablo Neruda and heirs of Pablo Neruda.

George Orwell: from *Homage to Catalonia*, by permission of A. M. Heath and Harcourt, Brace, Jovanovich, and by permission of the estate of the late Sonia Brownell Orwell and Martin Secker and Warburg, Ltd.

M. Pombo Angulo: from *La sombra de la bandera*, by permission of Planeta, S. A. Editorial.

Emilio Prados: "La Unión Soviética," from *Poesías completas* by permission of Aguilar S. A. Editores Mexico.

Gustav Regler: from *The Owl of Minerva*, trans. Norman Denny, by permission of Verlag Kiepenheuer und Witsch.

Antoine de Saint-Exupéry: from *Un sens à la vie*, by permission of Editions Gallimard.

Stephen Spender: "Ultima Ratio Regum," "Port Bou," "Fall of a City," "Two Armies," and "A Stopwatch and an Ordnance Map," reprinted from *The Still Centre*, by permission of Faber and Faber Ltd.; "The Bombed Happiness," from *The New Statesman and Nation*, 4 February 1939, by permission of *New Statesman and Society*.

César Vallejo: "Spain, Take This Cup from Me," and from "Hymn to the Volunteers of the Republic," trans. James Higgins, by permission of Francis Cairns (Publications) Ltd.

Sylvia Townsend Warner: "Benicasim," by permission of Carcanet Press Ltd.

Notes on Contributors

Elaine Barry is associate professor of English at Monash University, Melbourne, and is currently director of its Centre for American Studies. Her main field of research and publication is American literature. Her published works include *Robert Frost* (New York: Frederich Ungar, 1973), *Robert Frost on Writing* (New Brunswick, New Jersey: Rutgers University Press, 1973), and *Fabricating the Self: The Fictions of Jessica Anderson* (Queensland: University of Queensland Press, 1992).

Kevin Foster is lecturer in English and Communications at the University of New England, Armidale, New South Wales. He currently is completing a book on the discourse of conflict, and has published a series of articles on the literary treatment of the Falklands War. He has further research interests in twentieth-century fiction and postcolonial writing.

David Garrioch is senior lecturer at Monash University, Melbourne, where he teaches European History. He is the author of *Neighbourhood and Community in Paris* (Cambridge: Cambridge University Press, 1986) and currently is working on comparative urban history in early modern Europe.

Alun Kenwood is senior lecturer in Spanish in the Department of Romance Languages, Monash University, Melbourne. His main research interests are eighteenth-century Spanish poetry and contemporary Spanish literature and society. In addition to publishing articles in these areas he is coeditor of *War and Revolution in Hispanic Literature* (Melbourne: Voz Hispánica, 1990) and editor of *Love, Sex and Eroticism in Contemporary Latin American* literature (Melbourne: Voz Hispánica, 1992).

John Leonard is senior lecturer in the Department of English at James Cook University of North Queensland. He is the editor of two anthologies, *Seven Centuries of Poetry in England* (Melbourne: Oxford University Press, 1991 [1987]) and *Contemporary Australian Poetry* (Melbourne: Houghton and Mifflin Australia, 1990).

Colin Nettelbeck is associate professor of French at Monash University, Melbourne. He has published widely on twentieth-century French literature and cultural history. He is also active in the Centre for European Studies.

Pavel Petr teaches German literature at Monash University, Melbourne. His areas of interest include twentieth-century German and Czech literature, literary theory, and the sociohistorical background to literature. He has published on Gerhart Hauptmann, Franz Kafka, Bertolt Brecht, Anna Seghers, Stefan Heym, Jaroslav Hasek, and Karel Capek.

Index

Index

CPSIA information can be obtained at www.ICGtesting.com
Printed in the USA
LVOW12s1219070813

346673LV00012B/82/A